OUTLINES OF THE HISTORY OF
THE ENGLISH LANGUAGE

MACMILLAN AND CO., Limited
LONDON · BOMBAY · CALCUTTA · MADRAS
MELBOURNE

THE MACMILLAN COMPANY
NEW YORK · BOSTON · CHICAGO
DALLAS · SAN FRANCISCO

THE MACMILLAN CO. OF CANADA, Ltd.
TORONTO

OUTLINES OF THE
HISTORY OF THE
ENGLISH LANGUAGE

BY

E. CLASSEN, M.A., Ph.D.

GREENWOOD PRESS, PUBLISHERS
NEW YORK

Originally published in 1919
by Macmillan and Co., Ltd.

First Greenwood Reprinting 1969
SBN 8371-2547-2
PRINTED IN UNITED STATES OF AMERICA

PREFACE

THIS little volume does not pretend to furnish any new materials for the history of the English language. It is rather a modest attempt to present the well-known linguistic facts as illustrations of a consistent theory of the development of language, and in that way to invest them with a more human interest.

The author feels, and feels strongly, that the study of language has been too long divorced from the study of ordinary human life and thought, and that the traditional method of isolating linguistic material from the world of individual and social thought and emotion in which language lives can only be misleading.

The theory of development which is here put forward, and which the facts of historical English grammar serve to illustrate, is not orthodox. Indeed, in regarding sound change as the very last effect of a number of complex causes, it runs directly counter to accepted views. In other places, too, as in the explanation of the development of logical gender in Middle English, and of the -s plurals, the theory comes into conflict with current opinion.

The author is greatly indebted to Mr. O. T. Williams, of King's College, London, and to Mr. H. G. Wright, of the University College of North Wales, Bangor, for their kindness in reading and revising the proofs.

E. CLASSEN.

LONDON, *March*, 1919.

CONTENTS

OUTLINES OF THE HISTORY OF THE ENGLISH LANGUAGE

INTRODUCTION

BETWEEN the development of human civilisation in general and the development of human speech in particular there is a close connection which it is one of the objects of the science of language to elucidate. Human civilisation in all its manifold activities and in all its countless changes manifests itself only by means of works and by means of the expression of thought in language. We are justified in saying, therefore, that language is a mirror of civilisation, or we might perhaps better say that it, is the autobiography of the human race. And yet, though we all study our own political history, the history of our art and literature, etc., how few of us ever seek in the history of our language the evidences of the development of thought which the history of language alone can reveal.

All human progress is the result of co-operation between man and man. But without language such co-operation is not in the broadest sense possible. By language alone do we express our intentions, our wishes and our hopes and our thoughts. Language, then, is an instrument by means of which man may communicate with man. It is an instrument which may be of the very simplest or of the most complex nature and structure and that structure will necessarily depend on the nature of the work which it has to do. Children and savages, in the nature of things, have only simple needs and simple thoughts and their language will be simple accordingly. They will not require many words and the words which they use will have simple and elementary meanings, seldom tending towards the abstract. A highly civilised adult, on the other hand, could not go through his day's work with the limited language of the child ; his needs are so much greater and so much more complex. He has, therefore, modified his instrument according to his needs. In each of these two cases, however, language is a mirror of the world of circumstance and of thought in which the child or the adult lives.

If the sole function of language is the communication of thought it follows that every development of thought will produce also a development of language. What we require of language is, therefore, no small thing. We require of it that it shall give expression to every human activity, high and low, good and bad ; that it shall render all human knowledge, human emotion, human faith and human ambitions ; for the creative impulse in man will never rest until it has found its appropriate expression in words or deeds. We expect of language, therefore, that it shall give expression to every possible development of human thought, and the history of the literature in any particular language is the most convincing proof possible that language rises to the occasion and satisfies those demands. It is, indeed, much easier to demonstrate this fact in relation to the demands which we make of language in connection with material things than in relation to the demands which we make of it in connection with abstract thought. So, for example, in modern times, the great advances which have been made in the manufacture of synthetic dyes have led to the introduction of a host of new colour names, some of which are still purely technical but many of which have entered the language of every day. These new names are, however, a reflection of material progress and could never have arisen without it. Moreover, many of these new names of colours are only in common use among certain sections of the community, among women in particular, and their use is a mark of the particular interests and sharper observation of that class.

Nor can the claim of language to be a mirror of civilisation be set aside by the claims of literature, for the former reveals phases of the development of thought which are not revealed by the latter. The information which is afforded by language is often information concerning earlier mental phenomena than those reflected in literature, and is often more precise in its detail. We find, indeed, in the thousand and one ways in which language seeks to give expression to new thoughts some which take us back far beyond the earliest literary monuments ; we observe, for example, the tendency everywhere to express conceptions of length by means of the names of the parts of the body : " foot," " ell " (= forearm), and the decimal system based upon the number of fingers. At other times we discover in the changes of meaning of words evidence of the progress of civilisation ; the

word " hammer," for example, originally meant simply
a piece of stone ; the name has remained because the
function has remained the same, even though the
material and form may have changed.

From the example of the word " hammer " just
adduced it becomes clear that words acquire the meaning
which is pressed into them by the speaker; an instrument
made of metal may be used as a hammer just as well as
an instrument made of stone.   So long as the context in
which the word is used makes it clear that the function
of the instrument is referred to, it does not matter what
the instrument is made of.   Most names of material
things have such a long and interesting history behind
them and the reader would, in many cases, be surprised
to learn how different the objects originally designated
by names were from those which are now so designated.
But it is not only the names of things which bear such
interesting witness to the development of civilisation.
Just as often it is the way of thinking about objects
which is revealed.   We still speak of the sun " rising "
and " setting," even though we all know that it is the
earth and not the sun which rises and sets.   There is
evidence here of earlier conceptions which have remained
in the language, though nowhere else.   In the same way
we say that the dew " falls."

Much more difficult to analyse and to present clearly
are those changes in language which do not consist
merely in the change of meaning of a word but rather in
the manner of conveying an idea, or in the first efforts
to give an expression to a new conception.   Thus, for
example, Old English has a present indicative *ic macie*
which corresponds to the Modern English " I make " or

"I am making." The Modern English form "I am making" is the expression of a more precise conception, and
is the result of a deliberate analysis by which a distinction is drawn between making in general and the action
of making at a given moment. It is the equivalent of
"I make now." Or one may take as an example the
development of the definite or indefinite article. Primitive man has no need for the expression "a house";
the expression is too indefinite. He thinks only of his
own house or his neighbour's house or his enemy's
house, always of some particular house; with houses in
the abstract he has nothing to do, for he has not attained
to that objective and detached point of view in which
houses may be regarded as something outside purely
personal interests or desires. Hence the development
of an indefinite article is late in all languages. In the
same way it will be found that in English all the words
with more abstract meanings are of late origin, for
they are the expression of a developed civilisation which
alone could produce them.

But what we especially wish to emphasise here is
that language is a mirror of civilisation only because it
is the living instrument of human thought. So long as
man thinks and speaks, his language will adapt itself to
the quality of his thought and will be modified by it.
Material, mental and moral progress must find expression in speech, either by introducing new elements
of meaning into words or by modifications of that synthesis by which words are combined in sentences. We
must bear in mind, too, that we most of us learn the
names of things before we are fully aware of the things
themselves or of their exact nature, and that there is

therefore in each one of us a tendency either to extend or to restrict the original meaning of any particular word; we also learn the meaning of words under particular circumstances, so that very often a word has an emotional content to one person which it does not possess for another. We may imagine, for example, that the word "war" will have a very different meaning to the child of occupied Belgium and to the child of London. And though this may be an extreme case, it is nevertheless true that to some extent all words have slightly different meanings to different individuals according to the circumstances under which they were acquired and according to the associations, emotional and other, which have developed round them.

Language is, therefore, in a peculiar and intimate sense a history not only of material progress, but also of the mental, moral and emotional development of the people which speaks it. It is all the more surprising, on that account, that it is not more commonly studied. The reason for the neglect of the study of language, and more particularly of our native tongue, is to be found perhaps in the somewhat unattractive way in which the material is often presented. There is a tendency to regard language too much as a mere agglomeration of sounds or grammatical forms ; to regard it as a dead thing to be dissected rather than as a living thing to be described and interpreted. The study of sounds and grammatical forms, upon which the science of language is largely based, has been so extraordinarily fruitful in results that it has tended to obscure the fact that language is something more than sounds and inflections, and that behind these there are human creative forces at work. In this little book an attempt will be made to bear in mind these creative forces, and, whilst presenting the main facts of the development of English, to interpret them, or to suggest an interpretation, in the light of these forces.

Absorption in the classification of material has, too often, led to the easy blunder that ascertained facts are themselves causes, whereas, in fact, they may equally well be effects. Sound changes, changes in declensions and conjugations, etc., are only the external, apprehensible manifestations of inner forces which cannot be interpreted in terms of linguistic science at all. These inner forces are the human mind and the human heart, the thoughts and emotions of which find outward expression in words and sounds. No history of language can be complete, therefore, which does not take into account the relations which must necessarily exist between thought and emotions on the one hand, and their outward manifestation—language—on the other hand. This proposition is so evident that it needs no labouring. The language of the Fiji islander differs from that of the Londoner by just as much, neither more nor less, as the mental, moral, physical and emotional requirements of the two differ.

But if the proposition is a truism, its consequences in the interpretation of the history of language must be evident too. For if thought alone gives birth to language, then the history of language must be one chapter of the history of thought ; and unless we are prepared to admit that each separate sound in a word has an independent meaning attached to it, we must look to the higher units of language, to the word and to the sentence, for the reflection of the underlying thought. As a matter of fact, however, a thought is only rarely expressed in a single word, unless it be in an exclamation or a command. In language as it really exists as a means of communication of thought, words do not exist independently. We cannot stop a man in the street and say to him, " house " or " sixpence." If we did, he would with good reason enquire " What about it ? " In other words, he would demand a completed thought or a completed sentence. The consequence, therefore, of regarding the history of language as the history of one of the manifestations of thought is that we must in the first place seek to interpret the changes of sentence structure in language, *i.e.* the significance of stylistic and syntactical change. And just as it is the completed thought, or the completed sentence, which is the real unit of language, so also it is the sentence that determines which of the many possible senses of a word is to be understood in any particular context. The word " train " may have many meanings, but it is the context alone that determines which of these many meanings is intended in any particular sentence. It follows, therefore, that from our point of view, the development of meaning in words must be traced immediately after the development of syntax.

Changes of syntax, however, frequently react on the inflectional system of a language. One habit of thought may require a word order which depends for clearness on the presence of an elaborate system of inflections in nouns, adjectives, verbs, etc., whereas another habit of thought may require a different order of words and may, as has actually happened in English, render such an inflectional system unnecessary. The study of the development of words should therefore be followed by a study of the development of inflections.

In addition to changes in syntax, word-meaning and inflections there remain the changes which sounds undergo in language. These changes would seem, at first sight, to be independent of the changes we have so far noticed, in so far as they are not accompanied by, nor, so far as one can see, caused by, any change of meaning. These changes we shall consider in the last chapter, and shall attempt an explanation of the causes which are active in producing them. It will appear there that they too may be regarded as the last stage in a train of causation, and not, as is so commonly supposed, as the first.

CHAPTER I

THE BEGINNINGS

§ 1. ENGLISH is one of the West Germanic languages, like German, Dutch, Flemish and Frisian. There are two other groups of Germanic languages: the North Germanic, including Norwegian, Swedish, Danish and Icelandic, and the East Germanic, which includes Gothic and Burgundian. This threefold division is based on certain agreements, usually of sounds or grammatical forms, between the several members of each group. In the same way, by a careful comparison of the three main groups, it has been possible to postulate a common parent, Primitive-Germanic, for the three. Primitive-Germanic or Germanic is, in its turn, but one of several families of languages which are all descended from a common parent, Indo-Germanic or Aryan. The families of languages which together with Germanic constitute the Indo-Germanic group are: 1. Indo-Iranian, sometimes called Aryan, comprising Sanskrit, Persian and Zend. 2. Armenian. 3. Albanian. 4. Celtic, including (a) Gaulish, (b) Welsh and Cornish, (c) Gaelic. 5. Balto-Slavonic, including (a) the Baltic division—Old Prussian, Lettic, Lithuanian, (b) the Slavonic group—Russian, Polish, Bulgarian, Czech. 6. Italic, including Latin, from which the Romance languages, French, Spanish, Italian, Portuguese and Roumanian are descended. 7. Hellenic. It is not to be supposed when we speak of a Primitive-Germanic or Indo-Germanic language as being the parent of other languages that we have any actual records of them. They are really only hypothetical languages which have been built up and reconstructed by the help of a comparison of the materials which survive in the various languages which are descended from them.

§ 2. Where the original Indo-Germanic language was spoken we do not know with any degree of certainty, but the most widely held view at the present day is that it was somewhere in northern or central Europe, and not, as was for so long supposed, somewhere in the East. But whatever the original home of the Indo-Germanic or Aryan people or peoples, it is clear that sections of it migrated in all directions over Europe and Asia. Each of these bodies of emigrators took with it some of the common stock of the original language, and modified and developed it to suit its particular needs. It is natural, therefore, that since the linguistic foundation of each group of languages was the same, there should be some affinities between all the various groups, and it has been the work of comparative philology to discover and classify these affinities. There is no single group of the Indo-Germanic languages which has not some affinity with every other group. In some cases these affinities are more numerous than in others, but they exist in all. It is therefore inexact to represent the relationship of the various families of languages by means of a genealogical tree, because such a tree misleadingly implies that each of the languages or language groups is self-contained and completely excludes all the others, whereas in fact this never occurs. It is better, therefore, to think of the migrations as occurring in an ever widening circle from a fixed centre. As time goes on any particular point on the circumference becomes more and more remote from an opposite point, but it nevertheless always maintains some contact with it through the intervening areas.

§ 3. The parent Germanic language already shows certain well-defined characteristics of its own which differentiate it from the other groups of the Indo-Germanic family. The most marked of these character-istics, and at the same time one which is destined to play a very large rôle in the development of each of the Germanic languages, is the treatment of the accent or stress in words. In Indo-Germanic the accent was what is called " free." That is to say, sometimes it lay on one syllable of a word, and sometimes it lay on another. In Germanic, however, the accent becomes fixed on a certain syllable—the first, in uncompounded words—and always remained there. The consequences of this fixing of the stress are many, and some of them will be dealt with in a later chapter. For the present it may suffice to point out that since the first syllable is the more strongly stressed, the other syllables, being less strongly stressed, are apt to be slurred over in speech, and to lose in clearness of enunciation, with the consequence that sounds in such syllables change more freely and more rapidly than sounds in stressed syllables.

We do not know what is the cause of any particular principle of accentuation. All that we can be quite sure about is that there is a deep-seated natural impulse in man to perform all acts constantly repeated to a certain rhythm, and that this rhythm is determined partly by our physiological and partly by our psychological nature. It is very easy to convince ourselves of the psychological necessity for rhythm. If we attempt to read ten lines of prose in an absolutely even tone, without any difference in stress between syllables, and without any variation either in pitch of the voice or in tempo, it will be found that what we read is quite unintelligible. In fact, accent is the very soul of speech : without it human speech becomes lifeless and meaningless. It has been justly remarked that we can always tell by the tones of speech whether the speakers are a part of a funeral gathering or of a wedding party ; whether they are grave or gay. In exactly the same way various rhythms in poetry correspond to various moods. It would be impossible to write a light-hearted lyric in the measure of a solemn elegy. Accent, then, whether it be in the form of stress, which consists in a stronger breathing and consequent louder sounds, or whether it be in the form of pitch, which consists in a modification of tone, would seem to correspond to something inherent in man's nature. By means of accent in one or other of its forms we are able to impart to our speech something more than a mere meaning, something, indeed, of our feelings and emotions. It seems not unlikely, therefore, that the normal rhythm, or, what amounts to the same thing, the normal principle of accentuation in a given language corresponds to an average mental or emotional state in those who speak that language. Such a supposition accords very well, moreover, with our everyday experience; for the slow, even rhythm, and the even-toned speech of the English faithfully reflects a temperament which suppresses the emotions, and whose most marked characteristic is its reserve. On the other hand, the quickly changing tones of French or Italian are in like degree a reflection of a temperament which is more spontaneous in expression. Or we might make a similar contrast between the tones of children and adults. In the case of tone the relationship between speech and temperament is, it is true, much more clear than is the case with stress. But in those languages whose accent is mainly stress, the rhythm in all probability corresponds to temperament, though it is not so easy to demonstrate the fact.

However this may be, the parent Germanic language from which English is descended had a fixed stress, a peculiarity which it shares with the Celtic and Italic groups of languages as against all the others, which had free accent. A second characteristic of Germanic, which is already noticeable at this early stage of development, is that it has begun to use the analytical method of expression instead of the synthetical or inflectional method of the parent language. The synthetic system may be exemplified by Latin and Greek, in which the relation of one word to another in the sentence, as, for example, the relation of verb and subject or verb and object, was indicated by means of inflections. It is characteristic of a language which has a highly inflected structure that it at the same time has a free word order. In Latin, for example, one may write: *Romulus condidit Romam*, or *Romam condidit Romulus*, or *Condidit Romam Romulus*, or *Romulus Romam condidit*. The order in which one writes these three words is not of primary importance, for the inflections clearly show that *Romulus* is the subject of the verb *condidit* and that *Romam* is the object. In Modern English, on the other hand, the word order is, within certain limits, fixed. We can only say : *Romulus founded Rome.*

§ 4. In Primitive-Germanic, word order is beginning to be fixed. But parallel with this gradual fixing of the word order there is another development which is of very special significance for the development of English. This further development is the above-mentioned tendency to analytical expression. By the analytical method of expression the relation between words in a sentence is indicated by prepositions and auxiliary words instead of by inflections. Thus, instead of *þurh ieldra manna segene* we say in Modern English *by the stories* of *older men,* and the relation between the word *stories* and the word *men* is indicated by the word *of* instead of by the inflection of the genitive plural *-a.* We do not know whether the fixing of the word order was the effect of the development of the analytical method or whether it was the cause. Current theory holds that it was an effect. But if we turn back to the above example from Latin, it may appear that neither of these two phenomena is a cause and neither an effect of the other, but that both are the effects, either separately or conjointly, of the ordinary processes of thought and of the ordinary impulse to give expression to thought. The two sentences : *Romulus Romam condidit* and *Romam Romulus condidit*, though both equally clear, yet do not mean exactly the same thing. In so far as it is possible to give a precise translation, the first means : *Romulus* *founded Rome,* and the second means : *Rome was founded by Romulus.* In the first *Romulus* is more strongly stressed than *Rome,* and in the second *Rome* is more strongly stressed than *Romulus.* It appears, therefore, that even where there exists a free word order there is nevertheless a possibility of obtaining finer shades of meaning by the adoption of certain conventions of word order, and such conventions constitute the first stage in the progress to a fixed word order in which the whole of the meaning depends upon the observance of such conventions.

Just as a fixed word order may conceivably be conducive to greater clearness, or to greater expressiveness, so also may the analytical method of expression be conducive to these ends. For though a system of inflections may indicate in any particular sentence that a man is *in, at, from, by, on,* going *into, of,* etc., a house, yet there is a limit in practice to the number of inflections which can at a given time indicate all the possible relations of, say, one noun to another. The analytical method of expression indicates this relationship with greater precision, for even the eight cases of Sanskrit are not sufficient to indicate without ambiguity the exact relationship which is desired. Such an analytical syntax, therefore, is the effect of a striving to render as accurately as possible the thought which is present in the mind. There may be many other ways in which language adapts itself to thought, but it is sufficient if we notice these two, as being especially significant in the subsequent development of the English language.

§ 5. It is again characteristic of Primitive-Germanic, in comparison with Indo-Germanic, that the original inflectional system has already to a great extent broken down, more particularly in the verb. It has commonly been supposed that this break-up of the old inflectional system was the cause of the development of the analytical method of expression and of the fixing of the word order. It has been said that the " decay " of inflections rendered some alternative system imperative. But we have seen that both of these processes, *i.e.* the development of analytic syntax, and the loss of inflections, can be adequately explained by the very nature of language, and it need only be added in contradiction of this view that as late as Old English the analytic construction of cases by means of prepositions was already in operation long before the inflections had themselves disappeared. It would seem more probable, then, that the decay of inflections is due to the growth of the analytic method of expression, which rendered the inflections superfluous.

§ 6. If one compares Primitive-Germanic with Indo-Germanic, what strikes one perhaps most forcibly is the great simplification which has occurred in the grammatical forms. To some extent this is due to a cause already mentioned, to the fixing of the stress on the initial syllable. The change can be best understood by a parallel development in Modern English, when we add to the word " cadence " the prefix " de-." The immediate consequence of the shifting of the stress from the syllable *ca-* to the syllable *de-* is that the vowel of the former is weakened. In much the same way the relatively weak-stressed syllables of Primitive-Germanic were weakened and lost, especially in final inflectional syllables.

But this great change in the form of words need not

necessarily be due to this cause alone. There are indeed certain characteristics of the change which would seem to point to a different cause. Thus, for example, whole categories of words have disappeared, as, for example, whole tenses of the verb, three or four cases of the noun, and much more besides. Such a loss can scarcely be attributed to the effects of stress, which are limited in operation to the single word. Rather these fundamental changes are due to the conditions of life under which the Primitive-Germanic people lived and had their being. To take only one instance : the simplification of the inflectional system has already gone far in Primitive-Germanic, but everything which has been lost has by no means been replaced. Consequently Primitive-Germanic syntax has not the means of expressing clearly a complex thought; it has not developed the means of adequately expressing the finer shades of coordination and subordination in sentences. In this respect it differs strongly from Latin and Greek, and the surmise seems justified that the coarseness of the instrument is mainly due to the fact that it has nothing but coarse work to do. We can scarcely expect even the most cultured of the migrating Teutons to have had the thoughts of a Cicero, and if he had not the thoughts he cannot have had the language either.

An examination of the vocabulary of Primitive-Germanic points to the same conclusion. The vocabulary is that of a people which has not very varied needs, nor yet any great refinement or subtlety of thought. This, too, is the inevitable consequence of a peculiar mode of existence, and it accords with this view that so many original words were lost and not replaced until much later.

CHAPTER II

SYNTAX

§ 7. BEDE tells us that three Germanic tribes settled in Britain, the Angles, the Saxons and the Jutes, and that the earliest settlement was in 449. The *Anglo-Saxon Chronicle* repeats this statement. Nevertheless there is good reason for supposing that there were settlements earlier than this date. But however this may be, it is of interest to note that from the beginning of the settlement the invaders were not of one tribe, and an examination of the Old English texts reveals the fact that the language of the invaders was not uniform. We know, too, that these three different tribes had in their continental homes different political institutions. We may therefore presume that already in the Old English period (449 ?–1050) there existed in English the beginnings of the development of dialects. The Jutes settled in Kent, the Isle of Wight and the shores of Hampshire ; the Saxons settled on the banks of the Thames and occupied the territory south of that river, with the exception of the parts occupied by the Jutes ; the Angles occupied the rest of the country. Of these tribes it was the Angles who gave their name to the language of the whole country, for the name always found in English

19

texts is *Englisc,* and only in Latin sources do we find the names *saxonicus* or *lingua saxonum.*

§ 8. If we turn now to a brief examination of the syntax of the Old English period we shall find that it is in many respects clumsy and lacking in precision. Nor is this in any way surprising. A developed synt: *x* necessarily presupposes either a developed literature or a developed art of discussion and conversation. We have no evidence of the existence of the latter in the daily life of our Germanic ancestors, and, in the absence of evidence to the contrary, we may assume that the subjects of their conversation would pertain to a simple round of daily duties, whether in peace or in war. Their literature deals with accounts of heroic deeds in battle ; there is nothing of so complex a nature that it cannot be expressed in the simplest of sentences, though there is, it is true, within the Old English period a marked development of syntax, which corresponds to an advancing civilisation and a widening outlook on life.

§ 9. It is not possible to realise the character of the development of the English language without first taking a glimpse, however brief, at a specimen of the language as it was written at the earliest period. We shall first, therefore, before attempting any account of the development of the language, submit a piece of Old English prose and a piece of Old English verse, and point out some of the special features of the older language. Our first piece is an extract from King Alfred's Preface to his translation of Gregory's *Pastoral Care.* It begins :

Ælfred kyning hateð gretan Wærferð biscep his wordum luflice ond freondlice ; ond ðe cyðan hate ðæt me com swiðe oft on gemynd, hwelce wiotan iu wæron giond

Angelcynn, ægðer ge godcundra ge woruldcundra; ond hu
gesæliglica tida ða wæron giond Angelcynn; ond hu ða
cyningas ðe ðone onwald hæfdon ðæs folces on ðam dagum
Gode ond his ærendwrecum hersumedon; ond hu hie
ægðer ge hiora sibbe ge hiora siodo ge hiora onweald in-
nanbordes gehioldon, ond eac ut hiora eðel germydon.

Literally translated the passage runs :

Alfred (the) king bids greet Wærferð (the) bishop with his
words lovingly and with friendship ; and I bid to be made
known to thee that it has very often come into my mind
what wise men formerly were throughout England, both
of sacred and of secular (orders) ; and how happy times
(there) were then throughout England ; and how the kings
who the power had over the people obeyed God and his
messengers ; and how they preserved peace, morality and
order at home and also extended their territory abroad.

We next take a short extract from Beowulf :

Þa wæs on healle   heardecg togen,
Then was in the hall the hard-edged (sword) seized
sweord ofer setlum,   sidrand manig
the sword over the benches, many a broad shield
hafen handa fæst :   helm ne gemunde,
raised firmly in the hand :   helmet did not remember
byrnan side,   þa hine se broga angeat.
the wide burnie, when him the monster seized.
Heo wæs on ofste,   wolde ut þanon
she was in a hurry, (she) wished (to go) away from there
feore beorgan,   þa heo onfunden wæs ;
to save her life, when she was discovered ;
hraðe heo æðelinga   anne hæfde
quickly she of the warriors one had
fæste befongen,   þa heo to fenne gang ;
securely seized, when she to the fen went ;
se wæs Hroþgare   hæleþa leofost
he was to Hroþgar of the heroes the dearest
on gesiðes had   be sæm tweonum,
in his following between the seas,

rice randwiga,   þone ðe heo on ræste abreat,
a glorious warrior, whom she destroyed in his rest,
blædfæstne beorn.
a glorious warrior.

Several marked differences between Old English and Middle or Modern English appear in these passages. Beginning with the prose passage, we notice that the verb *hateð* has the inflection *-eð* and the infinitive the ending *-an* instead of the modern *to*. The next point is that the inflection *-um* of *wordum* is used instead of the modern preposition *with*. The second clause introduces suddenly a new grammatical subject, *I*, understood, for the earlier subject *Ælfred*. The change is indicated by the verbal form *hate*, which is first person and not third, like *hateð*. Notice also the omission of the pronoun *I*. In the next sentence the subject to the verb *com* is the clause beginning *hwelce wiotan*. Modern English uses a preparatory subject *it*, which is not found here. Observe also the Old English construction *com me on gemynd* = "came to me in the mind." In the sentence beginning "*ond hu ða cyningas . . .*" the verb *hersumedon* goes to the end of the sentence, because the whole clause is dependent on *I remembered*. Observe, further, how in the relative clause, *ðe ðone onwald*, etc., the verb *hæfdon* also follows its object and separates *onwald* from *ðæs folces*. In the two final clauses likewise, as being dependent, the verb comes at the end. It may also be noticed how clause is heaped upon clause with the help of the sole conjunction *ond*.

The verse extract illustrates one or two points which are not to be seen quite so clearly in the prose extract. The first of these is the great freedom of the word order.

This is perhaps best seen in the last two lines, where *blædfæstne beorn* is to be constructed with *þone þe* in the preceding line, to which it stands in apposition; and in the separation by a whole line of *hæleþa leofost* and *rice randwiga*. Noteworthy also from the point of view of syntax is the absence either of a definite or indefinite article in the whole passage.

Both extracts afford numerous examples of grammatical inflections of which there is not the least trace in the modern language: *e.g.* wæro*n*, gretan, hate, hwelc*e*, godcund*ra*, hand*a*, gesæliglic*a*, tid*a*, ð*am* da*gum*, God*e*, etc., etc. Some of these have no corresponding inflections in Modern English, as: godcund*ra*, hwelc*e*; others are represented by prepositions, as: *handa* = " in the hand," *æþelinga* = " of the æthelings." Observe also, in line 5, the omission of the verb of motion after the auxiliary *wolde*, a common construction in Old English, which has its parallel in Modern English " Let me (come) in."

§ 10. Old English syntax is visibly in a state of transition. The simple and undisciplined expression of thought which we find in the earlier prose monuments is that of ordinary everyday speech in which ideas are expressed just as they come to mind, and without any clear arrangement or perspective. Indeed one of the greatest difficulties of the study of Old English to the beginner is to discover the real drift and purpose of a passage of prose. The conjunctions do not make sufficiently clear what is principal, what is subordinate and what is coordinate; nor do they show the relative significance of the various clauses of a sentence. The reason for this is sufficiently clear. The oldest literature deals almost exclusively with narrative or the description of concrete objects ; it seldom goes beyond a relation of time or place. The finer and more complex relations which are introduced by the development of abstract thought could not be clearly expressed, because there was no need for them. For these a considerable mental development and discipline were necessary. A passage of Old English prose resembles very much in its incoherence, its indiscriminate stringing together of sentences and clauses, its abrupt changes of point of view and its sudden change of grammatical subject, the essays of a schoolboy. It is discursive, disordered and unclear, especially in its use of pronouns. All these faults are the faults of an undisciplined mind, of a mind which throws off one thought after another without any heed. of unity or coherence. Contact with foreign models did something to improve the crude Old English syntax, but the improvement, was a slow process, and it was not until the end of the Middle English period that there began to appear any real clarity in the writing of English prose. Perhaps the most marked feature of Old English syntax is the absence of signs of any kind of abstract thought. It is significant in this respect that there was in the older language no indefinite article, and that even the definite article still preserved much of its original demonstrative function. It was possible to say *the house,* or *one house,* but the purely abstract conception *a house,* meaning *any house whatever,* was not possible, for the need of it had never been felt.

§ 11. The syntax of Old English is visibly passing from the synthetic to the analytic structure. The grammatical relations of the noun are still for the most part

expressed synthetically ; the inflections of case are still
largely preserved even though the cases have been
reduced to four, with occasional traces of a vocative
and an instrumental. But the syntax of the verb is
distinctly analytic. The tendency to analysis, already
inherent in Primitive-Germanic, is strengthened, and we
find in Old English that the various compound tenses
of the verb are all expressed analytically by the help
of such auxiliaries as *habban*, " to have " ; *wesan*, " to
be " ; and *weorðan*, " to become." The passive is
similarly formed. Even in the declension of the noun
there are visible the beginnings of analytic syntax ;
already many relations are expressed by means of prepositions, as, for example, *ic wolde æt his fotum licgan*,
"I wished to lie at his feet" ; *ic beo mid eow eallum dagum*,
" I am with you always." Among the personal pronouns the accusative has almost disappeared in the
first and second persons singular and plural, *mec* and
þec give way to the dative forms *mē* and *þē, ūsic* and
ēowic to *ūs* and *ēow*. But as there still remains a
considerable number of inflections, the word order in
the sentence is still free as compared with Modern
English. Thus, for example, the number of cases in
which the subject follows the verb is considerable in
Beowulf, but it is very small in any average work of
more recent times. Certain conventions of Germanic
word order still remain, as, for example, that the verb
in dependent sentences goes to the end, as in Modern
German ; that the infinitive often holds the same
position. There are also still a considerable number of
verbs which govern a genitive or a dative case, and
which in Modern English must be constructed with a

preposition. Thus, for example, *he geweold ðæs folces,* " he ruled *over* the people."

But it is not so much in the syntax of the simple sentence that Old English differs from Modern English as in the syntax of the compound and complex sentence. Here we are dealing with more advanced and complex thoughts and reasoning processes, and it would appear that the earliest writers were not quite at home in such regions. There is in their writings a scarcity of those guiding words such as conjunctions, adverbs and relatives, which are so necessary to analytic syntax. The conjunctions *and* and *ðæt,* for example, have very many functions in Old English, and it is not always clear which of these functions may be implied in a particular case. At other times, again, it is not clear whether a conjunction has a coordinating or a subordinating function ; whether it is causal or concessive, and so on. It is here, indeed, that Old English syntax most clearly reflects the mind behind it and the lack of that clear thinking which comes only after long exercise of the faculties of the mind.

§ 12. The main development within the Old English period in the province of syntax is towards a fixing of word order and the development of the syntax of the compound and complex sentences. This development was aided, no doubt, to a considerable extent by the example of Latin prose and by the translations of Alfred. We can only speak with any certainty, however, of the literary language of the West Saxon court, for we have no materials to judge either of the other dialects, or of the spoken language.

§ 13. Certain peculiarities of Old English syntax which

are inherent in the synthetic system have been preserved in Modern English. We may note some of the more important of these whilst emphasising the fact that the regular lines of development throughout the history of the language show a constant tendency to modify existing syntax by analysis rather than by synthesis. In the matter of case in nouns we notice in the first place the survival of the Old English adverbial genitive in *He went his way*. This genitive was in common use in Old English either with purely adverbial function or in a complement. It survives also in such adverbial forms as " always," O.E. *ealles weges*. Sometimes the adverb so formed has become a preposition or a conjunctive adverb, as in " whilst," O.E. *hwiles*, " amongst," " amidst," etc., though all three of these have developed a final -*t*. In the same way the old adverbial dative ending in -*um* survives in " seldom " and the archaic " whilome." An old dative is also found in the construction with the reflexive pronoun " self," as in " himself," " themselves," as distinct from the construction with the genitive in " myself," " thyself," " ourselves," " yourselves." " Herself " might be either genitive or dative.

§ 14. There are also certain survivals of Old English syntax in the inflections of number in nouns. Modern English uses the construction " a five pound note," " a three foot rule," " a five mile walk," etc. It is sometimes said that these singular forms of the substantive are formed on the analogy of certain Old English neuters which were uninflected in the nominative and accusative plural. This assumption is quite unnecessary and at the same time improbable. There is a much simpler psychological explanation, namely, that in such expressions the five pounds or miles or the three feet are thought of as a single amount or quantity, or that they are regarded as a kind of collective. There is, however, another view of the origin of this construction. In Old English as in Indo-Germanic the numerals were regarded as substantives, just as in Modern English " a dozen," " a pair," and the noun dependent on a numeral was placed in the genitive plural, which always ended in -a. This -a would be lost in Middle English, leaving no trace. But that in itself would perhaps not have been sufficient cause for withstanding the normal tendency to inflect such nouns as plurals, if there did not exist some motive for keeping them in the singular. It should also be noticed that such numerals as " dozen," " score," " hundred," " thousand," " million," etc., still require the use of the indefinite article, and are therefore syntactically parallel with any other substantive.

§ 15. The most important syntactic innovation of Old English was the formation analytically of future and conditional tenses and all other compound tenses ; the future by means of the auxiliaries *sceall,* " shall," and *wille,* " will," and the conditional by *sceolde,* " should," and *wolde,* " would." Side by side with these analytic futures and conditionals Old English used, however, the present indicative for the future and the imperfect subjunctive for the conditional. This use of the present for the future is still quite common, especially in the colloquial language, in Modern English, as, for example, in the sentence : " he arrives to-morrow " for " he will arrive to-morrow." In the compound tenses Old English used the auxiliaries *habban,* " to have," and *wesan,* " to be." Intransitives were conjugated with *wesan* and transitives with *habban*. By degrees, however, in Middle English, *haven* becomes more and more common as the auxiliary to be used in such cases. The old practice of forming compound tenses with *wesan* still survives, however, in Modern English, especially in the conjugation of verbs of motion. For example : " He is gone," " they are come." But here it is to be noted that, as is usual where two constructions exist side by side, there is a tendency to differentiate their functions and meanings. Hence in Modern English, where both constructions survive, there is a difference in meaning. " He is come " and " he has come " do not mean quite the same thing. Another isolated survival of an O.E. construction is to be found in the occasional omission in Modern English of a verb of motion after an auxiliary, as in the sentence : *let me in* for " let me (come) in," or *he is off* for " he is (gone) off."

§ 16. One of the most marked features of the conjugation of the verb in Modern English is the development of the so-called continuous tenses : " I am, was, shall be writing." The beginnings of this analytical tense are already to be found in the older language. Thus, for example, we find in O.E. *hie wæron blissiende*, " they were rejoicing." This construction doubtless originated in the use of the present participle as an adjective, just as we can say " a running stream." Hence such an expression as *hie wæron blissiende* is intermediate between *hie blissedon*, " they rejoiced," and *hie wæron bliðe*, " they were happy." It has the additional advantage, however, of indicating that the state of rejoicing is not yet at an end.

§ 17. We turn finally to a brief account of word order in Old English. This order, as we have already seen, was still to a large extent free ; there was as yet no sign of the rigorous law of Modern English that words which are to be taken together in sense must not be separated by words which are not logically connected with them. In Modern English all qualifying words are, as a general rule, placed before, and as near as possible to, the words which they qualify. In Old English, on the contrary, qualifying words very often follow the words which they qualify, and are even separated from them by other words. Such a word order as we find in Modern English "water enough" or "Captains Courageous" is quite common in Old English : *his suna twegen,* "his two sons" ; *Ælfred cyning,* "king Alfred." Such sentences as : *ða se sealmsang gefylled wæs ðæs uhtlican lofsanges,* literally, "when the psalm completed was of the morning song of praise," would be impossible in Modern English. Such a separation of a noun in the genitive case from its governing noun is, however, quite common in the older language. Sometimes we even find that when a verb has two subjects one of them precedes and one follows the verb, as in the following sentence : *Cynewulf benam Sigebryht his rices and Westseaxna wiotan,* "Cynewulf and the Westsaxon councillors deprived Sigebryht of his kingdom." Such a word order is, of course, only possible so long as there are sufficient inflections to make clear the relations of the various parts of the sentence.

The post-position of qualifying words still remains in Modern English, as in Old English, in exclamations and in the nominative of address : "Father dear," "brother mine," etc. In other cases in the modern language its

origin is different, as, for example, in " courts-martial,"
where the word order is French, or in " the novel proper,"
where the post-position by the very fact of its being
unusual lends emphasis to the adjective. Again, Old
English has very often inversion of subject and verb,
especially where the sentence begins with an adverb,
as, for example, in the sentence : *Đa feng he to rice,*
" then he succeeded to the kingdom." In Modern
English this inversion is still necessary in a few cases, as,
for example, where the sentence begins with " scarcely,"
" hardly," " never," " nor," and a few more words.

§ 18. On the whole, Old English syntax corresponds
to the needs of those who wrote the Old English language.
It enables simple thoughts to be expressed with sufficient
clearness, but it is not an adequate instrument for the
expression of the finer shades of meaning or of more
complex thoughts.   Thus, to take only a single example,
the conjunction *and* has more than a dozen different
functions, or, as it would perhaps be more accurate to
say, it corresponds to what would be a dozen different
functions in the modern language.   Sentences and clauses
are strung together by the means of this conjunction
more than by any other, in much the same way as in
the first attempts at essay-writing by a modern schoolboy.   It is not to be supposed, however, that this is
true of the whole of the Old English period.   The translations of Alfred introduced a new world of thought,
much of it abstract thought, and thus emphasised the
need for some development, so that, as we approach the
Middle English period, there are distinct signs of greater
attention to sentence structure and to the coordination
and subordination of sentences.

§ 19. For the sake of comparison with the forms and structure of Old English it may be well to present here two specimens of Middle English prose, one early and one late. The first passage is taken from the later years of the *Anglo-Saxon Chronicle*, and represents the language of the end of the twelfth century; the second passage is derived from the writings of Sir John Mandeville, and represents the language of the middle of the fourteenth century.

Nu we willen sægen sum del hwat belamp (happened) on Stephnes kinges time. On his time þe Judeus of Noruuic bohton (bought) an Christen cild beforen Estren and pineden (tormented) him alle þe ilce (same) pining (torment) þat ure Drihten (Lord) was pined. And on long fridæi him on rode (cross) hengen for ure Drihtines luue, and sythen byrieden (buried) him. Wenden þat it sculde ben forholen (concealed), oc (but) ure Dryhtin atywede (showed) þat he was hali martyr; and þo munekes him namen (took), and bebyrieden him heglice (solemnly) in þe minstre, and he maket (made) þurh ure Drihtin wunderlice and manifældlice miracles, and hatte (is called) he Sanct Willelm.

And ʒow schulle understonde that Machamete was born in Arabye, that was first a pore knave that kepte cameles, that wenten with marchantes for marchandise; and so bifelle that he wente with the marchandes in to Egipt: and thei weren thanne cristene in tho partyes. And at the desertes of Arabye, he wente into a chapelle, where a eremite duelte, and whan he entred into the chapelle that was but a litylle and a low thing and had but a lityl dore and a low, than the entree began to wexe so gret and so large and so high, as though it had been of a gret mynstre, or the ʒate of a paleys. And this was the firste myracle, the Sarazins seyn, that Machomete dide in his ʒouthe.

In the first of these passages the word order is already approaching the word order of Modern English; there is little left of the freedom of Old English, and the order

—Subject, verb, object—is almost established. But there are still some clumsy constructions, such as, *pineden him þe ilce pining þat ure Drihten was pined,* and there is still the same heaping up of clauses connected by *and.* But the word order is, except for the three cases, *him on rode hengen* and *munekes him namen* and *hatte he,* the same as in Modern English. So also the definite article is in use and also the indefinite article, and there is no case of the omission of the subject of the verb such as we saw in Old English. There still remain, however, several of the older inflections, such as will*en*, sæg*en*, Stephn*es* king*es*, boht*on*, etc.

The second passage has no departure from the normal word order of Modern English, its inflectional endings are still fewer in comparison with the earlier passage, and its only link with Old English prose is in the unvarying use of the conjunction *and.*

§ 20. One of the most marked features of the transition from Old English to Middle English syntax is the gradual fixing of the word order. Two general principles may be observed at work. In the first place, there is a tendency to place all modifying words as near as possible to the words which they modify. This is the natural result of the tendency to analysis. If the Old English *dæges* is to become, as the result of the tendencies which we have noted in the last chapter, " of the day," it follows that the preposition " of " must be placed immediately in connection with the word " day," otherwise there is nothing to indicate the word with which it is to be constructed. Similarly, if the Old English *he him spræc to* becomes " he spoke to him," the word " him " is taken out of its former position and placed after " to " in order clearly to show that "to" governs "him." The practical outcome of all this was that the so-called pre-position, in which a modifier precedes the word which it modifies, was generally adopted. The fixing of the word order was the direct outcome of the general analytic tendencies of English syntax ; it was the consequence of the developed use of prepositions instead of inflections. It led, in its turn, to the fixing of the three most important components of every sentence in the order : Subject, verb, object or complement.

§ 21. The second marked feature of Middle English syntax is the tendency to indicate any syntactical concord once only. We see here the beginning of the tendency to reduce inflections to a minimum, and to indicate syntactical concords by word order and context, a tendency which has been developed further in English than in any other of the Indo-Germanic languages. If we look at the Old English sentence : *He hæfde, ða he ðone cyningc sohte, tamra deora unbebohtra syx hund,* and compare it with the Modern English equivalent : " He had, when he visited the king, six hundred unsold animals," we shall see that the accusative *ðone* has disappeared and that the accusative is indicated by the position of " king " after the verb. In the same way the genitive plural *deora* has become a plural " animals," but the inflections of the adjectives *tamra* and *unbebohtra* are lost because their position before " animals " sufficiently indicates both their number and their case. The inflections have become superfluous and were therefore dropped. It is exactly the same in other cases; everywhere we find in Middle English the tendency to replace inflections by word order and to reduce them to a minimum.

The article is reduced to a single form for all cases and both numbers, since the position in the sentence of the accompanying noun shows its case, and the plural inflection of the noun shows ́its number. The same is true of the indefinite article, and of adjectives. Inflections of person in verbs also disappear, except in the third person singular of the present indicative, for here also the pronoun or the position of the noun shows the person of the verb. Towards the end of the period it may be said that the only surviving inflections of the complex system of Old English are the third singular indicative present, "loves," the inflection of the plural and the possessive of nouns and a few survivals of very common words such as the pronominal forms "he," "him," "they," "them," "their," etc., and a few verbal forms such as "is," "was," "were." Every other concord formerly expressed by means of inflections has given way to the analytical method of expression.

§ 22. One of the consequences of the fixing of the word order was that each word in the sentence had its particular syntactic function according to its exact position, and that the survivals of free word order which were to be found in Old English disappeared in Middle English. For example, the finite verb is no longer placed at the end of a subordinate clause ; the infinitive or participle follows its auxiliary instead of being placed at the end of the sentence ; inversion of subject and verb becomes more and more rare, and such a word order as that which is to be found in the already quoted sentence : *Cynewulf benam Sigebryht his rices and Westseaxna wiotan*, becomes impossible under all ordinary conditions. Although, strictly speaking, it might appear that the loss of inflections of which we have been speaking belongs rather to the province of accidence than to that of syntax, yet it has been referred to here because it is the result of a purely syntactic change in the structure of the language. It is an effect rather than a cause of that change.

§ 23. The tendency which led to the replacement of inflections by a periphrase or by a convention of word order necessarily led to a considerable development in the use of prepositions and to a specialisation of their functions. Hence we find in the Middle English period a considerable development in the number of these words, new ones being formed either by the use of old material, usually adverbial, or by borrowing new pre-positional forms from French, such as *during, concerning, except,* and others. Scarcely less marked is the development in the Middle English period of new con-junctions and relatives. It was here, indeed, that Old English stood in greatest need of development, for it was poor both in conjunctions and in relatives, especially in the latter. It would seem, on the evidence, that the development of new conjunctions in Middle English was mainly due to the written or literary language, for it must have been there that the need was most acutely felt. The Old English conjunctions, such as *ond, swa, ðeah, ðæt, ægðer,* and a few more, sufficed perhaps for the expression of the simpler coordinating and sub-ordinating functions, but were entirely inadequate for the expression of the finer shades of meaning. This insufficiency must have been more and more felt when writers passed away from simple historical or epic narra-tive to the rendering of more abstract thought and reasoning. The spoken language, on the other hand, has less need of carefully differentiated conjunctions, and it is characteristic of this fact that even in the modern spoken languages conjunctions are used loosely and without a due sense of their precise function. Such conjunctions as *ðæt* and *and* had in Old English many functions which subsequently became specialised and were expressed by special words. But this specialisation has not even in Modern English penetrated into the spoken language. Thus, for example, *ond* in Old English might be merely copulative or it might be adversative. The copulative function still remains as the main function of this conjunction, whereas the adversative function is usually differently expressed. Old English has : *Seo sunne ymbscynþ þone blindan and se blinda ne gesihþ ðære sunnan leoman,* "The sun shines upon the blind man, *but* the blind man does not see the light of the sun." Nevertheless we see the old use of *and* in the line of Cowper :

God made the country *and* man made the town.

In exactly the same way the numerous uses of the conjunction *ðæt* in Old English were by degrees specialised, with the result that, on the one hand, we find in Middle English *in order that* = O.E. *ðæt,* and, on the other hand, it is often compounded with adverbs or nouns, *while that* = *ðæt.* The new conjunctions are almost all either compounded forms, such as *although, otherwise, nevertheless, whereas, as far as, sometimes . . . sometimes,* or else they are borrowings or adaptations from French, such as *accordingly, in case, consequently, finally, partly . . . partly, directly,* etc.

§ 24. Closely akin to the development of new conjunctions is the development of new relatives which serve to connect clauses. Here, again, Old English was insufficiently equipped, for it had no true relative pronoun at all. In Middle English we find that there are a number of what one might call experimental relatives, some of which have survived, and some of which have not. Thus we find such relatives as *the whose* = " whose," *whose that* = " whose," *which that* = " who," *what that* = " whichever," " whoever," and several more.

§ 25. An especially remarkable syntactical novelty of Middle English is the development of natural gender in place of the Old English grammatical gender. In later Middle English gender is no longer determined by the form of the word or by suffixes ; names of lifeless things can no longer be masculine or feminine, and names of living things can no longer be neuter as in Old English. This remarkable change, which is not paralleled anywhere else, is commonly attributed to the loss of the Old English inflectional endings, both in nouns and in the articles. It has been thought that when these inflections disappeared it was no longer possible to distinguish gender. But this explanation is in the highest degree unsatisfactory. For, in the first place, the loss of endings need not necessarily cause any such confusion as is alleged, since we learn genders—and everything else in language—only by use, and once the gender of nouns has been committed to memory no amount of subsequent change in a word will obliterate that memory. In the second place, there are clear signs of the transition to natural gender, or the determination of gender by sex, already before the inflections were lost, indeed already in the Old English period.

The transition to natural gender in Middle English would seem rather to be just one more manifestation of the broad general tendency which we have so often noted, to discard all grammatical categories and inflections which are superfluous, that is to say, which can be expressed by syntactic means. We have already seen how inflections of case could be represented by means of inflections or by virtue of the position of a word in the sentence. In exactly the same way gender would be expressed by the noun itself, or in the case of a pronoun by the feminine form of the pronoun. In later Middle English, as in Modern English, gender is only indicated by means of the pronouns, *he*, *she* and *it*, or by the few words such as *man*, *woman*, *boy*, *girl*, etc., which have different forms for the masculine and feminine. It is to be observed that even in the relative pronoun there is no distinction whatever of gender, because here also the antecedent noun indicates the gender with sufficient clearness. What would seem to have happened in Middle English is that with the general tendency to express a syntactic concord once only, gender simply disappeared, and in its place we find a clear conception, and a useful one, of the difference between lifeless and living things, the former all being expressed where necessary by *it* and the latter by *he* or *she*.

§ 26. Another development which occurred in Middle English, though the beginnings may be traced to the older period, is the development of the indefinite article. In Old English the numeral *an* is sometimes used with something of the sense of the indefinite article, though more often the word *sum* is used with this function. As a rule, however, the indefinite article is simply not used, the noun alone must be translated in Modern English by means of the article and the noun. Thus we read in *Beowulf :*

> Swa sceal geong guma   gode gewyrcean
> *so must a young man do good deeds*

In Middle English, however, the use of the indefinite article becomes more and more common. In English, as in other languages, the indefinite article develops at a late date, marking, as it does, a stage in the development of abstract thought, the power of thinking not, for example, of " the " man or of some particular man, but of man in general, any man whatever.

One of the consequences of the development of new conjunctions in Middle English was that these conjunctions gave expression to shades of thought which previously had been expressed by the inflections of mood in verbs. We find, in consequence, that the more we approach modern times the more the subjunctive mood tends to disappear from the language. In Middle English it still survives, just as it does in Modern English, but its range of use is much more restricted than it was in Old English, and we may perhaps infer from the fact that the third person singular of the subjunctive (the only case in which the subjunctive differs from the indicative) has practically disappeared from the modern spoken language, that this tendency was already operative in Middle English times.

CHAPTER III

VOCABULARY

§ 27. THE vocabulary of a people, like that of an individual, is a more or less faithful reflection of the mental, moral, emotional and physical world in which it lives. The vocabulary of a people consists of words which are the names of the objects, desires, emotions and general conceptions with which it is familiar. The more complex its civilisation, its social and political institutions and experience, the more advanced and developed its art, literature, philosophy and science, the richer its vocabulary will be. In addition to the words which are the names of things, there are in every language also words whose function is to bind together these significant and expressive words. Such are conjunctions, prepositions, and to some extent pronouns. These latter constitute the mortar of the edifice, whilst nouns, adjectives, verbs and adverbs are the real building stones. Or we may regard the mere relational words as instruments by which the main words are levered into position and securely held. The vocabulary of Germanic, as far as we can see from our reconstruction of it, was unmixed and contained only a very small number of words from non-Germanic languages. Of

41

its syntax, of course, nothing can be usefully said, for, in the absence of texts, we have no material upon which to base any conclusions. Certain loan words, however, from their occurrence in more than one of the Germanic languages at an early date may be presumed to be a common inheritance from the Primitive - Germanic period. These words are themselves instructive, for they throw some light on the connections of the Germanic peoples during the period of their migrations. Some of these loan words can be traced to other Indo-Germanic languages; some of them, on the other hand, cannot be so traced and are presumably derived from some tongue which is not of the Indo-Germanic stock. These latter are, however, very few, the most important being the word "silver," O.E. *seolfor*, Goth. *silbur*, O.N. *silfr*; and the word "hemp," O.E. *hœnep*, Gr. *cannabis*. From which language these words are derived we do not know, but they are not derived from any of the Indo-Germanic languages.

§ 28. The vocabulary of Germanic reflects, to some extent, the history of the people which spoke it, for there are successive layers of words which in some respects are as interesting as geological strata. These words give many an indication concerning early civilisation which is denied by either history or archæology. Among the words of Indo-Germanic origin one of the most interesting is the Germanic word for "snow" which is to be found in all the Indo-Germanic languages but curiously enough in the Asiatic branch its meaning is "damp." The conclusion has been drawn from this fact that the united Indo-Germanic people at one time lived in temperate climates, and that the Asiatic group

in moving south and east came first into regions of
melting snow and then into snowless districts. The
common words for *summer, winter* and *spring* would seem
to point to the same conclusion. Less conclusive is
the universality of the word *birch*, for this tree is almost
as widespread as is its name. Of similar interest is the
Old English word for " salmon," *leahs*, which is found
throughout the Indo-Germanic languages. Now in continental Europe the salmon is only to be found in the
rivers flowing into the North Sea and the Baltic ; it is
not found, on the other hand, in the rivers flowing
into the Caspian and the Mediterranean. Such words,
therefore, give us a clue, even if it is only a faint one,
to the original home of the Indo-Germanic people. It is
sometimes stated, as against this evidence, that we have
no common Indo-Germanic word for " sea " or " salt,"
and that the absence of such words in the language of a
people located near the Baltic and knowing the salmon is
strange. But such arguments *ex silentio* are dangerous.
We have, for example, no common Indo-Germanic word
for " hand " and many other things which were certainly
familiar to the Indo-Germanic people, and yet it would
be rash to argue from the absence of such words that
the Aryans either had no hands or had no name for them.

§ 29. There are other groups of words of Indo-Germanic
origin which give us some idea of the type of civilisation
which existed before the original stock split up into the
various groups. We know that Europe as early as
2000 B.C. was inhabited by a settled population engaged
in agriculture and cattle breeding. It is in accordance
with this fact that we find in the various Indo-Germanic
languages common words for " herd," " ox," " cow,"

" goat " and a word for " horse," O.E. *eoh*, Lat. *equus*. The development of family life is similarly shown by the common words for " father," " mother," " brother," " sister," etc. That the Aryans were a settled population is further shown by words for " door " and " thatch," which imply settled life in a house. An agricultural civilisation implies, however, a settled population, and this is further strengthened by the existence of the common root *sē* to be found in *sow, seed*, or Lat. *semen*, also by *mow* and *milk*. Many words, on the other hand, are peculiar to the European branch of the Indo-Germanic family, and as these mostly relate to agriculture, it may be presumed that the Asiatic group had moved away when these came into use. Such words are O.E. *erien*, "to plough," *acre, furrow, corn, grain, wheel, yoke, axle*. Other words belonging to the same period are *beech, pork, wasp, milk, mere, salt, bee, hornet, thrush*. Belonging to this earliest period also is the word O.E. *ǣr*, " ore," Lat. *ǣs*.

§ 30. But though the vocabulary of Germanic is in the main pure, yet it does contain a number of words borrowed directly from cognate Indo-Germanic languages, and these words are of very special interest as showing the kind of relationship which existed between the Teutons and their immediate neighbours. They also have the advantage of showing at what relative periods contact with other peoples was established.

History tells us very little concerning the centuries of migration of the Germanic peoples. Language tells us a good deal more. It shows us that the first race whose civilisation had any marked influence on the Germanic peoples was the Celtic race, and from the character of the words borrowed from Celtic it becomes clear that the civilisation of the Celts was superior to that of the Teutons, more especially in the arts of government and war. The Old English word *rīce*, which might mean " powerful " or " kingdom," was a very early loan and is found in all the Germanic tongues. The Celts, too, from their closer proximity to the civilisation of the Mediterranean and the Southern countries, were more advanced in the arts of metal working than were their Germanic neighbours, and they made earlier the important advance to the use of iron instead of bronze. They were in the position, therefore, to instruct their Germanic neighbours in these arts and to lend them the word *iron* and others of a kindred kind.

But it was especially in the arts of war that the Celts were superior to the Teutons, and this in spite of the fact that the Teutons, being a hardier race, succeeded in driving the Celts further into the West. The Germanic vocabulary is especially rich in terms relating to warfare, but it is surprising to note how many of them are peculiar to the Celtic and Germanic families of languages and have no cognates outside those languages. Thus two of the commonest words for " battle " in Old English, *heaþu* and *beadu* are both Celtic, as also the commonest word for " army," *here*, surviving in *harry*.

Another word of special interest borrowed from Celtic in the Primitive-Germanic period is the word *Welsh*. Originally the name of one single Celtic tribe, the *Volcæ*, this word was borrowed in the Primitive-Germanic period and came to be used for all the Celtic tribes. It also, however, developed the secondary meaning of " foreign," and traces of this meaning survive in the modern language. Thus the Old English *wealh* and its adjectival form *wielhisc* survive not only in the names *Wales* and *Welsh* and Corn*wall*, but also in the word *wal*nut.

§ 31. The Germanic peoples on the continent came into contact with yet another civilisation superior to their own, the Roman civilisation. The character of the loan words from Latin at this period is the clearest possible evidence of the inferiority of the Germanic civilisation. There is, however, one thing in common between the Celtic and the Roman influence on Germanic civilisation : that in both cases the exchange was not so much an exchange of ideas as an exchange of names of concrete material things. There is plenty of evidence among the loan words taken from Latin of acquaintance with material things, but there is no evidence of any borrowing of thoughts or of anything pertaining to the higher mental culture of the Romans, for the gulf between the two peoples was too great for any real contact of mind to be possible. This is shown just as much by the character of the words borrowed from Latin as by the contemptuous references by Latin writers to the northern barbarians.

But these barbarians traded with the Romans, and borrowed from them the names of certain weights, measures and coins. Our English words *ounce, pound, mile, mint,* and others, were all borrowed from Latin in the period before the Teutons invaded England. Germanic warriors also accepted service in the Roman legions and borrowed a number of military terms such as Old English *segen,* Lat. *signum,* " standard " ; O.E. *ceaster,* Lat. *castra* ; O.E. *strœt,* " street," Lat. *strata,* and others. From the Romans, too, the Teutons learnt

the art of building in stone and with it some of the commonest architectural terms such as *wall, post, port, tile,
mortar*, etc.   Of equal importance to the Teutons was
the knowledge they gained from the Romans of horti-
culture.   Names of fruits and plants are especially
common, as witness *pear, cherry, prune, pepper, cauli-*
(flower), *beet, imp*, etc.   Some words of this last category
would seem to point to Roman influence in the art
of cooking and the preparation of foods. The word
kitchen is itself a Latin word, as are also *cheese* and *butter*.
We should perhaps include here the names of certain
common domestic utensils such as *dish, candle*, and others.
Among miscellaneous words derived from Latin might
be mentioned *mill, copper, pit, anchor*.   From Latin,
too, we have the names of the days of the week : *Sunday
=dies solis, Monday=dies lunæ, Thursday=dies Jovis,
Wednesday=dies Mercurii*, except that in the two last a
Germanic God Thor has been substituted for Jove, and
Woden for Mercury.

§ 32. Trading connections are again shown by the
borrowing of words which point to the apparatus of
trade rather than to the actual objects of exchange.
In addition to words for weights and measures we notice
monger and *cheap*, from Latin *mango* and *caupo* respectively.   The latter word especially has had an interesting development in English.   Originally restricted in
application to those who sold wine—another Latin
loan word—it came to be used of buying and selling
in general and subsequently acquired the meaning of
" cheap " in Modern English, though something of its
older meaning is preserved in place-names such as
Chepstowe, Cheapside and *Copenhagen*.   Similarly the

names of some common vessels are Latin, such as *sack, chest, cannister, flask, cup,* and others. In some words on the other hand, the Latin word appears to have been literally translated into Germanic, as happened in the names of the days of the week. Thus *quicksilver* is a translation of *argentum vivum.* The borrowing was not, however, entirely one-sided, though the words which Latin borrowed from Germanic are not numerous. They consist of a few military terms such as *helm* and, curiously enough, the names of several colours such as *brown, grey* and *blue.*

§ 33. The vocabulary of the invaders contained already, as we have seen, a certain number of foreign words derived from Latin, Celtic and elsewhere. After settling in England the invaders again absorbed some foreign material. The people with whom they came into contact in these islands were Celts more or less Romanised, and from them a few more Celtic words were borrowed. It is nevertheless a remarkable fact that they borrowed as few words as they did. These words, such as *rasher* and *rug,* are, it has been pointed out, those which would mostly be used by women, and may indicate that the male population was exterminated or enslaved, and only the females spared. The absence of more Celtic words may, however, be due to the fact that the Celts were so largely Romanised before the Saxon invasions. The most numerous Celtic words are place-names, names of rivers, mountain ranges, etc. But one word should perhaps be specially noted : *Crīst.* In Old English, as in Modern English, the vowel of *Crīst* is long, whereas in Latin and the other Germanic languages it is short. In Celtic, on the other hand, it is long, and it is now generally supposed that this word came to us in Old English in its Celtic rather than its Latin form.

§ 34. The number of loan words from Latin in the Old English period is much greater than the number of Celtic loan words. Some of these were borrowed before the coming of St. Augustine, but most of them were borrowed later. This new accretion of Latin words in English has the same general characteristics as the earlier one in Primitive-Germanic times. It shows the contact of a superior with an inferior civilisation. It shows the undeveloped English borrowing the names of things which are new to their experience, and here again they are the names of material things and not of qualities or emotions or mental conceptions. The abstract conceptions of Christianity or of Roman philosophy could not be learnt in a day, and it was therefore a considerable time before they found expression in English. At first, indeed, they were translated into English, and it was not until later that Latin abstract terms were introduced. The new Latin words are almost without exception connected with the institutions of Christianity. We notice such words as : *engel*, " angel " ; *deofol*, " devil " ; *biscop*, " bishop " ; *munuc*, " monk " ; *mynster*, " minster " ; *nunne*, " nun " ; *abbod*, " abbot " ; and many more of the same kind, such as *regol*, (monastic) " rule " ; *mæsse*, " mass " ; *pæll*, " pall." The word *cyrce*, " church," however, which is common to the various Germanic languages, is clearly an earlier borrowing, and is derived from Greek and not from Latin. With the coming of Christianity there arose a need for the expression of ideas which were quite new to the English. These new ideas were not rendered by loan words, but by native material adapted as far as possible to the new needs. The adaptation was made partly by adding native suffixes to Latin loan words, thus creating hybrids, partly by derivation of new words from existing stems, and partly by composition, or the formation of new compounds. Thus from *prēost*, " priest," was formed *prēosthād*, " priesthood " ; from *Crīsten, Crīstendōm*. The Latin *trinitas* is quite literally translated *thrȳness*, and in the same way *hǣþen* may be a translation of the Latin *paganus*. Such literal translations are, however, the exception. As a rule the new conception is analysed and one or other of its more important attributes is selected and made to stand for the whole conception. Thus, " congregation " is rendered by *gesomnung*, a word which consists of a collective prefix *ge-* and a stem, since lost, meaning " together." The word " divine " is rendered by *godcund*, which is made up of the two elements " God " and " nature " ; to " baptise " is rendered by *fulwian*, which means " to fulfil " or " complete " (the consecration). Another word (a translation from Greek) which expresses the same thing, though from a totally different point of view, is the word *dyppan*, " to dip." This form is seen likewise in other Germanic languages : German *taufen*, Swedish, *döpa*, etc., so that it would appear that the act of immersion in the ceremony of baptism must have much impressed the people. The reason why the majority of these new ideas were expressed by native words is clear enough. The early Christian missionaries wished to impress upon an ignorant people the truths of the Christian religion, and they could, of course, only hope to do so by means of the native idiom.

Among the common people, however, there were none with a knowledge of Latin, and even among the rulers of the land there were very few. Alfred himself tells us how few there were in the country who could understand their services in Latin or who could translate a letter into English. It is evident, therefore, that there existed a very strong motive for the expansion of the native vocabulary. With Christianity there came also a knowledge of higher intellectual achievements outside the domains of religion, and this knowledge also impresses itself upon our language and leads to the formation of new words such as *efenniht*, " equinox " (literally " even night "), or *foresetnes*, " preposition " (literally " setting before "), from which new formations it appears quite clearly that the existing linguistic material was sufficient, when wisely used, to satisfy all ordinary needs. But the expansion of the vocabulary in the Old English period was so considerable,—especially in respect of words to express more or less abstract mental conceptions ;—and the process of abstraction such as one observes in the above-mentioned word *fulwian* implies so much deliberate creative thought ; that one is forced to the conclusion that very many of these words must have been formed by men of a superior education and were not words of purely popular origin. They nearly all bear the stamp of learned or semi-learned origin, in the endeavours of early preachers to teach the new religious doctrine to the people in words which, because they were formed from common and familiar stems, would be intelligible to them.

§ 35. If we look at that part of the Old English vocabulary which consists of native words brought over to

England by the Angles, Saxons and Jutes, we shall find that it forms a very accurate mirror of the civilisation of early Saxon England. Syntactically, as we have already seen, the language is imperfect and undeveloped. In respect of vocabulary it is very highly developed in respect of those activities in which the people were especially interested, and of which the oldest literature gives us a picture. The society which is revealed is one organised for war, and in which warlike prowess, personal bravery and physical strength are the chief claims to honour. There is an elementary simplicity of conduct, combined with a vigorous physical life, which are characteristic of the heroic age. The emotions portrayed are likewise of the simpler order : love, hate, revenge ; the chief virtues are those of the warrior : personal bravery and unflinching loyalty. The social life and amusements of the people consist of gatherings in the mead hall for drinking and singing. The vocabulary reflects all this. There are many words for warrior, and still more for the chief virtue of the warrior, his bravery in battle. There are many words too for the weapons and armour of the warrior, and for other things connected with warfare. Add to these words descriptive of features of natural scenery, which were perhaps more necessary then than now, words to denote the material objects with which people were familiar, words for the simple legal, political and social institutions of the time, and the vocabulary is exhausted.

We should not forget, however, that, well within the Old English period, the vocabulary was very much enlarged by the influence which Christianity exerted in every sphere of life. King Alfred's translations from

Latin introduced a large number of new words reflecting a new world of abstract thought and of more highly developed life. Christianity modified profoundly the conditions of life in England, and it would be strange indeed if the new moral system, the new outlook on life, and the new learning had not been reflected in the vocabulary of the language.

§ 36. Interesting sidelights on early English civilisation and of Germanic civilisation in general are to be found in the investigation of proper names, whether of persons or of places. Names ending in -*stead*, though in England they cannot, of course, be older than the Anglo-Saxon settlements, are on the Continent of great antiquity, pointing as they do to settlements on marshy ground where pile-driving was necessary, the pile being the "stead" or support. Other names, like Thursley, point to the pagan Germanic gods. An examination of the Anglo-Saxon place-names, again, shows clearly that England in those days was a land covered with forests. The evidence is unmistakable, for there is a very large number of place-names in which the second element is a common noun denoting a clearing of some sort in a wood or forest. Such are names in -*field*, -*thwaite* and *ridding*; -*gill*, -*holt*, -*lund*, -*clough*, again, all mean some sort of wood or copse. Other place-names show the pioneer at work; -*leah*, as in "Staveley," "Bradley" meant "pasture land," *tun* meant "enclosed land." The settler next picks out the chief landmarks and the most striking features of the landscape. These, as we know from old charters, were used for describing the boundaries of land and enter very largely into the formation of place-names. Such are *stream, ridge, ford, bank, burn, mere* and many more, usually compounded with some descriptive adjective such as *deep, high,* etc. Some of these compounds have a special interest, as they reflect early conditions of life. Compounds with *-ford* in particular deserve notice. In the days before far-flung bridges, rivers were very serious obstacles and fords were of the utmost importance. Hence we find throughout Germanic Europe the regular recurrence of place-names in *-ford*, and naturally they are found beside rivers. But not only was a ford in itself important, but the very nature of the ford was of importance. Some were deep, too deep for cattle to pass ; others, again, would admit of the passage of oxen, and hence we find several *Oxfords.* Others, again, would only allow swine to cross, and hence we have our *Swinfords* in England and *Schweinfurts* in Germany. More convenient still were those shallow fords into which one could cast stones over which to pass, the " stone-fords " or *Stamfords.*

After the first settlements had been made, men began to congregate in villages, both for the advantages of communal life and for purposes of defence. We find, therefore, a newer and later stratum of place-names ending in *-by*, meaning a " village," a sense which it still retains in *bye-law*, or "local law." The numerous place-names ending in *-burgh* or *-borough* or *-bury* point to the fortification of such places and are interesting parallels to the earlier names in *caster.* So also we read in the *Anglo-Saxon Chronicle* that the Danes sailed up the Thames and built a fortification (O.E. *geweorc*) south of the river opposite London. This was the *Sūþgeweorc*, or *Southwark.* An advancing civilisation is also shown by the introduction of place-names compounded with -*mill* and the numerous names ending in -*bridge*. Much more might be added to show how the various phases of our development are illustrated in our place-names. We might point to the various Celtic names ; to the place-names ending in -*church, -kirk,* or -*minster* as evidence of the arrival of Christianity ; or to names such as *Beaumaris* and *Chapel-en-le-Frith* as evidences of the Norman Conquest.

§ 37. Scarcely less interesting, for the same reason, are the Old English personal names. Especially do they show the preoccupation of our forefathers with war. The number of personal names in which one or other of the elements denotes some phase of warfare is extraordinarily great. A glance at such a collection of names as is to be found in the Old English *Liber Vitæ* shows how common are the names beginning or ending with one of the following words : *sige,* " victory " ; *here,* " army " ; *helm,* " protector " ; *hild,* " battle " ; *bald,* " bold " ; *ecg,* " sword " ; *beorn,* " warrior " ; *hadu* or *haþu,* " battle " ; *mund,* " protector " ; *heard,* " brave " ; *wald,* " ruler " ; etc., etc. In later times Christianity is responsible for numerous baptismal names, and the development of the arts and crafts produces such personal names as *Weaver, Webster, Baker, Tinker, Marchant, Smith, Chaucer,* etc.

§ 38. Of special interest as showing something of the cultural conditions of Primitive-Germanic times are the words for reading and writing, and the word *book* itself. Our modern word " write," O.E. *wrītan,* meant originally " to scratch," and this in its turn is an indication of the materials originally used in writing, for the scratching was done on wood or stone. In some of the Germanic languages this word has been replaced by the Latin word *scribere*, since the Germanic runic alphabet was an adaptation of the Latin alphabet for the special purpose of making writing on stone or wood more easy. Similar evidence is afforded by the word *book*, for this word is the same as the word *beech* and therefore corroborates the evidence afforded by the word *write*. The word *read* likewise throws a most interesting light on the workings of the popular mind, for its original sense, or one of its original senses, was that of explaining or interpreting a thing, and the thing which was to be explained was the rune, which word might mean either a letter of the alphabet or a mystery. Reading, then, meant to interpret a mystery.

MIDDLE ENGLISH

§ 39. The general character of the English language undergoes a very great change in the Middle English period, a change which is equally marked in the provinces of syntax, accidence and vocabulary. The influences which were at work in re-moulding the language were both numerous and complex. Some of them were already operative in the Old English period and some of them were peculiar to the Middle English period. The Scandinavian invasions, culminating in the monarchy of King Canute ; the Norman Conquest and the subsequent political and ecclesiastical reorganisation of the land ; the closer contact with the world of continental thought : all of these exercised a powerful influence on English thought and literature, and therefore on the English language also.

It would indeed be strange if the complete transformation of English life ; if the newer and wider outlook ; if the new worlds of thought and imagination had not, in seeking expression in language, laid a very heavy strain upon its resources. One could perhaps best realise the nature of that strain by supposing in modern times a backward race with limited and narrow traditions to be conquered by an advanced race and yet seek to adapt its language to the needs of the advanced civilisation of the conqueror. Nevertheless, this is what happened in Middle English. The older language, sufficient perhaps for the simpler needs of an older civilisation, was inadequate for the expression of the more complex conceptions of Christian doctrine, and still more inadequate for the expression of social and political ideas which differed so fundamentally as did those of the England of the Heptarchy and the England of Norman feudalism. Contact with the literature of the Continent must in the same way have imposed upon writers of English the necessity of developing their language.

When one considers what a great and sudden revolution the Norman Conquest effected in English life, and when one considers the urgent and pressing need which stimulated the development of the English tongue, one is tempted to seek in the social and political re-organisation of Norman England the causes of the most marked features of the development of English. After the Conquest English became the language of a subject people, and its fate might well have been the same as that of the Celts in Britain or in France. But something of that national stubbornness which, in social

and political life, prevailed ultimately against the conqueror must have been at work also in the preservation
of the national tongue.   Even so, it could only survive
at a price, and the price, was that it should so adapt
and transform itself as to remain a worthy instrument for
the new work which it had to do.   It is certainly significant that it was not until the national vitality had
proved itself in the peaceful struggle with the conqueror,
and not until Englishmen had begun to hold important
positions in Church and State, that there appeared
French words in considerable numbers in the English
language.

§ 40. It is a pity that at this distant date we cannot
possess any accurate knowledge of the mental processes
which lay behind every step or stage in the adaptation
of English to its new needs, but we can safely assume
that the human mind obeyed the same fundamental
laws then as now.   Whether it was a question of giving
a name to a new thing or whether it was a question of
giving more precise expression to a thought, the linguistic means available and the mental processes which
selected or modified those means were the same.   It is
therefore not improbable that Englishmen in the Middle
English period when confronted with a number of new
thoughts, new conceptions, new institutions and new
systems behaved in exactly the same way as an Englishman in modern times would do.   He would be obliged
to look the new fact full in the face and to analyse carefully its significance and its precise import before he
could give expression to it in his own language.   In
other words, the advent of this entirely new type of
society, with its thousand new associations, coupled

with the imperative necessity either of making English an effective instrument or of being it die out, forced the English into a habit of analysis in regard to their speech which has remained its dominant characteristic from that day to this. It is true that the analytical tendency was already to be seen in the Old English period, but it is in the transition to Middle English that it becomes most marked.

That the English language survived at all is due to the nature of the Conquest and to the nature of the English people. It was of the nature of the Conquest that it permitted the subsequent fusion of the two races, a fusion so complete that at a later date the English by virtue of their numerical superiority were able once again to assume the government of their country. But it was also of the nature of the Conquest and of the feudal institutions which it introduced that such a fusion was possible. A less close intermixture of the conquered and the conquerors would not have permitted that free interchange of ideas which is the necessary condition of such numerous borrowings of words as took place from French to English. But it was the national virility which, profiting by the opportunities afforded by the feudal organisation of society, and at the same time developing its language commensurately with its new functions, succeeded at last in ousting the language of the conqueror.

Without this social fusion of the two peoples it is scarcely conceivable that such large numbers of French words should have been taken up into English. For it is to be noted that the new words are not merely the names of material objects ; they are also the names of abstract ideas and of abstract qualities, and these latter would scarcely have been understood by the English except as the result of prolonged intercourse and familiarity with the world of thought to which they belong. One can understand that such words as *pork, beef* might be borrowed by people who were in utter subjection and had no other relation to the conqueror than that of servant and master ; but the borrowing of such words as *circumstance, dignity, familiarity* and hundreds more of the same sort point to relations of a more finely graded kind. The great majority of the French loan words in Middle English must have been in use by the Normans in England for a considerable time before they became a part of the English language, for they would scarcely have been understood by the English until after the lapse of many years. Such understanding could only come, moreover, as the consequence of that fusion of the peoples which the peculiar institutions of the Conquest rendered possible, and of the stubborn virility of the English. It is for this reason that French loan words in English do not begin to appear until a very long time after the Conquest. In the century after the Conquest there are, for example, only a bare dozen French words in the *Anglo-Saxon Chronicle*.

§ 41. Concerning the Scandinavian influence on Middle English, which is of earlier date than the Norman influence, little need be said in this place, since it is an influence not so strongly felt as the latter. The Scandinavians did not bring with them any fundamentally different social institutions, nor any fundamentally different ideals of life. Their vocabulary and syntax was, moreover, closely akin to that of English, so the

influence which they exerted over English was, in the
nature of things, limited in extent to single words or
single sounds and inflections. These will be considered
in a later section.

§ 42. The Norman Conquest brought England into
the main stream of European culture, so that from the
Middle English period onward there are visible in the
English vocabulary traces of the religion, philosophy,
art and scholarship of Europe. But another important
movement of the Middle Ages—the Crusades—also
shows its influence on the language in the numerous
words of oriental origin which were introduced. These,
however, are almost all names of concrete things, and
therefore only affect the vocabulary of the language
and not at all its structure or its syntax.

But if the fusion of the English and the Norman
peoples opened the gates to the numerous sources of
continental culture and continental thought, and if in
consequence, there flowed into the English language
various fertilising streams, yet the contact of English
with French under such peculiar conditions had the
further important result of determining to a very great
extent the methods by which the language was to be
enriched in future centuries. The familiarity with words
of classical form, which the English acquired from their
knowledge of French, not only rendered it more easy
for them to continue to draw upon French sources, but
also facilitated the borrowing of words in their Latin
as distinct from their French forms. We may attribute
to this same cause the profound influence of French
upon English literature and the readiness with which
French forms and French idioms were assimilated. But

it is chiefly in preparing the ground for the reception of new words of Latin origin that the Norman Conquest has affected Modern English, for without that familiarity with French words which c. me from the intimate association of Norman and Englishman it is inconceivable that at subsequent periods—at the Renaissance and in the eighteenth century—such large numbers of Latin and French words should have been introduced.

§ 43. In Middle English the vocabulary was enriched from three main sources : Scandinavian, French and Latin. Of these the Scandinavian influence was the earliest and began already in the Old English period, though it is not until we come to Middle English texts that Scandinavian words become common, and even then they are not found in equal numbers in all parts of the country. In the middle of the ninth century the Danes were firmly established in England, and, considering the extent of territory which was comprised in the ancient Danelaw, and the power and influence of King Canute, it is perhaps at first sight surprising that the influence of the Scandinavian tongues on English was not greater than it appears to have been. But appearances here are deceptive, for in the first place, owing to the common descent of English and Danish, or Norse, the two languages had numerous words and forms which, if not absolutely identical, were yet so similar that they might freely pass from one language to another. Hence the task of disengaging the Scandinavian loan words from the native words is one of very great difficulty and delicacy. In the second place, there was so much in common both in language, character and institutions between the native English and the invaders that there was not the same pressing need for loans as there was in the case of French.

§ 44. One of the earliest loan words from Scandinavian is to be found in a patriotic poem descriptive of a battle with the Danes, *The Battle of Maldon.* Here we find the word *call.* In the *Anglo-Saxon Chronicle*, in the later parts, we also find a number of Scandinavian loan words such as: *feolaga*, "fellow"; *lagu*, "law"; *brydlop*, "bridal"; *husting*, etc. The Danish settlements have left numerous traces in the elements of place-names, such as those ending in *-by*, *-thorpe*, *-thwaite*, *-dale*, *-beck*, which are most frequent in the northern and eastern counties of England. Sometimes the Scandinavian word already existed in English in a slightly different form. In this way doublets arose and the two forms were differentiated in meaning at a later date. Such has been the fate of *shirt* and *skirt*, *-less* and *loose*, *rear* and *raise*, *shriek* and *screech*. Sometimes, again, the two forms continue to exist side by side, as in *church* and *kirk*, with the same meaning. In all of these cases the first form is the English and the second the Scandinavian. As a rule, however, one or other of the two forms has been lost in the standard language. Thus the Old English *giefan*, "to give," appears in Chaucer by regular development as *yive*. In the Northern dialect, on the other hand, under the influence of Scandinavian, the form with was preserved and subsequently spread over the whole country. Similar words are *gift*, for English *y ft*; *get*, for English *yet*; and others. The Old English word *ǣg* gave in Middle English *ey*, but this form was abandoned in favour of the Scandinavian form *egg*.

In other cases it is not so much that a Scandinavian word has been borrowed, as that the English word has taken the meaning of the corresponding Scandinavian word. Thus the word *vi'zing*, although it existed in English before the viking age, took on the meaning which attached to it in Scandinavian, and which it preserves to the present day. Its original meaning was "pirate." In the same way the O.E. *plōh*, which meant a measure of land, took the Old Norse meaning of "plough." Much more difficult to account for are those loan words which supplanted Old English words, and which are among the words most commonly used in the language. That the Danish *dǿja*, "to die," should have been borrowed in the form *deyen* in English is perhaps natural, for it corresponds in form to the English words *dead* and *death* more closely than do the Old English words *sweltan* or *steorfan*, "to die." But that words in such common use as personal pronouns should be supplanted by strangers is somewhat remarkable. Nevertheless this is what happened to the Old English Nominative *hie*, Accusative *hie*, Genitive *hiera*, Dative *him*. These were replaced, first in the north, and then, by degrees, throughout the country, by the Scandinavian forms *they*, *their* and *them*. It may be that they gained currency because of the dentity of the initial sound *th*- with the initial of other native pronominal forms such as *this*, *that*, *the*, *those*, etc.; but this does not seem an adequate explanation of the phenomenon. Among other common words borrowed at this time should be noticed also the words *ill* by the side of *sick* from O.E. *seoc*, and *same, skull, skin, skill, scream, scowl, skulk* and others in *sk-, loose, wrong, ugly, rotten, meek, hit, cast, take, sky.*

It is not possible from an examination of the words borrowed from Scandinavian to form any conclusions as to the nature of the influence exerted by the Danes on English thought and institutions. From the fact that such common words as *die, take, they, till* and others were borrowed, it would appear that the fusion of the two peoples must have been very complete. If we were to look only at the words which were borrowed in the older period and not merely at those which have survived, the list would be very much longer, and it would appear that the invaders exercised an influence at least upon our legal system, though many of the words which bear evidence to this influence were subsequently swept away again when the whole administration of justice passed into the hands of the Normans. The most important surviving words in this category are the already-mentioned *law* and its compound *bye-law* = " village-law," containing the same word as is to be found in such place-names as *Whitby,* etc. ; O.E. *thriding* = " riding," " a third part " (*North, East, West Riding*), *thrall* ; also in *ransack* = " to search a house " (for stolen goods). There are also in the older language a few words relating to ships and war, but these have not, as a rule, survived in modern times.

With the exception of these few law terms there is nothing, then, to justify any generalisation concerning the relationship between the Danes and the English. There is nothing to point to any marked superiority of culture of the one over the other, and in this respect the Scandinavian loan words tell a very different story from that which is told by the loan words from French. All that we can see from them is that the two peoples when they intermixed were on an equal footing, for it is only on this assumption that words such as we have noted could have been universally adopted.

§ 45. Vastly more numerous and vastly more significant are the words which were borrowed from the Normans. These point to a profound influence exerted in almost every sphere of social and political activity. There is scarcely a single walk of life which remains unaffected by the activities of the new-comers. From the king right down through the social scale until we reach his cook, all alike modify and enlarge their vocabulary by means of words derived from the language of the conqueror.

There are several problems which arise in considering the influence of French upon English. It is a remarkable fact, and one which calls for some explanation, that although French is a language not nearly so closely related to English as are Danish or Old Norse, and which must have been quite unintelligible to the Englishman who heard it for the first time, yet it has contributed very much more to our vocabulary than the Scandinavian languages did. That this should have been so, in spite of the seeming probabilities, was due to the different characters of the Danish and Norman occupations. The former was not in the nature of a conquest, and it was made by a people enjoying a very similar civilisation. The latter, on the other hand, was a conquest of the whole country effected by a people very much superior to the English in culture, who imposed upon the country all their institutions of government and law.

Though an alien race, they were yet the ruling class for several centuries ; they were both numerous and powerful and they brought with them all the blessings of the superior civilisation of the Continent. Nor did they abandon their connection with their continental home, but rather attracted more and more immigrants as the years passed. Moreover, as unchallenged rulers in all departments of the state, they were able to impose their language upon the people of this country. A knowledge of French was necessary, not only on grounds of what Jespersen has called snobbery, but as the sole and essential means of obtaining promotion in any of the higher walks of life. French was for a long time the language of the Court, of Parliament and of the Church. Education was only to be had through the medium of French, so that for all these reasons it was imperative that the English, whether of the upper or of the lower classes, should be familiar with it. The incorporation of French words in the English language was not, therefore, as the incorporation of Scandinavian words had been, a more or less spontaneous and voluntary assimilation, it was rather necessitated by the sheer force of circumstances.

It is true that French had a number of words of Germanic origin which may still have been recognisable as such by the English, and for that reason have been more easily assimilated, but the number of these cannot have been very great. The majority were probably assimilated for different reasons. There is, for example, a certain grim significance in the circumstances of the appearance of some of the very earliest of the French loan words in English. Thus we find in the *Anglo-Saxon Chronicle* under the date 1123 the word *prisune*, and still earlier the word *castel*. But the bulk of the words did not appear until a century or a century and a half after the Conquest. Nor was the geographical distribution of these loan words uniform ; some writers employ them more freely than others. In one Middle English text, the *Ormulum*, French words are very rare ; in another, almost contemporary with it, the *Ancren Riwle*, they are extremely common. Something of the educational process by which the English became familiar with French is, indeed, visible in Middle English texts—especially those of a didactic character— in the habit of joining together a French word and its English equivalent for the benefit of the uninstructed. Thus the *Ancren Riwle* has : *that beon malicious and lithere again othere, nimingee of husl . . . other sacrament.* Further evidence of a widespread bilingualism or even trilingualism is to be found in the numerous songs of the *clerici vagantes* in which lines in English alternate with lines in French or in Latin, as, for example :

> Scripsi hæc carmina in tabulis
> Mon ostel est en mi la vile de Paris ;
> May y sugge namore, so wel me is ;
> Yef y deye for love of hire, wel hit ys.

There is another point of some importance which should be noticed in connection with these loan words. Just as familiarity with French words must have been for many Englishmen the result of the deliberate learning of the French language, so also it may reasonably be assumed that a very large number of the words borrowed by such educated people were introduced only into the written language and not at all into the language of everyday speech. These words would probably be the majority. Certainly at the present day a very large number of the loan words in English from French, or from Latin through French, are words of the literary language and are not in common use in the spoken language at all. Words like *philosophy, astrology, logic*, which came into English in the Middle English period, were quite certainly confined in the main to the language of literature and science, and the same is true of a large number of terms less technical than these. *Avidity* still remains a purely literary word by the side of the colloquial *greed, perspicacity* has not replaced *clearness* in the spoken language. That this should have been the case is, of course, entirely natural, for writers in the fourteenth and fifteenth centuries addressed themselves to a very limited audience which was already familiar with French. They therefore felt themselves at liberty to use French words freely, and the temptation was all the stronger since Middle English literature leant so heavily upon French literature and consisted to a considerable extent of translations from French.

§ 46. When we turn to examine the various classes of loan words from French we are able to see in how many different ways French civilisation and French culture influenced English. It becomes at once apparent that the Normans are the ruling race and that they have remodelled all the English institutions according to their own pattern. In the province of government, although the native words *king* and *queen* remain, the names of most of the officers of State are French : *chancellor, minister, justice, councillor*, etc. So also the names of governing bodies and their activities : *state, estate, realm* (though the native word *kingdom* survives), *govern-*

ment, parliament, country, sovereign, exchequer, people, nation, emperor, empress, countess, peer, peerage, prince, noble, squire, baron, marshal, constable, chamberlain, and the names of many more of humbler rank, such as *page, servant,* and its doublet *sergeant, person,* etc. Similarly the names of the officers of the Church are French, *clergy, cardinal, hermit, palmer, pardoner, prophet,* etc. Many other words more or less directly connected with the Church are likewise French : *pray, prayer, preach, sermon, religion, order, sacrament, miracle, trinity, penitence, absolution, paradise, relic* and *rule.*

§ 47. Among the first words to be introduced were those relating to war and military affairs such as *battle, armour, assault, banner, standard, fortress, tower, enemy, company, lance, captain, lieutenant, officer, colonel, soldier, force, guard, war.* Turning now to the province of law, we find that there are a great many terms derived from French, most of which were originally technical terms, though many of them have passed into everyday speech and have taken on new meanings. We notice in the first place *court, judge, justice, suit, plea, plead, damage, debt, entail, bailiff, assize, session, heir, heritage, felony, robbery, traitor, treason, rebel, crime.* Technical are still such words as *larceny, petty, attorney,* and others. Feudalism is reflected in such words as *fief, vassal, feudal, homage,* and in the names of persons of rank such as *prince, peer, duke, marquis, baron, viscount,* and their feminines.

§ 48. The conquerors were also the leaders of fashion in dress, as may be seen from such words as *costume, dress, robe, cope, garment.* In architecture, too, they introduced a number of technical terms including *palace, castle, tower, chamber, arch, column, pillar, porch, choir, cloister,* etc. Especially noticeable are the names of various cooked foods such as *bacon, beef, mutton, pork, veal, venison,* even though there existed native words for the animals from which these meats are derived. Similarly, the methods of cooking are indicated by French words, *boil, fry, broil, roast,* and the names of two of the meals are likewise French, *dinner* and *supper.* To this same category belong such words as *spice, soup, jelly, sauce.* There are also other words pertaining to domestic life, including *lamp, lantern, table, chair, carpet, master, servant, butler, bottle.* Trade, industry, the professions and vocations are also well represented in the French loan words, as witness *merchant, merchandise, riches, carpenter, mason, mariner, painter, joiner, tailor, butcher, profession, money, custom, tax, rent.*

§ 49. Among the arts we notice that the word *paint* is French, as are also the words *art, ornament, design, colour. Music* and *melody, lute* and *tone* are of the same origin. Especially common are the words relating to the amusements of the conquerors. In the world of sport the word *sport* itself is a French word, as are also *chase, quarry, falcon,* and the names of numerous animals, whether or not objects of the chase, such as *lion, unicorn, dragon, panther, scorpion, turtle, pigeon, eagle, pheasant, partridge,* etc. Finally, among the names of concrete things we should notice the names of relationships outside the closer family relationships : *uncle, aunt, nephew* (though this may have been influenced by the O.E. *nefa*), *niece, cousin, ancestor.*

§ 50. The words which have so far been noticed are mostly the names of things which would be brought to the notice of everybody, whether Englishman or Norman ; many of them are the names of new objects or new institutions, and it is therefore natural that with the preservation of those things and institutions these words should have been fully assimilated in the language. The influence of French was, however, by no means restricted to such words. There is abundant evidence in the language, even if there were none elsewhere, to show what a profound influence the civilisation of the conqueror exerted in less material spheres. The vocabulary of science and scholarship was so greatly enriched by words from French that it is impossible to make any sufficiently short selection which would be representative. Words like *astronomy* and *astrology*, *physician* and *medicine*, *scholar*, *study* and *clerk* indicate some only of the various departments of thought which were affected, while the great majority of names of abstract qualities are of French origin and very often supplanted those which existed in the native tongue. We may notice, for example, *vanity*, *abstinence*, *contemplation*, *reflection*, *patience*, *honesty*, *virtue*, *vice*, *adversity*, *ignorance*, *hypocrisy* and dozens more.

§ 51. More interesting as representing the complete fusion of the two languages in the speech of the people are those words which are neither technical in origin, nor yet the names of new things, nor yet the names of abstract conceptions. It is surprising, for example, that the Old English ordinal *ōþer* should have yielded to *second*, or that while all the names of the parts of the body should have been preserved, yet *face* and *voice* replaced the native words. Similarly some very common adjectives gave way to French words, such as *large*, *feeble, poor, gay, false, dangerous.* It is curious, however, that whereas the other Germanic languages have adopted the Latin word *scribo*, for " write " (German *schreiben*, Swedish *skriva*) yet English should have kept the native word. This is the more remarkable since the bulk of the scribes in the Middle English period were Normans, and other words connected with the art of writing are French in origin, as, for example, *parchment, pen, letter, page* and *pencil.* Other words which may be included in this category and are in common use are, *language, forest, nature, custom, metal, manner, measure, choice, sound, part, cry* and many more.

§ 52. No doubt many of the loan words from French which came into English after the Conquest were first introduced into the language as technical terms and were only very slowly taken up in ordinary speech. Many have remained technical even in modern times. The word *larceny* is still a legal term, though it is no longer felt to be foreign, as is the case with other fossilised technicalities in the legal terminology, such as *malice prepense, escheat, estopper* and many more words which have remained only in a technical sense. Some of them, again, still keep their technical sense side by side with the ordinary sense which has developed out of them. Such, for example, are *order, lesson, discipline.*

§ 53. One of the consequences of the wholesale introduction of French words by the Normans was that there arose a considerable number of synonyms, more particularly in the case of names of material things, and of the simpler qualities and emotions. Where both words have survived in modern times it will usually be found that the native term is the one in common use, because it has its roots in the deeper traditions of the race ; it is, as a rule, more expressive, in consequence of its older and more varied associations, and it has a subtler emotional colouring. *Friendly* is much warmer than *amicable, lonely* is more expressive than *solitary*. But in other cases the difference of meaning would seem to be due to other causes. Especially in the names of material things the native word expresses a simpler and more unassuming variety of the thing than does the loan word, which seems to retain a certain dignity and formality which does not attach to its brother. Thus *house* is humbler than *mansion*.

In addition to synonyms, there also appeared in English numerous doublets as the result of borrowing from French. These doublets, however, invariably have different meanings, and not merely meanings closely related, as in the case of synonyms. These doublets may arise in different ways. For example, a Germanic word may have been borrowed in French and have developed there independently in meaning. Thus the English word *crab* was borrowed in an early form by the French from Germanic and assumed the form *crevice*, Modern French *écrevisse*. The Old French form then passed into English where it was not at all recognised and, since the accent in French was on the last syllable, it assumed in English the form *crayfish*, so that we now have the two forms *crab* and *crayfish*, with different meanings. Such doublets are not numerous. The second type of doublet arises from the fact that a word may be borrowed from French in a popular and in a learned form, or in an early and a late form.

Thus, for example, the word *frail* represents the form which developed regularly in popular French, but the word *fragile* represents a direct borrowing from Latin into French or into English. Doublets of this kind are quite numerous, as, for example, *blame* and *blaspheme*, *reason* and *ration*, *chapter* and *capital*. In these doublets, however, it is frequently difficult to determine whether the later form, the *mot savant*, which is usually the longer form, is in English derived from French, or whether it was taken direct from Latin, as the forms would in many cases be the same in English. The third class of doublets arises when a word has had a different development in the dialects of French. Just as in English we have double forms of the same word, according to the dialect from which it is taken (as in *dint* and *dent*, *church* and *kirk*, *brigg* and *bridge*) so also in French a word might have different forms according to the dialect in which it was found. The most important dialectal differences affecting loan words were those between Central French of Paris and Northern French. Thus *catch*, *warrant*, *lance*, *cattle*, are from Northern French, and *chase*, *guarantee*, *launch* and *chattel* are from Central French, and were introduced later.

§ 54. What is most important about the *mots savants* in French is that when they were introduced into English in such large numbers, they familiarised the English people with Latin forms and thus made it much easier for them to borrow directly from Latin and Greek. It is very largely for this reason that the borrowing from those languages has continued until the present day. No other Germanic language has borrowed so freely from Latin and Greek as has English, and the reason is to be found in the conditions we have just been describing. Had it not been for the Norman Conquest and the consequent familiarity of the English with French and Latin forms it is certain that the English vocabulary would have been just as pure as German or Swedish or Danish.

§ 55. Finally a few words should be said concerning the treatment of these loan words after they had been adopted in the language. In French the stress did not fall on the first syllable as it did in native words, but on the last syllable. This stress was also preserved for some time after the word had been adopted in English, though there is evidence that the native principle was also operative at an early date. In the poetry of the Middle English period the rhythm sometimes requires the stress on the first syllable of such words, just as if they were English words ; but very often it requires the stress on the last syllable as in French. It was, of course, a great advantage to the poet to be able to stress a word in either way, and he often avails himself to the full of that advantage. *Virtue, dignitee, matere,* to take some examples at random, are all stressed on the last syllable in Chaucer. We see the varying stress in such lines as :

> ye woot that every evangelist
> That telleth us the peyne of Jesu Crist,
> Ne saith nat al thing as his felaw doth,
> But natheles, hir séntence is al sooth,
> And alle accorden as in hir senténce,
> Al be ther in hir telling difference.

Here both principles are in operation, for the word *sentence* is stressed once according to native principles and once according to French principles. We find even as late as, and later than, Shakespere that this variable stress is still maintained, and some words have retained the French stress to the present day. Notice, for example, *hotel*. In other words, the difference of stress has been turned to good use in order to differentiate meaning, as where *present* with the stress on the first syllable means " gift," and with the stress on the second syllable it is a verb meaning " to give." Notice also the difference between *absent* with the stress on the first and with the stress on the second syllable.

Otherwise words adopted in the language are subject to exactly the same laws of development as native words. They may change their meaning in exactly the same way as the latter, and they may change their form. The sounds in such words undergo the same changes as the corresponding sounds in native words. So also they are inflected in the same way as native words, except that in a few cases in the older language adjectival plural forms are preserved for a time even though such plural inflections of adjectives had disappeared in English. Nouns were usually taken over in the French accusative form and not in the nominative, which ended in -*s*, as seen in the exceptional forms *Charles, James* and a few more. So also the form *sire* is a nominative, of which *seigneur* is the accusative, and *senior* the learned formation. Verbs were usually adopted in the form of the stem of the plural of the indicative in French ; thus in words like *flourish, nourish, punish, finish*, etc., the -*sh* corresponds to the -*ss*- of French *punissons*, etc. The infinitive when it was borrowed usually had the function of a noun.

§ 56. It is characteristic of the complete assimilation of French words in English that derivatives are freely formed from them, either on the model of English or French originals. Thus to the French stem *beauti-* is added the English suffix *-ful*. Hybrids thus formed are very common. We have grate*ful* and *un*grate*ful*, grace*ful* and grace*less*, plenti*ful*, lecture*ship* and governor-*ship*, false*ness* and false*hood*, total*ly* and superb*ly*, preach*ing* and pray*ing*, in all of which the suffix or prefix is native and the stem foreign. Sometimes, on the other hand, the stem is native and the suffix or prefix is foreign. Thus, for example, shepherd*ess*, seamstr*ess*. One of the most fertile of the Romance suffixes of this kind is the suffix *-able* which can be added to all sorts of words in order to form adjectives. Thus we have *unforgetable, loveable, laughable,* and many more. Another suffix is *-ous*, which enters into the formation of words like wondr*ous*. In other words a derivative is formed on the model of numerous existing words, even though there is no actual antecedent either in French or in Latin. Thus the word *chastise*, though the stem *chast-* is to be found in French, or in the Latin *cast-*, has no antecedent in either of these languages, and is a new formation on the analogy of such words as *suffice, baptise,* and many more. Similarly, the word *reliable* has no counterpart either in French or in Latin, but is a purely English formation, though compounded of exclusively French elements. This tendency to coin words independently of the language from which the elements are derived creates additional difficulties in determining whether a word has been derived from French or Latin, for in many cases though a parallel

form may exist in French, the English word need not
necessarily have been derived from it, but may be an
independent coinage. It is worth while noticing, too,
that a word once borrowed may have a much more
interesting history in the land of its adoption than in
the land of its origin. It may develop new meanings
which never attach to it in its original home, or it may
be the starting point of a number of derivatives which
in the manner of their formation or in the meaning which
attaches to them would be quite contrary to the spirit
of the language from which they were borrowed.

§ 57. We have already alluded to the fact that after
the Conquest the work of copying manuscripts was very
largely done by Norman scribes. So long as they were
copying French texts this was no doubt all to the good,
but when they were copying English texts the same can
scarcely be said. Being unfamiliar with the sounds
of English and with the forms of English, and meeting
many combinations of sounds which were quite strange
to them, and unknown in their own tongue, it is scarcely
to be wondered at that they should have taken some
liberties with English spelling, especially since there was
no such thing as an accepted spelling, and since most
people wrote, or tried to write, as they spoke. The
endeavours of the Norman scribe to spell English
phonetically were not always successful, as every student
of Middle English knows. Their errors, however, have
not left many traces in the modern language, so there is
no need to detail them here. But there were certain
innovations made by these Norman scribes which
have become a recognised part of our Modern English
orthography, and these may perhaps be best con-

sidered here, even though they do not affect the actual vocabulary.

Among consonants the most important changes which they introduced were the substitution of *th* for the old runic symbol þ and for ð. So also the old runic symbol p was replaced by *w*, which originally consisted of two v's interlaced. They also introduced the symbol *v*, which did not exist in Old English, though the sound for which it stands was quite common. Of the old symbol þ there are still traces in the form *ye* in such pseudo-archaisms as *ye olde English hostelry*. The spelling *gh* which is so common in English in words like *light, sight, bright, night,* etc., is also probably of similar origin, though the sound for which it originally stood (a velar or palatal spirant) has since been lost. The Norman scribes also made some important modifications in the representation of vowel sounds. Thus the Old English sound which was represented by the symbol *y* and which had much the same sound as the vowel in French *sur* was written by them *u*, and the Old English sound which was represented by the symbol *ū* and had much the same sound as *oo* in Modern English *school* was by them written *ou*, the symbol always used for that sound in French. This *ou*, however, was frequently written *ow* at the end of a word, so that we now write *now, how, cow,* but *house, mouse, louse* (O.E. *nū, hū, cū, hūs, mūs, lūs*). The short *u* sound, represented in Old English by *u* was kept, however, except that in words in which it was followed or preceded by *m, n, v, w,* it was written *o*, though keeping the sound of a short *u*. Thus it comes about that in Modern English we have the two words *son* and *sun*, differently spelt, but with the same pronunciation, though both in the older language had the same root vowel. So also words like *come*, *some* and others, are written in Modern English with an *o*, though the sound which is pronounced in them is a *u* sound. In other cases the normal English spelling was influenced by the French spelling. Thus, for example, the sound *s* was often in French represented by the symbol *c*, as in *face, place*, etc. This spelling was not only preserved in French words which were borrowed in English, but it was even extended to some native words such as *ice, mice, twice, thrice,* etc., where Old English had *s*. French also is the spelling *ie* in words like *field*. Other consonant changes were the substitution of *ch* with its French value of (tsh) for the older *c* ; *k* with the value of *k* was written before the vowels *i, e, kin, ken* and *c* before *a, o, u, can, come, cut*. The older *cw* was replaced by the French *qu*. French also is the symbol *z*, which did not exist in Old English, and also the spellings *sh* and *wh* for O.E. *sc, hw*.

§ 58. The large number of French words which entered into the language made the English people so familiar with Latin stems that there was no difficulty in introducing words in their Latin rather than in their French form. In some cases, as we have already noted, the form of a word would have been the same whether taken direct from Latin or through French. But the bulk of the Latin words which were borrowed directly from the Renaissance onwards are easily recognisable by their form, and very often by their meaning. The word which was taken direct from Latin usually had a longer form than the one which first passed through French ; thus, for example, the word *blaspheme* is much nearer to the

Latin original than is the word *blame*. The former is
nearer to the Latin form and preserves its original sense ;
the latter has undergone various changes in French
before passing into English. With regard to the direct
loans, however, it should be noticed that French also at
the same time was borrowing new words from Latin,
the so-called *mots-savants*, and these might have precisely the same form as they would have when taken
straight from Latin into English. It is therefore difficult,
and often quite impossible, to tell by which route a Latin
word has passed into English.

The Latin words which were borrowed during and
after the Renaissance are, in the great majority of cases,
words with an abstract or technical sense. They
represent more remote and complex conceptions than
are ordinarily found in the language of everyday speech,
and it is therefore characteristic of them that they are
found mainly in the language of literature. These words
began to appear in the language as early as the fourteenth century, and they became exceedingly numerous
in the sixteenth and nineteenth centuries. At the
present day the borrowing still continues, though for
purely technical terms Greek seems to afford more words
than Latin. Even from the early days of the Renaissance borrowings from Greek have been frequent, though
Greek words have usually been Latinised before adoption
into English.

It is not easy to account satisfactorily for this long-
lived habit of turning to Latin and Greek for the elements
of new words in English. The cause is probably complex. It would be rash to assume that the easy adoption
of classical words in English is an indication that the

English have pursued the study of the classical languages with greater zeal than have other peoples. The explanation is to be found rather in the fact that the Norman Conquest had not only made the English people familiar with the form and meaning of Latin words but had also, owing to the dependence of English Literature on French literature, created the habit of looking to Latin and Greek for new words. Tenacity in habits and traditions is a notoriously marked characteristic of the Englishman, and speech-forming habits are among the most persistent and deep-rooted habits of man. Moreover the habit of using certain words for the expression of thought is evidence that the thought itself tends to run along particular lines. We can very well understand, therefore, that fourteenth century writers—and we are here mainly concerned with the vocabulary of literature—who were nourished on French literature should have found in words of French or Latin origin the symbols of their thought, and that in the progress and development of their thought new associations of ideas should seek interpretation in symbols akin to those which already served for the interpretation of the simpler elements of their thought. Or, differently expressed, language is thought and thought is language. Therefore, when for any reason whatever an individual or a people contracts the habit of thinking in a particular language it is the most natural thing in the world that it should continue to do so and should develop its language uniformly in the same direction. The presence of large numbers of classical words in English is evidence, therefore, of a very profound influence of the genius of the Latin language or of the genius of Roman thought upon the English language and English thought. It is not merely a superficial influence, as might be inferred from the use of such terms as "borrowings" and "loan words"; it is rather the consequence of a general sympathy in outlook and manner of thought, a sympathy which is clearly seen in the predominantly political and practical character both of the Roman and of the Englishman. It is doubtless for the same reason that Greek words before being adopted into English were made to assume a Latin dress.

But though the habits of thought formed after the Norman Conquest and during the Renaissance may be responsible for the addition of large numbers of Latin and Greek words to our vocabulary, yet the conditions of English life and English education in later times also had their influence in preserving those habits. It may well be that it was our national conservatism of character which kept alive the tradition of Latin as the language of learning longer in this country than elsewhere, and the classical training even of our scientists in more modern times has made them prone to turn to the classical languages for new technical terms.

§ 59. One of the first consequences of familiarity with Latin authors during the Renaissance was the reshaping of French words which had already been adopted in the language. Many of these were respelt in conformity with the Latin word from which they were derived, more particularly when the etymology was obvious. Thus the word *descrive* was rewritten *describe*, a *b* was reintroduced into *debt* and *doubt* and a *c* into *verdict* and *victuals*. *Langage* was mixed up with *lingua* and the result of the mixture was *language*. In other cases

the resemblance between the two words was not so
obvious, as in *peinture* and *picture*.

§ 60. Another consequence of the introduction of words
in their Latin forms was that there arose once again
doublets, though not necessarily with the same meaning.
Side by side with the older French *assoil* we find the
Latin *absolve*, and *benediction* is only a Latin form of
benison. So also *antecessor* is the form from which
ancestor was derived in French ; the word *grace* appears
in its French form, but in *grateful* and *gratitude* we have
the Latin form. In other cases the different words
develop different meanings, as has happened in the case
of *hostel, hotel* and *hospital*, or in *jealous* and *zealous*.
Words like *ambition, antecedent, difference*, and many
more, might equally well be derived either from French
or from Latin.

§ 61. It would not be possible to give within the limits
of this book a systematic analysis of the various categories of words borrowed from Latin since the fourteenth
century, for there is no department of thought and there
is no activity the vocabulary of which is not affected to
some extent by the influence of Latin. We must content
ourselves, therefore, with a brief survey of the material.
One of the most important sources of the earliest Latin
loan words in Middle English was the science and pseudo-
science of the schoolmen. From them we have the words
grammar, logic, metaphysic, rhetoric, astronomy, and the
technical terms of the seven " arts " of the universities
such as *comedy, tragedy, history, philosophy*. Here, too,
should be included a number of terms originally technical
but which have since assumed a more general sense,
such as *subject, object, individual, premise, assumption*,

general, special, universal and many more. To scholarship and science belong words like *physic, equator,
philosophy*, and to astrology such terms as *influence,
conjunction, aspect, astrolabe, horoscope, lunatic*. From
the language of medieval medicine we have *dropsy, gout,
poison, medicine, palsy, melancholy, humour* and many
more. From the sixteenth century onwards a large
number of words were borrowed or coined to furnish
a vocabulary for all branches of knowledge. Thus, of
political terminology, we have *anarchy, democracy* and
politician from the sixteenth century ; *diplomat, natura-
lise* and *neutral* from the seventeenth ; and *diplomatic,
nihilism* and *communism* from the eighteenth and nine-
-teenth centuries. Literary terms were also freely
borrowed in the sixteenth and seventeenth centuries as
may be seen from the words *drama, pantomime, rhyme,
rhythm, critic, biography, orthography, obituary, poem*.
From Latin in the seventeenth century come *education*
and *instruct*. Since the sixteenth century hundreds and
hundreds of new words have been borrowed from Latin
or coined from Latin materials in the vocabulary of all
the sciences and for the names of those sciences themselves : *analysis, parallel, parabola, geology, physiology,
psychology, biology*. Most of these latter, it is true, are
ultimately of Greek origin but have Latinised forms.
Among words of more recent origin we may notice
monograph, calisthenics.

§ 62. But while words were thus freely taken from
Latin and Greek sources, borrowing was by no means
restricted to these languages. Throughout the centuries
new words have constantly been taken from French.
Especially during the reign of Charles II. borrowings

were frequent. From that period we have *corps*, *chagrin*, *campaign*, *cannonade*, *caprice*, *miniature*, *hautboy*, *fusilier*, *pontoon*. From French of a slightly earlier period we derive further the words *commerce*, *factory*, *manufacture*, and in the eighteenth century we took the words *finance* (in its modern sense), *consol*, *budget*, *banking*. The French Revolution, in its turn, gave us *aristocrat*, though the word *aristocracy* already existed in the language, and the word *conscription*. The same century gave us *palette* and *pastel*. Somewhat later are *chateau*, *critique*, *environs*, *liqueur*, *douche*, *connoisseur*.

§ 63. The classical languages and French have not been the only foreign sources of the English vocabulary. From the Middle Ages onwards all languages far and near have contributed something to the enrichment of the English vocabulary. More particularly the contact between East and West which was established by the Crusades brought to Europe and to England words of Eastern origin. Some Eastern words, however, reached England before the Crusades. Such are, for example, *India*, *Saracen*, *pepper*, *silk*, *sugar*, *orange*. From Arabic or Persian we have *crimson*, *scarlet*, *azure*, *caravan*, *assassin*, *chess*, *bazaar*. From India come the words *indigo*, *chintz*, *bungalow*, *calico*, *cashmere*; from Hebrew, *balsam*, *cherub*, *shekel*, *ebony*. From Chinese comes *tea*; from Malay, *lemon*. Other Arabic words which may have reached us by roundabout routes are: *alkali*, *azimuth*, *algebra*, *admiral*, *arsenal*, *antimony*, *cotton*, *coffee*, *mosque*, *Sultan* and *cockatoo*. Tartar gives us *cossack*, *horde* and *turquoise*. From different parts of Africa have been taken the words *banana*, *fez*, *morocco*, *gorilla*. From the American languages we have *hickory*, *toboggan, pemmican, tomahawk,* from the Indians; through the Spaniards we have received *chocolate* from Mexico, *cannibal, canoe, hurricane* and *tobacco* from the West Indies ; *alpaca, quinine, guano, puma* and *llama* from Peru. Many of the words of Oriental origin only came by very indirect routes into English, thus *asparagus, musk, paradise, tiger, rice* all passed first through Latin and Greek before they reached English from Persian, and *tulip* and *turban* appear to have passed through both Turkish and French.

§ 64. Turning to the Slavonic languages we notice the words *sable, slave, steppe, polka, mazurka* and others.

§ 65. Among the remaining languages of Europe the one which has contributed most to English is Italian. A considerable number of words was borrowed from Italian in the sixteenth and seventeenth centuries and these words are interesting evidence of the nature of the close relationship which existed between England and Italy. Many of them are musical terms such as *adagio, andante, opera, piano, sonata, soprano.* Others, again, are literary terms such as *stanza, canto,* or architectural terms such as *cupola, portico, casino,* etc. The words which came to us from Italian more frequently, however, passed first through French, as for example, *sonnet, carnival, concert, facade, escort, parapet, parasol, porcelain, corridor, colonnade,* etc. The common words *maccaroni, vermicelli, influenza, soda, volcano* come direct from Italian.

Spanish and Portuguese words are not nearly so numerous as Italian words and most of them have come into English through contact with the Spanish and Portuguese colonies. Among the words in common use from Spanish we notice *cigar, anchovy, armada, domino, lasso, mosquito, negro, sherry*; and from Portuguese *madeira, port, molasses, verandah.*

§ 66. Since the Middle English period borrowings from a related Germanic language have not been common. The Scandinavian borrowings almost ceased after the Middle English period, though such new words as *tungsten, dahlia, slag* have appeared. More numerous are the words which were borrowed during the great trade and maritime rivalry of the English and the Dutch. These, as might be expected, are largely sea-faring terms such as *boom, derrick, dock, lighter, marlin, reef, skipper, yacht.* Other words in common use are *brandy, knapsack, landscape, loiter, veldt.* Words borrowed from German are still less numerous, the commonest are *quartz, meerschaum, landau, plunder, waltz, nickel.* In modern scientific terminology there are many more, as, for example, such grammatical terms as *Umlaut, Ablaut.* Others, again, are much disguised owing to the fact that they have first passed through French. Thus *fauteuil* is nothing more than the German word *faldstol* or "folding stool."

§ 67. In consequence of these numerous borrowings from different languages at different periods it often happens that a word is borrowed twice over with different forms according to the language from which it is derived and according to the period at which it was borrowed. Thus there arise new doublets in the language. We have, for example, the word *sir* or *sire* in its French form, but we have also the Latin form *senior*, and the Italian form *signor*, and the Spanish *senor*. *Army* comes from French, but *armada*, which is originally the same word, comes from Spanish ; *cargo* is the Spanish form of *charge* ; *influenza* is the Italian form of *influence, madonna* the Italian form of *madame* ; *papyrus* is the Latin form from which *paper* is derived ; *portico* is from Italian and *porch* from French ; the Latin *superanum* appears in two distinct forms, firstly in its French form *sovereign,* and secondly in its Italian form *soprano. Carmine* is probably the Spanish form of an Arabic word and *crimson* the French form of the same word.

CHAPTER IV

HOW NEW MEANINGS ARISE

§ 68. Nowhere can the activities of the mind in the development of language be seen more clearly than in the development of new meanings in words ; for the process is everywhere a faithful mirror of thought. Whatever may have been the origin of language, one thing is quite certain about the earliest human speech : its first words were either exclamations or the names of things or actions perceived by one or other of the five senses. The forces of environment and the more urgent needs of primitive life would leave their impress on all early vocabularies. We should expect to find in such a primitive vocabulary words for " man," " woman," " dog," " cow," " eat," " drink," " sleep," etc. The things which were seen or felt or heard would receive names first, and it is natural, therefore, that the most primitive forms of words are always found to be either verbal or substantival stems.

But if primitive man has names for " dog," " cow," " tree," etc., these names are the names of specific objects. There is no word, such as *animal*, which includes both dog and cow ; for the creation of the word " animal " shows that men had begun to think, and to think somewhat

91

deeply about the nature of a dog and of a cow ; that they had begun to observe that there was something common to them both—that they lived and moved, had four legs, etc. Such an analysis of the nature of things and of the resemblances between things presupposes considerable reflection and it is, therefore, a mark of an advancing civilisation if we find in a language a large number of such generic terms.

Another kind of reflection upon the nature of material things is seen in the gradual ability to distinguish the various qualities of material things, as, for example, that grass is green, that the sun is bright, etc. The existence of such words also points to a process of thought which detaches certain qualities of things and then compares them with something else in order to name them.

A much more advanced stage in the development of human thought is reached when men are able to conceive and name immaterial things. We may best illustrate the process of thought by considering the history of a word which shows the various stages of development. We may imagine that primitive man saw before his eyes things growing and that many of these things, such as grass, trees, etc., were conspicuous by their colour. We find, then, in the Indo-Germanic languages a stem which appears in the English words *grow, grass* and *green*. We may assume, for the sake of discussion, that the stem originally meant something which grew, such as grass, or growing things. Then it was observed of some other thing, which did not grow, that it had the same colour as these growing things. Let us suppose that this new thing was the sea. Now one of the most striking features of the sea is its colour, and whenever the necessity, or the desire, arose to describe this feature of the sea, a comparison was made in the mind between the sea and growing things, not, of course, in respect of shape or texture, but only of colour. The result of this comparison was the evolution of the adjective green. It is a significant confirmation of this process that adjectives in Indo-Germanic are derived from nouns and were originally declined exactly as if they were nouns. The psychological process underlying this development, moreover, still operates fully in modern times ; for just as our more primitive man may have made a mental comparison of growing things and the sea, so the modern Englishman has made a mental comparison between a certain colour which he has produced and the sea and has called it " sea-green." So also we have " sky-blue." A further stage of abstraction is reached when such a quality of a thing is conceived as something distinct from the objects with which it is usually associated, and we speak of " greenness," " whiteness." In the same way the adjective red is connected with the Sanskrit word rudhira, which gives us the necessary clue to its origin, for the Sanskrit word means " blood."

Such abstractions as whiteness, greyness, etc., have their obvious origin in the names of concrete things. But other abstractions such as justice, right, wrong, animation, and all the rest of them, have a similar origin. They are all based upon an act of the mind comparing, consciously or not, two distinct things and associating them in speech. The word right, for example, literally means "straight" and therefore signifies a purely visual image, and it is curious to note that in Modern

English we use the word " straight " in a similar sense
when we say of a man that he is " straight." Similarly,
the word *wrong* meant " twisted " or " crooked," and
here again the image of crookedness has been visualised
in " a crooked character," or a " crook." *Animation* is
derived from a stem which meant " breath." *Prudence*
is derived from *providentia*, " a seeing before." And so
with other abstracts, they are derived from stems
which originally had concrete meanings, and they are
the result of a gradual abstraction which reflects a
developed faculty of thought.

But now if we return to our original example of *green*
we shall be able to see the conditions under which all
changes of meaning arise. Let us assume that the stem
which underlies *green, grow* and *grass* originally meant
" grass." (It may have meant something else, such as
" tree " or a growing thing, but that does not affect the
discussion.) Now that word as applied to grass was the
name of a specific thing ; it meant grass in its entirety,
including its colour, its shape, its uses and so on. But
when it was first used in association with the word *sea*
it must have been evident even to the most primitive
intelligence that the resemblance between sea and grass
was only one of colour and not one of shape or consist-
ency. In other words, the association of grass and sea
in speech immediately had the consequence of shutting
out from consideration all the elements of meaning of
the word *grass* except that of colour. It is therefore
only when the word *grass* is used together with another
word that the particular sense in which it is to be
understood becomes clear. The same condition is
present in all intelligible speech and it is a condi-

tion *sine qua non* of every change of meaning in a word.

It cannot be too much emphasised that the meaning of all words depends upon the context in which they are found. Let us illustrate this from Modern English. We may say : *He was obliged to resign for reasons of health,* and we may also say : *His health permitted him to undertake such arduous work.* In both of these sentences the word *health* occurs ; in the first it means " bad health" and in the second it means "good health." But there is absolutely nothing in the word itself to tell us which sense is implied. The context alone tells us that. Or let us look at the sentences : *He broke his arm.   The right arm was fur-lined.   He leant on the arm of his chair.* In no case can we know what is meant by *arm* unless we first hear the context, but once we have heard the context all those elements of meaning which the word *arm* may suggest are excluded except the particular one which fits in with the context.   Or we may take one more example to illustrate the general principle.   In Old English *health* meant only " good health," " the state of being whole."   Now so long as the word had such a meaning it was obviously impossible to say *bad health,* for that would involve a too flagrant contradiction in terms.   But one can very well conceive of such an association of ideas as " lost health " or " injured health," in which the sense is perfectly logical.   But whilst still being logical the context makes a subtle implication that what was good health is now a state which can no longer be described as good.   There is in such collocations a somewhat modified conception of health ; it now means " state of health."   But once this meaning has become familiar there is no difficulty in saying " ill health." Yet it is to be observed that since the adjective *healthy* could not be used in such a context it has retained its original meaning of " being in good health," though even here we can now speak of a person as being " indifferently healthy." Such changes of meaning as we have seen in this word, which may mean two opposite things according to the context, are by no means uncommon, and such a logical contradiction as is really involved in the expression *ill-health* is by no means peculiar to English. An excellent example of it is afforded by Swedish, which has the word *bläck* for " ink." The word is the same as our word *black* and its origin requires no further comment. But what is remarkable is that where the context makes it perfectly clear that the word means " ink " it is possible to speak of *rött bläck*, which means " red black."

Sufficient examples have now been given to illustrate the general principle that a change in the signification of a word is only possible because the surrounding words make it clear what particular modification of the original sense is intended. Indeed one may not inappropriately liken a word to a piece in a jig-saw puzzle. Standing by itself it is useless and meaningless. It is only when it fits into its proper place that its significance appears, and it can only fit into its place if it has the correct form and content. It is because a word has so many elements of meaning that it is capable of entering into association with other words. If we take such a simple everyday word as *house* we shall see how much more complex is the thought of which it is a symbol than is the symbol itself. The word *house* may mean a " place to dwell in," but it may also conjure up a vision of walls, of a roof, of windows, staircases, rooms, bricks and other things. But in using the word *house*, we do not necessarily think of all these things. Some of them are not necessary to our immediate purpose. When we say that we have just moved into a new house, we think of a house as a dwelling place and the other elements of meaning of the word are not brought prominently forward in our consciousness. If we say " a white house " we call up images and associations of quite a different kind ; we think of the outer walls, their colour ; but we do not think at all of such details as the kitchen, the bathroom or the staircase. When we speak of a well-fitted house we think rather of certain accidentals of decoration and fittings. In each of these cases the context acts as a sort of guardian on the threshold of consciousness which permits certain elements of meaning to come forward, while the rest slumber on in the recesses of the mind. Moreover, it is not only the immediate neighbour of a word which determines its meaning in a particular sentence ; it is the whole of the context also. Thus in the sentence, *I moved into a new house*, it is not the word *new* which brings forth the meaning of dwelling house ; a " new house " means something different ; it conjures up the vision of new bricks, new woodwork, new paint, etc. It is the rest of the context together with the word *new* which gives the word its particular meaning in this context. So it is with all words. Each one has the power of calling up numerous images, sensations and meanings. Each one of them has innumerable associations, and it is the subtle combination of any one of these associations with any association of any other word in the context which makes it possible for language to keep pace with the development of thought. The mind is stored with the memory of all our thoughts and experiences and each one has as its symbol a word or a group of words. These thoughts and experiences combine, associate, group and regroup themselves in the mind and find expression in words which, by their fine shades of meaning, reflect something of the process which brings them forth.

The great masters of language are those who have learnt the secret of these inner meanings of words, meanings which shift and change according to the company which they keep. There are some writers who know well how to harvest the surplus of meaning which comes from the association of words, and who are able to combine them in the way which yields the maximum of suggestion :

penitent Zephyrus
fondles a flower amid the sobbing rain.

The mental processes at work in the modification of the meaning of a word are exactly the same as those which are at work in the formation of new words. They are everywhere the same. Wherever we look we find that new meaning is the result of a mental comparison between two things, and it is often instructive to compare words in different languages in order to see what the comparison is which underlies the meaning of a particular word. Thus, for example, the word *blood* in English corresponds to an Indo-Germanic stem *bhlo*, which is seen in the Latin *fluo* and meant " to flow." The other Germanic languages also have this word, Ger. *blut*, Goth. *bloth*, Swed. *biod*, etc. But this comparison with

something that flows does not stand alone. We find
in O.E. a form *drēor* and in Old Norse *dreyri*, both of
which words come from a stem meaning "to drop."
There is also a word *swāt* in O.E. (*heaþu-swāt*) O.N.
sveiti which means "sweat," and though this word is of
much later origin with the meaning of blood, it nevertheless shows that the process of comparison is still at
work. But what struck others in naming "blood"
was not that it was "dropping" or "flowing," but that
it was "red," Sanskrit *rudhira*. Similarly, although
the word *body* is of doubtful origin, there exist in Old
English and other Germanic languages words which
point to various associations of ideas. Thus O.E. has
a word *līc*, which later came to mean a "corpse" and
is still seen in *lich-gate*. The underlying meaning here
is that of "likeness" or "image." It was also used
in combination with a word *hama*, which meant originally "covering" or "dress," and this same stem also
appears with a different sense in the Latin *camisia*,
English *chemise* and German *Hemd*, "shirt." In addition
to these, Old English has numerous compound descriptive names of its own, such as *feorh-hūs*, "life-house,"
feorh-bold, "life dwelling," *bān-fœt*, "bone vessel,"
bān-hus, "bone-house" and many more. Especially
interesting in this connection are the names for "hand."
Both *hand* and *fist* are derived from a stem which originally meant "to grasp." The word *right* in "right hand"
means "straight," but in some of the Scandinavian
dialects we find, instead of "right hand," "soup-hand."
Old English uses a word *swīþ*, which originally meant
"strong." Gothic, like Latin, used a word which meant
"fit," "suitable." The meaning may be seen by a

comparison of the word *dexterous* and the substantive *decor*.

The development of meaning in words being such as we have seen, it is natural that there should be in the history of word meanings some traces of the material conditions and of the mental conceptions which gave rise to them. This expectation is indeed amply justified, for there are a number of words in English which throw a particularly vivid light on earlier conditions. One of these is the O.E. word *fōn*. Its original meaning was "to seize," but in Old English it has the meaning "to succeed" (to a throne) and this meaning throws interesting light on the political history of the Germanic peoples. In much the same way the word *king*, O.E. *cyning*, is made up of two elements of which the first is O.E. *cynn*, "tribe," and the second a suffix denoting origin. A "king," therefore, is one of the tribe, or else the son of the tribe, and the underlying conception may be compared with that which is to be found in the Latin *rex*, which means "one who rules." Interesting, too, are the numerous words in Old English for "companion," all of which have been lost in Modern English. They all of them point to various forms of social life, in exactly the same way as the word *companion* itself means "one who (eats) bread with somebody." The Old English words signify those who travel together (*gefēra*), those who dwell in the same room or building (*geselda*), those who enjoy something together (*genēat*). Another word which reflects an earlier, pre-industrial society is the O.E. *feoh*, which survives in *fee*. Its original meaning is "cattle," a sense which it still preserves in Old English. But since cattle were one of the most important forms of wealth, they came to be used as a medium of exchange, and the word *feoh* came to mean also a means of exchange or "money." In a restricted sense, that of a payment of money for a certain service rendered, it survives in *fee*. It may be observed that the Romance word "cattle," from Latin *capitale*, also contains the stem *caput*, "head," but was extended in meaning to include other forms of wealth, until its sense in Latin and French came to be that of "property." In English, however, in the form *cattle*, it was again restricted in meaning, to one form of property, "cattle," whereas a doublet derived from Central French, in the form *chattel*, kept the original sense of moveable property. These two words afford an additional example of the constant tendency in language to discriminate in meaning between, and to differentiate, synonyms.

It happens not infrequently that, in consequence of the gradual change in the signification of a word, all sense of its original meaning is lost, though in another word derived from the same stem the original meaning is faithfully preserved. We have noted one such case in *health* and *healthy*. An excellent example of this phenomenon is afforded by the history of the word *humour*. Whereas the adjective *humid*, still preserves the sense of "damp" or "wet," the substantive *humour* is now never used in this sense. From its original sense of "moisture," this word came to mean one or other of the bodily fluids which in medieval physiology were held to determine a person's temperament ; it came then to mean "temperament" and "mood." In the sense of "mood" it came further to signify a special mood or disposition, or a whim or caprice, and finally it reached its modern sense. But it is curious to think that we can now say a " dry humour," which is a contradiction in terms, without anybody feeling that there is the least incongruity in the phrase. In the same way the word *quarantine* originally meant a period of forty days during which a person might be isolated in order to prevent the spread of a contagious disease. But now we can speak of " ten days' quarantine." The word *horn*, among its many developments, came to mean a vessel out of which one might drink, but in the course of time it became possible to speak of a " silver horn," or one can also speak of a silver " shoe-horn." A *steel pen* seems a perfectly natural name, if one does not happen to know that *pen* is the Latin *penna*, " feather," a sense which it still has in Middle English ; German and the Scandinavian languages, on the other hand, have translated this word (German *Feder*), but nevertheless they too can speak of a " steel pen " or *Stahlfeder*. It is again curious to notice that the meaning of the word *valetudinarian* has run a course somewhat similar to that of *health*, though the route has been somewhat different. Being derived from the Latin *valere* it meant "to be well" and thus meant " health " ; from this sense it came to mean one who was solicitous for his health and hence an " invalid."

§ 69. The kinds of change which occur in the meanings of words have been variously classified as consisting in expansion, restriction, deterioration, etc., of meaning. We may give a few examples in order to illustrate each one of these changes, but it may be pointed out that the classification is entirely artificial and does not correspond to anything fundamental in the nature of the

changes noted. In the first class, then, there are words
the meaning of which undergoes a progressive deterioration in sense ; that is to say, from having had a good
sense they come to have a bad sense. An excellent
example of such a change is afforded by the word *silly*,
which in Old English was *sælig* with the meaning
"happy." The word is derived from a stem *sæl* which
meant "happy," "well." A similar development is to
be seen in the word *cunning*, which is etymologically
connected with the verb *can*. Its earliest sense is that of
"knowledge," "learning" or else the faculty of knowing,
"intelligence" ; then it takes on the meaning "skill,"
"dexterity" ; then "craft," "artifice," "deceit." But
the adjective, when used in such a phrase as "a cunning
device," still keeps its earlier meaning. The word
craft, again, from having the sense "strength," a sense
which it still retains in the other Germanic languages,
has come to signify "cunning" by stages closely resembling those by which *cunning* came to have its present
meaning. Here, too, the older meaning has been preserved in a context which makes the meaning clear, as
in *craftsman*, though the forms *crafty* and *craftily*
have only the bad sense in Modern English. The cause
underlying many of these changes is the desire to present
an unpleasant fact in as pleasant a way as possible ;
a word used as a euphemism by degrees loses its force
as a euphemism and in the course of time takes on the
pure meaning of the unpleasant fact. Other words,
again, while not exactly taking on a bad sense, yet
lose their good sense, by being overmuch used. This is
especially the case where words originally emphatic are
used in every possible context and thus lose their em-

phatic force. Such has been the fate of *pretty*, which originally meant "clever," "skilful," and gradually came to be used as an epithet of general approval, with a very vague sense. Sometimes a word is used ironically, and in such a use we find a cause of deterioration almost as potent as the euphemistic use of a word : "a pretty mess." Another word which has had a similar development in meaning is the word *fine*. Its original sense was "finished," "perfect," and this sense may now be rendered by its etymological derivative "finished." It then passed through various stages of meaning such as "pure," in "fine gold"; "delicate" as in "fine feeling," "fine distinction," "fine texture"; until ultimately by overmuch use it came to be used, just like *pretty*, though with somewhat greater force, as a general term of approval or admiration. To the same class belongs the word *nice*, which is in even commoner use than *fine* or *pretty*. Its original sense was that of "foolish," in English. In this sense it still shows its connection with the Latin *nescius*, from which it is ultimately derived. In the sixteenth century it had the meaning of "fastidious," "particular," "precise," senses which may be seen in the phrases "nicely balanced," a "nice distinction" in the sense of a fine distinction ; later still the word has the meaning "pleasant," "acceptable," and it is in this sense that the word has become worn out until in the modern spoken language it signifies a vague sort of appreciation.

The changes of meaning which are due to restriction are common in all languages. The process of restriction is to be seen at work, as we have already observed, on nearly all words when they are used in a sentence ; for the context restricts their application. Sometimes, again, where a word has many meanings the intelligence of the reader or of the hearer goes swiftly behind the spoken or written word and guesses at the thought, either restricting or expanding the literal meaning of the word. But there are some words which, from being habitually used in the same context, come definitely to retain the meaning which they have in that context, whilst losing all other meanings. Such has been the case with the word *town*. Its original sense, as may be seen in the German word *Zaun*, was that of a "fence" enclosing some ground. We can easily understand how, when the word was used in the phrase "in the fence," or "inside the fence," the word gradually came to mean "enclosure," or all that was within the fence or wall, hence "village" or "town." The same change of meaning can be observed in the word *pit*. It is now used to designate a certain part of the theatre, but it is also used to designate that part of the audience which is seated in the pit. The only difference between the development of meaning in the words *town* and *pit* is that whereas *pit* retains its other senses and is still commonly used with those senses, the word *town* has lost its original sense. Similarly, the word *yard* has become restricted in sense to a piece of ground attached to a building or else used for some industrial purpose as in *farm-yard*, *dock-yard*, *court-yard*. Yet originally it is the same word as *garden*, as may be seen in *vineyard* or *orchard* from *ort* (Lat. *hortus*) + *geard*, "garden."

The opposite of restriction of meaning is expansion of meaning. Some examples of expansion we have already noticed, as, for example, where *feoh* from meaning

" cattle " also came to mean " fee." In fact, by far the greatest number of changes in the significations of words are due to expansion of meaning. This is quite natural, for, as we have seen, such developments of meaning are all due to a comparison of the properties or peculiarities of things, and in so far as we are all constantly seeing new resemblances between things these perceptions are reflected in our use of words and in the modification of their meanings. So, to go back to our example, *craft*, we see that quite recently it has been used as a collective in the compound *air-craft*, though hitherto it had only been used in this sense in reference to ships. But since it could be thus used of *water-craft*, it was not a very difficult transition to use it of craft which moved in the air, the more so since the word *air-ship* had already preceded it.

But it is when we turn to the words in most common use in language that we find the principle of expansion most active. Words like *draw, drive, sink, go* illustrate from their numerous meanings how active is this principle. Thus *draw* originally meant " to pull by force," but since there are many ways of pulling, and many effects of pulling, we find all of these gradually entering into the signification of the word. Thus we can speak of " drawn features," " drawing the breath " into our lungs. Then, too, the drawing may be effected by mental or moral force as well as by physical force, as in " to draw a conclusion " or in the sentence, " the promised speech drew a large audience." The word further develops the general sense of " to obtain," as in " to draw money from the bank," " to draw a salary." From the sense of drawing a pencil across a surface, we have the modern sense of drawing lines, figures, etc., and in a figurative sense the drawing of a word picture. Such are a few only of the extremely numerous expansions of meaning which this word has undergone, and the same principle might be illustrated with equal fulness from the history of words like *drive* and *give* and many more of the commonest words in the language. Such words as these are, in the very nature of things, the richest in associations and in potential meanings ; they therefore lend themselves most readily to the process of expansion.

Excellent examples of the process of expansion are also afforded by the names of the parts of the body. We may take two or three of these as illustrations. The word *eye* originally meant the organ of vision ; it was early applied to the sun as the " eye of heaven." It was then used to describe the action of the eye, in " to make eyes at " ; it further enters into a number of phrases with still something of its earlier meaning, as in " to have an eye to," " in the eye of " the law, etc. But it was then applied to objects resembling the eye in shape or function, the " eye " of a needle. Similarly *arm*, from meaning merely a limb, comes to mean a power or authority in the " arm " of justice, of the law ; and further comes to mean that which covers the arm as in the arm of a coat (cf. *leg* of a pair of trousers). It is then further used of things resembling arms, such as the " arm " of a chair, an " arm " of the sea, the " arm " of the linotype machine, etc. In the same way the word *body* departs from its original sense and may be used in the sense of the most important member, the " body " of the book, or it may be used in the sense of " person " as in *anybody, nobody*.   By a similar expansion of meaning the word *arm*, when used in the plural, is used of defensive and offensive weapons.

One of the most fruitful sources of expansion in the meaning of words is to be found in the use of metaphor. A change which is due to metaphor is born of the perception of the similarity of two things in some respect. The developments of meaning which are due to metaphor are therefore in a very special sense a reflection of the working of the human mind, and are to the same extent a measure of the mind's activity as well as an indication of the character of its activity.   It is therefore no accident that the language of the sailor is full of words and expressions which are based upon his experience of ships and of life at sea ; or that the vocabulary of American English is rich in words which testify to the hurry of life in the United States.

It is usually by means of metaphor that abstract nouns are formed, as they always are formed originally, from concretes.   We have already noticed in this connection the development of the meanings *right* and *wrong*.   The word *influence*, again, originally meant merely an " influx," a " flowing in," but in medieval astrology the word was used to signify a particular " flowing in " of a fluid from the stars, which was supposed to influence men's disposition.   Such " influence " was invisible and secret, and a similar influence was then attributed to men over men.   Curiously enough this new-formed abstract has again become concrete in another form, *influenza*, a word which was borrowed from Italian, where it had been used to denote a disease of unknown and invisible origin.

Very common metaphorical expansions of meaning are those which are based upon the transference of the sensations of touch, taste, sight, etc. Thus we speak of a *warm* reception, a *cold* comfort, a *bitter* grief; and we have side by side the metaphorical *acute*, in " acute understanding," and *acid*, both of which words are from the Latin stem found in *acer*, " sharp."

CHAPTER V

WORD FORMATION

§ 70. IT has already been remarked in previous chapters that the main cause of the development of English, as of the development of any other language, is the action of the human mind seeking ever finer and more precise expression in language. The same principle may be seen to be active in the changes which remain to be considered in this chapter on derivation and composition. Perhaps nowhere else in language do we find such a clear manifestation of the mental act remodelling language as in the formation of compounds. We have seen, indeed, how changes of signification in words reveal something of the mental processes, but such changes do not show quite such a clear and unmistakable comparison of two things as we find in the composition of compounds such as *daylight, sunshine*, and still more in such Old English compounds as *synwracu*, " sin punishment " ; *swīþmōd*, " strong of heart," " brave." Such compounds represent a real economy of effort in expression, how great an economy can only be seen when the functions of such compounds are examined in detail. Thus in the compounds *country-life* and *headache* the first element denotes the position of the thing

110

mentioned in the second element; in *day-dream* it indicates the time; in *godsend* it indicates the starting point; in *church-goer* it indicates the direction; in *five-pound* note, it indicates the value; in *dress-circle* or *arm-chair* one of the distinguishing attributes. In others, again, the first element as it were contains the second, *nutshell, flower-stalk.* In *loaf-sugar* the first element indicates the form of the second element; in *birth-right* and *sea-sickness* it indicates the cause of the second element; in *fireplace* and *post-office* the function; in *steam engine* and *windmill* the instrument; in *beeswax, banknote* and *rainbow* the origin; in *gas-works* and *sugar-beet* the product. And so one might go on multiplying examples to show the various relations in which one element of a compound stands to another. But what is significant about all of these compounds is that they are economical, not one of them could be rendered except by a phrase. They are obviously a very great convenience and simplify the communication of thought.

§ 71. One can perhaps best realise the forces at work in the fashioning of new words if one examines the formation of one or other of the words which have recently been added to the language and compares it with a similar new word in another language. An admirable example for our purpose would be the word *airship* in English as compared with *dirigible* in French. We have in the airship one of those new things with which a progressive civilisation is always confronting the maker of language. It is very obvious that the name *airship* is the result of a deliberate contemplation of the nature and functions of this new object. Here, as in everything else which we call new, it is found that the object is not entirely new, or at any rate the human mind refuses to regard it as such. On the contrary, the human mind perceives that this new object has in fact resemblances to certain pre-existing things, and the imagination builds upon these resemblances in fashioning a new word to describe it. Why " airship " ? Because it was remarked that the function of this new thing is to float in a fluid medium, because it has certain external resemblances to a ship, as, for example, that it is propelled by a screw resembling a ship's screw ; that it is steered by a rudder. The resemblances are so striking that the name seems most natural and appropriate. But it should not be forgotten that if the word *airship* is an indication of *one* way of looking at the new thing, it is by no means the only way. An airship has peculiarities other than these, and it is quite possible that other peculiarities may be uppermost in the minds of persons differently constituted. We observe, indeed, that in connection with aerial locomotion, though not so much in connection with the airship as with the aeroplane, that the image of flying was present in the mind of some people, even though the aeroplane is also propelled by a screw and steered by a rudder and floats in a fluid medium. That which makes the difference in the two conceptions is possibly the shape of the object. But if we restrict our remarks to the airship, it is noteworthy that to the French the most striking peculiarity of the airship is that it can be steered and navigated. The resemblances to a ship no doubt occurred to the Frenchman just as much as to the Englishman, indeed they could scarcely escape him, but his mind was so constituted that these peculiarities did not strike him with the same force, or

else they did not make the same imaginative appeal
as did the fact that this new thing could be steered.
One is tempted to think that perhaps the Frenchman
regarded this thing as merely an improved balloon,
which in essence it is. When we bear in mind that the
French had been long engaged in the problem of finding
a balloon which could be steered, we shall realise that it
was natural for them to exclaim " dirigible " when at
last the problem was solved. One might perhaps draw
further conclusions from these two names concerning
the mental habits of the two peoples, but that might
take us on to less secure ground. But at least these
two words illustrate sufficiently for our present purpose
that new words, like new meanings and new syntax,
actually reflect the working of the human mind
and the habits, environment and traditions of that
mind.

§ 72. English, as we have seen, has been able, throughout the various periods of its history, to enrich its
vocabulary by copious borrowings from other languages,
and it still continues to do so. In more modern times,
however, it has not added to its vocabulary very many
new words formed from native material, if we except
those new formations which have been created by the
help of suffixes and prefixes. Most of the new stems are
those of loan words. Indeed, the vocabulary of English,
after so many centuries of borrowing, has become so
rich in material that it is scarcely necessary, except for
the purpose of newly discovered materials and processes,
to go outside the existing vocabulary ; for the possibilities of meeting new requirements by the ordinary
change of meaning of existing words, or by the formation

E.L.   H

of new words by means of affixes, are so great that no further material is required.

§ 73. In the earlier stages of the language words were coined very much more freely from pre-existing native material, though many of them have since been superseded by foreign words. Of the numerous Old English compounds such as *ætīewnes*, " manifestation " ; *blōdgȳte*, " bloodshed " ; *ceasterwara*, " citizen " ; *egesful*, " terrible " ; *lǣcedom*, " medicine," many have been lost because one or other of the elements or both have disappeared from the language in the ordinary course. Thus the *īewan* of *ætīewan* has been replaced by *show*, *gȳte* by *pour*, *ege* by *fear*, etc. But perhaps the majority of the older compounds have disappeared owing to the long supremacy of French as the spoken language of the educated people of the land. This is especially true of those compounds which are names of abstract things or thoughts, for these would naturally be found on the lips of the educated classes, with their Norman traditions. There are, nevertheless, cases in which a native compound has been replaced, even when it is the name of a concrete thing, by a word which is not of French origin, as for example the Old English word *ēagþyrel*, which meant an " eye-hole " (*þyrel* is preserved in *nostril*= nose-hole), was replaced by *window*, a Scandinavian word meaning " wind-eye."

§ 74. The means by which the language extended its vocabulary before it was able to draw upon French or Latin were the means which are still available in the modern language. They are, first, the creation of entirely new stems. In fact, very few such new words are created, mainly because the existing language

material is sufficient for all needs, without having
recourse to this means of word formation. The words
of this kind which have been formed in recent times are
nearly all imitative, the so-called onomatopœic words,
and most of them are imitations of sounds, such as
buzz, whizz, pop, bow-wow, etc. Such imitative words
were doubtless originally deliberate attempts to render
as nearly as possible the sounds which they imitate.
They have, however, a further interest in that they are
evidence that the mind does associate certain sounds
with certain things, or that one word by virtue of the
sounds which it contains expresses more fitly an action
than does another. There can be little doubt that it
was a full consciousness of this association of sound and
sense which inspired the line,

> Five miles meandering with a mazy motion;

or

> The ice was all around:
> It cracked and growled, and roar'd and howl'd
> Like noises in a swound;

or

> The fair breeze blew, the white foam flew,
> The furrow follow'd free:
> We were the first that ever burst
> Into that silent sea;

or

> Down dropped the breeze, the sails dropt down,
> 'Twas sad as sad could be.

§ 75. The second method by which new words are
formed is by combining two independent words into one.
Such a compound word has the merit of being economical
in expression, and on that account is the result of one of
the commonest impulses in language, the impulse to

economy of effort, wherever such economy does not
sacrifice clearness.   In a word like *handbook*, for example,
we avoid the necessity of saying a " book which can be
carried in the hand."   It is of the essence of the true
compound that it stands for a single conception and not
for the two conceptions expressed by the separate
elements.   Thus *handbook* makes us think of a single
thing which is neither " hand " nor " book," but an
indivisible single thing.   *Father-in-law* and *draughtsman*
or *tradesman* are likewise the names of single and
indivisible things, in the first we do not think
separately of " father " and " law " and in the last
we do not think of " trade " and " man."

The order of words in compounds follows the usual
word order of the language, that is to say, if the first
element of a compound is an adjective or a noun with the
function of an adjective it will precede its noun like any
other adjective, and in the same way any qualifying word
will precede the word which it qualifies.   In English,
however, we have compounds which are not native
compounds and in these the word order of the elements
is of course the word order of the language from which the
word is derived.   Thus, in English, we have with the
normal English word order such compounds as *race-
course, blue-gray, sky-blue, motor-car, steam-engine, long-
lived* ; but we have also *legislator, jurisprudence, knight-
errant, court-martial*, showing the word order of Latin
and French respectively.

It is usually easy to distinguish the older from the
newer compounds either by their pronunciation or by
the way in which they are written.   The newest compounds are usually felt to be the product of the com-

bination of independent words, and this consciousness
finds expression in the fact that they are usually written
with a hyphen combining the elements of which they are
composed. The oldest compounds, on the other hand,
are distinguishable by their pronunciation, for since
they have been long in the language they have in pronunciation fallen into the regular rhythm of the language
and are stressed, like other words, on the first syllable.
The consequence of this is that the remaining syllables
have a weaker stress and tend to become unrecognisable
as independent words. In such a word as *fret*, for example, though it was originally a compound composed of
the elements *fra-* and *etan*, "to eat up," "devour,"
and was used of the eating of animals only, there is no
longer the least consciousness of its being a compound,
partly owing to the fact that the prefix *fra-* no longer
exists as a prefix, and partly because the meaning of
the word has changed so much that its original signification is no longer recognisable. In the case of some older
compounds the spelling does not so completely disguise
the elements of the compound as in the word *fret*, but
the pronunciation of the second or weak-stressed element
nevertheless reveals its age. In such a word as *husband*,
for example, the second element does not differ very
much in spelling from its earlier form *bond*, but in pronunciation it is very much weakened. Compounds
which are neither as old as Old English nor are yet as
modern as compounds like *tram-car*, are still to be
recognised by a degree of weakening not so great as that
in *husband*. The word *blackbird*, for example, retains
the spelling of its two elements and is not written with
a hyphen, nor is the vowel of *bird* reduced as much as is

the vowel in the second syllable of *husband*.   But nevertheless the stress on *-bird* is not as strong as in the
independent word *bird* in "a black bird." Broadly
speaking, therefore, the age of a compound can be
judged by the amount of wear and tear which it has
suffered through use, and this wear and tear is to be
seen in the pronunciation rather than in the meaning.

§ 76. Languages vary in the extent to which they make
use of compound nouns.   Old English, like Modern
German, made a very free use of them, but Modern
English has not formed nearly so many.   The reason
is perhaps to be found once again in the tendency of
English to analyse rather than to synthesise, for the
formation of compounds is at bottom the converse of the
process of analysis.   In forming compounds a language
is really reverting to the process by which, originally,
inflections were formed, and there can be no doubt
that an excessive formation of compounds tends to
deprive a language of something of the flexibility which
it acquires from the analytic mode of expression.   The
excessive use of compounds tends to overload the significant content of a sentence unnecessarily and we find
therefore a tendency to revert from a compound to a
simpler term as when we say a "motor" for a "motor-
car," or a "tram" for a "tramcar."

In English compounds, as a rule, the first element
restricts the sense of the second element as in *blackbird*,
ice-cold, *tramway*.   The reluctance of Modern English,
as compared with Old English and Modern German, to
form new compounds of certain types is probably not
alone due to the fact that such a method of word formation was unfamiliar to French.   It is due to an even

greater extent to the normal syntactical development of the language which gave us a fixed word order and an analytical syntax instead of an inflectional syntax. It is for this reason that we instinctively feel that certain compounds are contrary to the spirit of the language. Mr. Bradley points out that we cannot form compounds of the type of the German *Schadenfreude*, "joy in mischief," or *Vaterlandsliebe*, "love of country." We cannot say *country-love* or *mischief-joy*. Our instinctive dislike of such compounds can only spring from a consciousness that they are not in accord with the normal practice of the language. And in fact they are not. Such a word as "country-love," if it existed, would naturally mean a love peculiar to country in the same way as "mother-love" is the kind of love peculiar to a mother. There is abundant precedent for "mother-love" from the earliest periods of English to the present day, O.E. *huskarl, husbonda*, etc., Modern English *coach-house, railway-station*, etc. In such compounds the first element merely narrows the meaning of the second element, but in the proposed compound *country-love* the action implied by "love" passes back to the first element, the first element is the object of the activity implied in the second. *Mother-love* could be expanded into "mother's love," a phrase which would be quite in accord with normal syntax, but *country-love* could not be expanded into "country's love"; it could only be expanded into "love of country." "Country's love" would immediately be felt as unusual and would shock the linguistic consciousness. Hence there are no new compounds in which the first element is the object of the second or in which the first element cannot be expanded into an adjective.

It is the same with such a compound as the German *Schadenfreude*. Here the second element, "joy," is not restricted by the first element, "mischief." It is not a case of a mischievous joy, which it would have to be in the corresponding English compound, but a quite ordinary joy which is inspired by the contemplation of mischief—a very different thing. If, therefore, in English we can freely form compounds such as *tramcar* or *motor-car* it is because the first element can be used with adjectival function and take the position which is allotted to the adjective in the normal sentence. Those compounds, on the other hand, in which, like the German *Vaterlandsliebe*, an adjective cannot be substituted for the first element, and which therefore require an inflection to indicate the relation between the two elements of the compound, are foreign to the spirit of English and cannot be formed. Words like *tradesmen* are mere exceptions which prove the rule, and are, as a rule, survivals from a time when the ordinary syntax would admit of such formations.

Undoubtedly there are many compounds in the language, such as *sunrise, daybreak,* etc., in which an adjective cannot be substituted for the first element of the compound and in which the first element does not limit or restrict the meaning of the second, but in so far as these are nouns they are usually survivals from the earlier language and had an inflection which showed the syntactic relation between the two parts. *Daisy,* for example, still shows the genitival *-s* of the original *dæges-ēage*="day's eye."

A very large number of the compounds which are to be found in the other Germanic languages are the names of abstract conceptions. Many of them existed in Old English, but since they were words only to be found in the speech and writings of the upper classes they were replaced by the corresponding French or Latin words and the habit of forming them was lost. Hence, in Modern English, very few compounds are formed from native material to express such abstract conceptions. We have *philology* and not *speech-lore*, *geology* and not *earth-lore*, etc.

One may say as a general rule that the formation of new compounds is based upon the ordinary usage of the language both as regards word order and syntax, and that the compounds existing in the Modern language, which do not agree with the syntax and word order of Modern English, go back in the great majority of cases to a period of the language in which they did so agree. The remainder are subsequent analogy formations, which tend to become less and less numerous. We can say *inroad*, though the order of words is contrary to modern order, but the formation is made on the analogy of words like *income*, *downfall*, etc., which are relics of the period of English when the adverb might either precede or follow its verb. We cannot, however, say *out-road*, and as Mr. Bradley points out we say *lighting-up*, because, of course, we always say *light up*.

When once a compound has been formed, and when the two or more elements which are contained in it have completely fused in a single meaning, such a compound is subject to the same developments and to the same treatment as any other word in the language. It may change its syntactical function, as when *horsewhip* is used as a verb and as a noun ; or it may be the starting point for a new compound as where *horseman* enters into the compound *horsemanship*. Or in other cases one of the elements, though it continue to exist as an independent word in the language, will change its meaning owing to its association with a particular word in a compound. Thus, for example, we have numerous compounds formed with the word *stone* as the first element. We say *stone-deaf, stone-blind, stone-dead, stony-broke*, etc. In these the word *stone* has come to be a mere intensive equivalent to " absolutely " or some such word. But originally it was used in a compound with its literal sense as in *stone-hard*, or, figuratively, *stony-hearted*.

A type of compound which has become increasingly common in the Modern English period is that in which the first element is a plural noun, such as *newspaper, newsagent, painstaking, clothesbrush, thanksgiving, honours-school, prisons Bill, savings bank*, and very many more, though such compounds were comparatively rare in the older stages of the language. So-called group compounds are also more numerous than formerly, and arise, as a rule, from stereotyped phrases such as *bill-of-fare, man-of-war, mother-of-pearl, Board of Trade, right-of-way, son-in-law, cat and dog*. Sometimes, again, we find an existing compound noun shortened and used as a verb, even though compounds with a verb as the second element are strange to the genius of the language. Thus from *housekeeper* there is a verb sometimes used *to housekeep*, and from *typewriter* a verb *to typewrite*.

§ 77. The third method of word formation is the formation by derivation, in which a word is combined with an affix. Many, and possibly all, of these affixes were originally independent words, so that there is, fundamentally, no difference between this method of word formation and the one which we have just been discussing. But in so far as these affixes are no longer felt to be independent words there is not the same difficulty in forming derivatives by their aid as there is in the case of true compounds.

§ 78. Just as there are a number of words in Modern English which are completely disguised compounds, such as *fret, fortnight,* for " fourteen nights," *bridal* from *brȳd-ealu,* "bride ale," and others which are partly disguised, such as *manhood,* so also there are derivatives in which the derivative element is completely disguised. The cause is the same as in the case of the compounds : the derivative element has ceased to exist independently in the language and has so coalesced with the rest of the word as to be indistinguishable from the stem. A word such as *health* or *gift* contains a derivative suffix, originally used in order to form nouns from verbs or adjectives, and thus these two words were derived from *hāl,* " whole " and *giefan,* " to give." For the formation of nouns Old English had the suffixes *-ock, -kin, -ling, -ing, -er, -el, -m, -n, -nd, -th,* as illustrated by *hillock, napkin, duckling* (all diminutives), *king, sail, finger, helm, heaven, friend, length* respectively. Among the Old English suffixes still in use may be noticed *-en* to form adjectives from nouns as in *golden, wooden,* etc. ; *-ed* to form adjectives from nouns or verbs, in the latter case it is merely the inflection of the past participle, *gloved, graded, studded; -er, singer, weaver ; -ing, dwelling, hunting ; -ish, foolish, bookish, shortish.* This suffix gives the sense either of *-like* or else it implies a mild contempt. *-ness* is commonly used to form abstract nouns from adjectives, *goodness, badness, greatness ; -y,* O.E. *-ig,* is used to form adjectives from nouns, *stony, hilly,* etc.

§ 79. In addition to these suffixes, which did not exist as independent words in Old English, we have some which were still independent : *-hood, boyhood, manhood ; -craft, air-craft ; -dom, kingdom ; -kind, mankind, woman-kind ; -ship, friendship, professorship.* The suffixes *-lock, -red* and *-ric* are now lost as formative suffixes, *wedlock, kindred, bishopric.*

Of the native suffixes used to form adjectives the one in commonest use is *-ly,* O.E. *-līc.* It is also used to form adverbs from adjectives, O.E. *-līce.* In both cases the original meaning was "like," *goodly, manly.* Another common suffix is *-less, careless, fearless.* The only adverbial suffix in common use is *-ly, fully, badly, tolerably.*

§ 80. Among prefixes the commonest native ones are *be-* which is used to make intransitive verbs transitive, *bespeak* ; to form transitive verbs from adjectives and nouns, *befoul, bedew ; mis-, miscarry, mistake ; un-,* which has the sense of a negation as in *unkind, untrue,* or it has the sense of reversing the action implied in the word to which it is prefixed, *undo, unburden.* The principal Old English prefixes surviving in the modern language, but which are no longer active are : *a-,* which is of various origins, in *abed, afoot, anew, against ; for-, forbear, forsake ; mid-,* with its old meaning of " with," *midwife ; with-,* with its old meaning of " against," *withstand.*

The Romance suffixes, living and dead, are too numerous to be mentioned here. They fully make up for the poverty of native prefixes and suffixes and they are freely used in the formation of derivatives from native words as well as from Romance words.

§ 81. When the use of a derivative suffix or prefix is once established such a prefix or suffix is liable to all the changes which may affect full words. Though it may originally have been a foreign affix and was only attached to words of foreign origin, it will in the course of time be affixed to native words also, and in the same way a native affix will be added to foreign words. Or, from association with certain words, its meaning may be modified and thus new derivatives may be formed from a word of which it is a part. Thus we find a derivative *feverish* containing a foreign stem and a native suffix, and from it is derived a new word *feverishness*.

§ 82. Suffixes and prefixes of Romance origin have been much more fertile in forming new derivatives than have those of English origin. One or two of them are especially noteworthy in this respect ; *-able* we have made quite our own. Originally used only to form adjectives from verbs of French origin, it was soon added to native verbal stems, *breakable, bearable*, where it may have owed some of its popularity to confusion with the independent word *able*. But since some verbs which formed derivatives with this suffix had nouns of the same form corresponding to them, the suffix was also added to nouns, *saleable*. The suffix is now so common that we feel that we can use it on any occasion where an adjective is required. It is of special interest to note that it can also be added to the stems of verbs which are constructed with prepositions. Thus we can say it is *laughable*, though the sentence containing the pure verb would run, " it is fit to be laughed *at*." In some cases the form in -*able* has nevertheless established itself, as in *laughable, reliable, accountable*, though in others it has not. We may say that a man is *loveable*, but not that a house is *liveable*. In the latter case the loss of the preposition *in* would be felt.

Another very common adjectival suffix of Romance origin is the suffix -*ous*, with the sense of " full of," " of the nature of." This suffix is the regular development, through French, of the Latin -*osus*, but was used in French to form adjectives from native French nouns where there was no corresponding Latin adjective in -*osus*. Thus, though *copious* and *famous* correspond to Latin *copiosus* and *famosus*, words like *joyous, slanderous* have no equivalents in Latin. Just as French used this suffix to form new adjectives from native stems, so English used it quite freely to form adjectives from all sorts of Latin stems as in *capacious* from *capax*, and many more, such as *igneous, stupendous, sonorous*. The suffix was also extended to native English words, such as *wondrous, murderous*. The suffix also exists in a few words in its Latin form, *morose, grandiose, otiose*.

The suffix -*al*, with the sense " pertaining to," " of the kind of," is also in very common use in the formation of adjectives and nouns. It is found both in adjectives and nouns which already had it in Latin as *mortal, equal, vernal, rival, animal*; and also in words which did not exist with this suffix in Latin as *national, proportional, arrival*. The suffix is even found in combination with native stems as in *bestowal, betrothal*. Similarly, the suffix -*age* is found first in words in which it is original, as in *voyage*, Latin *viaticum*, but when it came into common use it was freely used to form new derivatives from words of any source. Thus we find it is used to form new nouns from existing nouns as in *bandage, brokerage, poundage, luggage*; or to form nouns from verbs as in *usage, marriage*. It is also frequently added to the names of persons as in *baronage, parsonage, vicarage, personage*, etc. All of these living formative suffixes have become so completely a part of the language that they may be combined with great freedom one with another or with native suffixes. Thus in such a word as *comically* we have no less than three suffixes, *-ic, -al* and *-ly*, one being Greek, one Latin and one English. Just as we have a combination of two English suffixes in *consciencelessness* so also we have two foreign suffixes combined in *pomposity, monstrosity*, etc.

§ 83. There is yet another method of derivation which consists neither in the formation of compounds nor in the addition of affixes, but in the converse process of reducing or shortening an existing word. Some of these shortened forms are still new and may scarcely be said to have gained admission into the standard language; others, again, are firmly established. Thus *cab* from *cabriolet, mob* (*mobile vulgus*), *edit* formed from the substantive *editor, bus* from *omnibus* are well established. Less secure, in varying degrees, are *Jap, Matric, pub, straw* for *straw hat, fire office* for *fire insurance office, bike* for *bicycle*. American English has *an urge* for an "*urgent* letter" or "reminder."

§ 84. In the methods of composition and derivation which we have so far noticed, old material is used with its ordinary meaning. There is, however, one method of word formation in which the old material is not so used, but in which it assumes a new meaning, not because there is any association of ideas, but because there exists a resemblance in sound between the new word and the word from which it is derived. This is what occurs in the so-called popular etymology. In such a word as *crayfish*, for example, the first syllable is meaningless and is a mere adaptation of the initial syllable of the French word *écrevisse*. In the same way the word *asparagus* is often pronounced *sparrow-grass*, and the Old English *weremōd*, when the first element was no longer understood, was pronounced as if it were made up of the elements *worm* and *wood*. Similarly, the French *perruque* came to be pronounced *periwig*, and the Old English *brȳdguma* which contained the word *guma*, " man," was refashioned *bridegroom* after the word *guma* had disappeared from the language and was no longer understood. So also O.N.F. *caucie* appears in *causeway*.

An extreme case of shortening which is very common in Modern English, and which is certainly due to the desire to economise effort, is to be found in the very widespread practice, a practice which becomes more common every day, to use initials of words found in titles in very common use. Thus, whereas not very long ago M.P. and J.P. and a few more were the only common initials so used, we now have P.R., I.L.P., L.N.W., G.E.R., and we even find such initials formed into a word as in D.O.R.A.

§ 85. There is one cause of change of meaning which has been very active throughout the later periods of the history of English, and that is the change of grammatical function when a word which was a noun becomes a verb or an adjective or some other part of speech. This was a process which was especially easy in English after the inflections of Old English had disappeared, for there was nothing to show the difference, so far as form was concerned, between a verb and a noun or an adjective.   Owing to the complete formal identity between verbs and nouns there was therefore nothing to prevent the one being used with the function of the other if the meaning was clear.   The noun *brand*, for example, differs in no respect from the verb *burn* in grammatical form, and it is therefore not surprising that *brand* should be used as a verb and that *burn* should be used as a noun. Such a change of function of words was not unknown to Old English, for adjectives could be used, and frequently were used, as nouns, and nouns often had the function of adjectives.   Similarly, in Old English, adjectives were freely used as adverbs.   The number of words which in Modern English may be two or three, or even four distinct parts of speech is very large indeed, and it is only because there are no inflections to distinguish these parts of speech that this is possible.   Words like *coin, thatch, house, hunt, eye, arm, coal, bridge,* though all of them nouns in origin, may now be used quite freely as verbs ; and words like *call, visit, burn, move, make, fit, feel,* though verbs by origin, may be used as nouns.   So the word *like* may be a verb, a conjunction or an adjective, and *home* may be an adverb or a noun ; *back* may be a noun or an adverb, etc.

CHAPTER VI

ACCIDENCE

§ 86. OLD ENGLISH was still a highly inflected language. Nouns and adjectives were inflected in four cases and two numbers, with traces of a fifth and even a sixth case. Pronouns likewise were inflected for case and number, but also for gender. The verb had fewer inflections, but still more than in Modern English. Nevertheless there were traces already in the earliest Old English of the falling off or weakening of inflections. This loss of inflections is usually attributed to the ordinary processes of sound change and is at the same time deemed to be the cause of the grammatical innovations which later took the place of the lost inflections. No doubt these inflections were weakened and even lost owing to the fact that they were unstressed, just as in Modern English the vowel " o " in the first syllable of " photograph " is weakened in the word " photography " because it occurs in a syllable which has become unstressed. But if in Modern English we say "to the day" instead of "dæge" it is doubtless for other reasons than the loss of the inflection -e, and the same might be said of other similar innovations. The loss of such a dative inflection as -e in the singular, or of such an

130

inflection as -*en* in verbs may be due to the fact that it is unstressed, but that cannot be the only cause, for if it were, we should expect the final syllable -*en* to disappear in words like "heaven" "often," "oven," "even" and many more. It would seem more in accord with the facts to say that the loss of these particular inflections—and of others—took place because new methods of expressing grammatical relationship were found more convenient. In nouns, for example, the four cases became overburdened with functions and on that account they must have become ambiguous. They might indicate that an object suffered the direct action of a verb (accusative) or the indirect action (dative) or that a thing was in the possession of somebody (genitive), etc. To these elementary relations were gradually added others, until in time, with the growing necessity of precision and increased subtlety and analysis of thought, mere inflections could not clearly express all possible relations unless their number was considerably increased. The need for precise expression would doubtless be felt most acutely when an emphatic statement was required, as, for example, when it was desired to emphasise that a thing was, let us say, *in* the wood and not *by* the wood, both of which relations were originally expressed by the simple dative or ablative.

Greater precision was attainable, as we have said, by increasing the number of inflections and increasing the number of cases. But there was an alternative, and one which was in harmony with the general tendencies of thought. That alternative was to analyse the new thought and to give expression to it by using separate words to express the new relation. It so happened that the material for this purpose existed in prepositions, so that it was possible to write or say : "to the man," "from the man," "of the man" instead of *mannes, manne.* These prepositions were originally adverbs and expressed the manner of action of the verb. But it was very easy to confuse the function of adverb and preposition and to substitute one for the other. Thus, for example, in Old English one could say : "*he him spœc to,*" "he him spoke to," in which *to* indicates that the speaker did not merely speak (to the air) but that his speaking was of a particular kind, of a kind intended to affect a certain hearer. *To* in this sentence is an adverb. But if we change the order and say, as one could say in Old English : "*he spœc to him,*" *to* becomes a preposition. In this way the growing needs of language were satisfied and the analytical cases, which replaced the inflectional cases, and were capable of indefinite expansion, were formed. The real cause of the change is therefore the mental impulse which underlies all speech, and it is this cause, much more than the weakening of sounds in unstressed syllables, which produced the change, though perhaps the latter was to some extent a contributory cause.

This view of the processes of development is confirmed, moreover, by the fact that the analytic cases constructed with prepositions, and the analytic tenses of verbs, formed by the help of auxiliaries, are to be found in Old English long before there is any sign of the loss or even the weakening of inflections. We are perhaps justified in saying, therefore, that it was the development of these analytical forms which made the inflections superfluous in the great majority of cases, and that this superfluousness, combined with the weak stress, led to their disappearance entirely.

§ 87. In treating of Middle English syntax and the changes which it had undergone in the transition from Old English we noted one tendency in particular : the tendency to represent a syntactic concord once only by means of an inflection. This tendency, combined with the development of the analytic cases in nouns, made a very deep impression on the inflectional system of the language, for it rendered superfluous the inflections of nouns, except the inflection for the plural ; it rendered unnecessary the inflections of the article, since the accompanying noun showed whether a singular or plural was to be understood. In the same way the forms of the indefinite article were reduced to one. The possessives stand in the same category as the articles, for here, too, the accompanying noun shows whether it is to be taken as singular or plural. With regard to the concord of personal pronoun and verb, this might be shown either by keeping the personal endings of the verb and discarding the forms of the pronouns, or by keeping the forms of the pronouns and discarding the personal inflections of the verb. As a matter of fact, the latter occurred, and the beginning of the process is to be seen earlier than the Middle English period. Already in Old English, as we shall see, the personal endings of the three persons of the present plural had been reduced to one, -aþ in the indicative, and -en in the subjunctive. In Middle English the process is carried still further, in so far as the personal endings disappear altogether, both in the present and past tenses, indicative and subjunctive, with the sole exception of *-s* in the third person singular of the present indicative. So also in the past participle there is a tendency to drop the final *-en*, as in *sing, sang, sung,* though there are still a number of participles which preserve it, as in *drive, drove, driven.* The only forms in which syntactic concords are still expressed twice are the demonstrative adjectives such as *those, these,* and the auxiliary verbs. Here, in such a sentence as " These inflections disappeared," the plural idea is expressed once in the plural inflection of the noun, and once in the plural form of *this.* The reason for the survival of the plural forms *these* and *those* is not difficult to find. It is due to the fact that these two words are also used as pronouns and therefore require a plural form just as much as do the personal pronouns, in order to indicate number when they are the subject of a verb. It is interesting to notice in this connection that the article *the,* when it had abandoned its pronominal function—which it had in Old English—also abandoned its plural forms, since these, under the new syntax, were superfluous.

§ 88. The second case in which a syntactic concord is expressed twice by means of inflections is where certain auxiliaries are used. Thus for example we say : " The books are cheap," or even " These books are cheap," where the concord is expressed three times, once in the adjective, once in the noun, and once in the form of the verb, *are* instead of *is.* Such forms are, however, extremely few in number, though they are in very common use, and perhaps for that very reason have survived. The only forms which still preserve this distinction between singular and plural are *was* and *were, is* and *are.* The other auxiliaries and modal verbs do not make this

distinction.   Thus we say *I have* and *we have, I can* and
we can, I do and *we do, I dare* and *we dare, I ought* and
we ought, etc.   The survivals *is* and *are*, etc., do not
invalidate the theory that inflections disappeared
because they had been rendered superfluous by the
general lines of development of the language.   As a
further confirmation of the view here advanced it may
be noticed that the relative pronouns, though they may
be subjects of verbs and might, therefore, be expected to
have plural forms like those of the personal pronouns
and the demonstratives *these* and *those*, yet have none.
In fact, however, the plural inflection is superfluous
here also, because the antecedent, whether noun or
pronoun, has already indicated the number and thus
renders an inflection unnecessary.

§ 89. The loss of case endings we have already discussed and have seen to be due to the development of
the analytic expression of the cases by means of prepositions.   There is, however, one survival of a case ending
in Middle and Modern English, and that is the inflectional
-'s and its substitute, the apostrophe, of the genitive
singular and plural.   This survival is not, however,
parallel with the survival of forms like *is* and *are*, discussed above, for these do not introduce any new shade
of meaning.   The distinction between the genitive in
-'s and the genitive in *of*, on the other hand, corresponds
to a useful distinction in meaning.   It serves in part
to remove the ambiguity which arises in such an expression as *God's love*, and it corresponds to the reluctance
with which an Englishman would speak of a *house's roof*.
In other words, in the latter example, it is a reflection of
the conscious distinction in English between living and

lifeless things which has been responsible for the transition from grammatical to natural gender.

§ 90. We may now summarise the main tendencies of development in Middle English, so far as accidence is concerned, by saying that there is a tendency to reduce inflections to a minimum and to substitute for them either a fixed word order in which the syntactic function of a word depends upon its position in the sentence, or a periphrastic, analytic construction in which the syntactic relations and the sense are brought out by means of prepositions, auxiliary verbs, etc. But not only is the number of cases in which a syntactic concord is expressed by inflections very much reduced, but also where inflections are still preserved there is a tendency to reduce the variety of such inflections. Thus, for example, not only are the old inflections of the accusative and dative lost, but the various inflections of the nominative plural of nouns are reduced to one or two. Old English, as we have seen, had various inflections to indicate the nominative plural ; it had *-as, -an, -u, -e*, etc. These, by the end of the Middle English period, were reduced to a single inflection, *-(e)s*. Similarly, in the verb, Old English had three distinct weak conjugations, which are reduced to one. In the strong verb the distinction between the singular and plural stem, as in *sang* (sing.), *sungon* (plur.) disappears.

It is not to be supposed, of course, that these important changes took place all at once. Language does not change its forms in that way. There is always a period in which one form is seen to be struggling against another, as may be seen in the competition which is going on at the present day between the various words for *cinematograph*.

In the Middle English period there is ample evidence of the gradual settling down to the inflectional system which has passed into Modern English, and when we speak of the great simplification of the older inflectional system, we refer to the final results which appear at the end of the period.

§ 91. The Old English noun differed in one very important respect from the Modern English noun. Its gender was determined not at all by sex, but by form. Nouns might be masculine, feminine or neuter without any regard to whether they were the names of living or lifeless things, and without any regard to whether they were names of male or female things. Thus *wīf,* " woman," was a neuter, and *hand* was a feminine ; *mœgden,* " girl," was neuter, and *Crīstendōm,* " Christendom," was masculine. Nevertheless, in respect of the names of living things, Old English gender differed very little indeed from Modern English ; the great majority of names of male things were masculine and the great majority of the names of female things were feminine. Such exceptions as *bearn,* " child," have their parallel in the modern language and are neuter in the literal sense of not belonging to either masculine or feminine because they may be either. It is in the gender of the names of lifeless things that Old English differs from Modern English, for such nouns might be either masculine, feminine or neuter. It would seem, therefore, that already in Old English natural gender, or gender determined by sex, was established, and this would seem to imply a growing consciousness of the distinction between living and lifeless things, that is to say, a long stride had been made towards the Middle English natural gender. More will be said on this point in the section on Middle English, but for the present it may be of interest to note that the chief exception to the rule of natural gender in Old English, namely *wīf*, is also found as a feminine. But if we are justified in assuming a sense of the difference between lifeless and living things in Old English, we may at the same time draw important conclusions from it, with regard to the breakdown of the system of declensions in Middle English.

§ 92. There are one or two more interesting points to be noted in Old English concerning grammatical gender. In the first place, there are many instances of nouns having different genders, but it is remarkable that nearly all of these are the names of lifeless things. The genders of nouns expressing living things are, on the other hand, stable. This would seem to confirm the view that a sense of the distinction between lifeless and living had grown up, for on that assumption the hesitation between two genders for the name of a lifeless thing would be quite natural. In the second place, we observe that where a noun changes its gender the change is seen in the first instance, not in the article or the adjective which qualifies the noun, but in the pronoun (usually the personal noun) which follows it. That pronoun is invariably the neuter pronoun *hit*. This fact goes to show that the pronouns *he* and *heo*, " she," which were most commonly used for man and woman, or for male and female—since natural gender for the names of living things already existed—had come to be restricted, in consequence of the above-mentioned distinction between lifeless and living things, to male and female. *Hit*, " it," on the other hand, came to be

used more and more in reference to nouns indicating
lifeless things. Hence, even where a noun is preceded
by an article in the feminine, the pronoun with which it
is constructed is in the neuter. Thus, for example :

> " Eal the murhthe the me us behat, al hit sceal beo god
> ane."

Here *murhthe* is feminine in Old English, but it is
used with the neuter pronoun *hit*. Similarly,

> The king Vortigerne
> haxede his cnihtes
> wat were the speche
> *that* the maide speke
>
> (LAYAMON, *Brut*, 529-532)

in which *speche*, feminine in O.E., is followed by the
neuter *that*. These examples, which might be multiplied,
are from Middle English texts, but they can be paralleled
from Old English, as in

> " Me sægde thæt wif hire wordum selfa " ;
>
> (Genesis, 2648)

where the article *thæt* is in the neuter, but the pronoun
hire is in the feminine.

§ 93. It need only be added concerning this point
that this is not the usual view of the cause of the development of natural gender in Middle English. The change
is usually attributed to the decay of inflections and the
consequent confusion of forms, so that it was no longer
possible to distinguish the genders. The gravest objec-
tion to this view is that there need have been no confusion
whatever, because, assuming all inflections to have been
lost, the only possible case in which gender could be
shown was where nouns were constructed with pronouns,

and these still showed the gender quite clearly. There is, therefore, absolutely no reason whatever why we should not to this day refer to a woman as *it* and to the hand as *she*. The only possible reason why we do not is that we have developed a sense of the distinction between lifeless and living things, and between male and female. We have seen the most unmistakable evidence of the development of this sense as early as Old English, and we have surely better reason for attributing such a momentous development to a natural cause, rather than to any imaginary and in fact unreal confusion of forms or suffixes.

Gender in Old English might be expressed by means of suffixes, by means of inflectional endings or by using different words for masculine and feminine. Thus *god* is masculine, *gyden* is feminine ; *mǣg*, " kinsman," is masculine, *māge* is feminine ; *hyse*, " boy," is masculine, *mægden*, " girl," is neuter ; *mon* is masculine, *wifmon* is feminine. All these methods of forming a feminine, survive in Middle and Modern English.

THE NOUN

§ 94. The Old English noun had four cases : nominative, accusative, genitive, dative, and traces of a vocative, locative and instrumental ; and two numbers. As in Latin, there were several declensions, which were classified into strong and weak, according as the stem of the word ended in a vowel (a, i, ō, u) or a consonant. The normal inflections of strong nouns, though they were often combined, as in Modern English, with prepositions, were :

STRONG.

	Sing.			Plur.		
	Masc.	Fem.	Neut.	Masc.	Fem.	Neut.
Nom.		(*-u*)		*-as*	*-a, (-e)*	(*-u*)
Acc.		(*-e*)		*-as*	*-a, (-e)*	(*-u*)
Gen.	*-es*	*-e*	*-es*	*-a*	*-a*	*-a*
Dat.	*-e*	*-e*	*-e*	*-um*	*-um*	*-um*

WEAK.

	Masc.	Fem.	Neut.	Masc.	Fem.	Neut.
Nom.	*-a*	*-e*	*-e*	*-an*	*-an*	*-an*
Acc.	*-an*	*-an*	*-e*	*-an*	*-an*	*-an*
Gen.	*-an*	*-an*	*-an*	*-ena*	*-ena*	*-ena*
Dat.	*-an*	*-an*	*-an*	*-um*	*-um*	*-um*

These inflections in Old English already show a confusion of declensions as compared with Primitive-Germanic, and this confusion is itself only one more manifestation of the tendency, already referred to, to simplify the grammatical forms and categories of the parent language. Surveying these inflections, we find that already a great simplification has taken place. The inflections of weak nouns are the same for nouns of all genders, except in the nominative and the accusative neuter of the singular. Further, the inflections of the strong genitive and dative plural are the same for all nouns of whatever gender or declension. In effect, therefore, all that is left of the original declensions, in which all cases, numbers and genders had separate and distinct inflections, is that in the singular of strong nouns the feminine has separate inflections and in the plural of strong nouns all three genders have separate inflections in the nominative and accusative. The simplification has indeed already gone a very long way.

§ 95. There were a few special declensions outside these in Old English, but not many words followed them, and of these only a small fraction has survived in

Modern English. We note here only the latter. The most important, from the point of view of Modern English, are the so-called Mutation Plurals :

	SING.	PLURAL.
Nom. Acc.	*monn, fōt, gōs*	*menn, fēt, gēs*
Gen.	*monnes, fōtes, gēs*	*monna, fōta, gōsa*
Dat.	*menn, fēt, gēs*	*monnum, fōtum, gōsum*

§ 96. Five names of relatives were also specially declined, as follows :

Nom. Acc.	*mōdor, brōþor, dohtor*	*mōdru, brōþru, brœþru, dohtru*
Gen.	*mōdor, brōþor, dohtor*	*mōdra, brōþra, dohtra*
Dat.	*mēder, brēþer, dehter*	*mōdrum, brōþrum, dohtrum*

Of the other peculiarities of declension in Old English practically nothing remains in Modern English, and already in the Middle English period these declensions have been considerably simplified.

§ 97. The general tendency in the inflections of Middle English is to reduce all O.E. inflectional vowels to a uniform -*e*, and to reduce the final -*m* of the dative plural to -*n*. The resulting development of the scheme of inflections given on page 141 was therefore as follows :

STRONG NOUNS.

SINGULAR.

	Masculine		Feminine		Neuter	
	O.E.	M.E.	O.E.	M.E.	O.E.	M.E.
Nom.	—	—	-(*e*)	-(*e*)	—	—
Acc.	—	—	-*e*	-*e*	—	—
Gen	-*es*	-*es*	-*e*	-*e*	-*es*	-*es*
Dat.	-*e*	-*e*	-*e*	-*e*	-*e*	-*e*

PLURAL.

Nom.	-as	-es	-(e), a	-e	-(u)	-e, -
Gen.	-as	-es	-(e), a	-e	-(u)	-e, -
Gen.	-a	-e	-a	-e	-a	-e
Dat.	-um	-en	-um	-en	-um	-en

WEAK NOUNS.

SINGULAR.

Nom.	-a	-e	-e	-e	-e	-e
Acc.	-an	-en	-an	-en	-e	-e
Dat.	-an	-en	-an	-en	-an	-en
Dat.	-an	-en	-an	-en	-an	-en

PLURAL.

Nom.	-an	-en	-an	-en	-an	-en
Acc.	-an	-en	-an	-en	-an	-en
Gen.	-ena	-ene	-ena	-ene	-ena	-ene
Dat.	-um	-en	-um	-en	-um	-en

§ 98. These inflections are all found in the early Middle English period, but with the gradual disappearance of all but the nominative case there only remain the following inflections :

		SINGULAR.			PLURAL.		
		Masc.	Fem.	Neut.	Masc.	Fem.	Neut.
Nom.	Strong	—	-(e)	—	-es	-e	-e,-
	Weak	-e	-e	-e	-en	-en	-en
Gen.	Strong	-(e)s	-e	-es	-e	-e	-e
	Weak	-e(n)	-e(n)	-e(n)	-e(n)	-e(n)	-e(n)

§ 99. It appears, therefore, that irrespective of gender, nouns had either -es, -e or no inflection at all in the singular, but that in the plural there were three possible inflections : -e, -es, -en, of which -en might be added to nouns of all genders, -e to feminines and neuters, and

-es to masculines. But with the disappearance of grammatical gender there lay a choice between *-es* and *-e* for strong nouns. It so happened that the number of nouns regularly taking the inflection *-es* was greater than the number of nouns taking *-e*, for a number of old neuters—the long stems—had no inflection in the plural. In effect, therefore, the choice lay between *-es* and *-en* as the regular inflection of the plural of nouns. During the Middle English period we do actually witness a conflict between these two inflections. In the Northern and Midland dialects the favourite inflection is *-es*, but in the Southern dialect the favourite was *-en*. Ultimately, as we can see from Modern English, the *-es* inflection prevailed.

§ 100. What it was which determined the choice of the one or the other of these two inflections in the different dialects we cannot at this late hour discover. All that we can see is the marked general tendency in all dialects to reduce the number of inflections. The most probable cause of any particular choice is that words with a given inflection, say *-en*, were more numerous, or were more often used in the Southern dialect than in the Northern, and on the other hand words in *-es* were more numerous in the Northern dialect than in the Southern. There was, however, one influence at work in the Northern and Midland dialects which seems to have been overlooked in this respect, and that is that in the Scandinavian languages the nominative plural of the weak declension—from which the inflection *-en* is derived —did not exist and was therefore unfamiliar to people of Scandinavian origin in the old territory of the Danelaw.

§ 101. Another explanation of the spread of the -*es* inflection is that it was fostered by the parallel -*s* inflection which was to be found in French nouns. This explanation is unsatisfactory in the first place because the tendency to use -*es* instead of -*en* occurs too early in the North to be attributed to Norman influence; and in the second place if the impulse had come from Norman French we should expect to find its influence in southern territory where the Norman influence was strongest, rather than in the northern territory where it was weakest, whereas exactly the contrary took place.

§ 102. Of the remaining nominal inflections mentioned on page 142, the mutation plurals are preserved in Middle English. Thus the forms corresponding to the Old English forms are :

Sing. *man, foot, mouse.*   Plur. *men, feet, mice.*

The names of relatives, *mother, brother, daughter*, on the other hand, are treated like other nouns and take -*s* in the plural. The sole exception is *brother*, which has a second plural in -*en*, with the Old English change of vowel preserved, *brethren*, though it should be noticed that here too a variant form has a different meaning from that which is conveyed by the normal form. In early Modern English and Middle English there were more survivals of the -*en* plurals than there are now. The form *hosen*, though now obsolete, was common in Middle English and represents an Old English plural, *hosan*. The Middle English *children* also contains the plural suffix -*n*, though it was not found in this word in Old English. The O.E. plural was *cildru*, in which the (*r*)*u* was a plural inflection. In Middle English, however, -*n* was added to the form *childre*, just as happened in *brethren*. Another noun with an -*n* plural in Middle English was *kine*, the plural of *cow*. In Old English this noun formed its plural just like *mūs—mȳs*, but to the plural form *cȳ* was added -*n(e)*, in which -*e* is not a part of the inflection, but merely indicates that the stem vowel is long. Finally, Middle English has the plural *shoon*, which may either be a reformed plural in -*en* or it may be a survival of the Old English genitive plural *scēona*.

§ 103. Middle English also preserves, as late as Chaucer, a few case endings, especially of feminine nouns. Thus, for example, we find *Ladye day* for *Lady's day*, surviving in the Modern English *Lady-day*.

§ 104. In Old English, as a reference to page 141 will show, there were certain strong neuters which were uninflected in the nom., acc., plural. Some of these remain uninflected in Middle English, as, for example, *deer, sheep, swine, year, head*, etc., though some of these took the usual -*s* inflection also. These uninflected neuter plurals may be regarded as mere survivals of uninflected neuter plurals in Old English, but it is nevertheless remarkable that whereas the majority of such originally uninflected plurals should have taken the ordinary -*s* inflection in Middle English, these few should not have done so. The reason may possibly be that most of these nouns would generally be used with an accompanying numeral which would indicate plural number and thus render the inflection superfluous. It is difficult to understand how, if there were not some such underlying reason, nouns which originally were inflected should have lost their inflection as if on the analogy of these neuters. If we look at the instances in which these nouns are still used in the modern language in an uninflected form, we shall see that it is always when constructed with a numeral. Thus we have *fortnight* and not *fortnights*=fourteen nights, though *night* in Old English was not a neuter and was inflected in the plural. So also we say, *a three-foot rule, a five-pound note, a six-mile walk, a ten-ton yacht*. Another explanation may be that certain of these words were regarded as collective nouns and thus, like all collective nouns, were used in the singular. Or they may be survivals of the O.E. genitive plurals, which were used after numerals.

§ 105. Of the special suffixes used in Old English for forming feminine nouns from masculines, the two, *-en* and *-stre, -stere* are seen to be already going out of use in Middle English and are replaced by the Romance feminine suffix *-ess*, which was found already in Old English in forms like *abbudesse*. The suffix *-en* survives in the form *vixen*, which is a Southern dialect form of *fixen* from Old English *fyxen*, the feminine of *fox*. The suffix *-ster* still survives in early Middle English as a feminine suffix in such words as *webster*, feminine of *weaver*; *baxter*, feminine of *baker(e)*; as also in *songster, huxter*, etc. But in the later period it became *-stress*, by contamination with the Romance suffix *-ess*, thus giving such forms as *seamstress, songstress*. In one word, however, it preserved its feminine force throughout the Middle English period, though in this word, *spinster*, feminine of *spinner*, it is the change of meaning which has preserved the feminine sense.

§ 106. Of the various O.E. inflections which survived

in Middle English, there only remains one in regular use in Modern English and that is the -*s* of the nominative plural and of the genitive. These are the inflections which are added to new nouns, except such as retain their foreign plurals. This -*s* is a voiced consonant when it follows a voiced sound, as in *trees*, *rugs*, *cinders*, but it is voiceless when it follows a voiceless consonant, as in *books*, *boots*, *caps.* It retains the earlier form -*es*, however, when it is preceded by (s, z, ʃ, dž, tʃ), *houses*, *roses*, *plushes*, *judges*, *churches*, etc. Words ending in -*f* usually voice the -*f* in native words, *loaves*, *thieves*, but preserve it in Romance words, *griefs*, *proofs*, *chiefs*. The voicing of the -*f* in native words is not, however, really a modern change, but is a regular inheritance from the time when the inflection was -*es* and -*f*- was voiced between vowels. Originally -*s* was treated in the same way when it was final in the stem of a word, but here it has sometimes come into the singular by the analogy of the plural, as in *rose*, which should be pronounced to rime with *close* (adj.) in the singular and *roses* in the plural. In the same way *glove* should be pronounced *glof*, just like *wolf*, in the singular, but the pronunciation of the plural has been carried into the singular, presumably because the plural form is the one in most common use.

§ 107. Of the other methods of forming the plural in Old and Middle English none has survived as an active principle, though there are isolated survivals in the modern tongue. Mutation plurals, though not so common as formerly, still survive in *feet*, *teeth*, *mice*, etc., and there are one or two plurals in -*en* such as *oxen*, and the special plurals *kine*, *children*, *brethren*. The old uninflected neuters such as *deer, sheep* also survive, and their number has been increased to some extent by the addition of some collective nouns such as *cattle, poultry, fish, fowl,* and some names of measures, quantities, etc., such as *pound, dozen, foot, mile,* in phrases such as *five-mile walk, ten-pound note.* Foreign nouns sometimes retain their foreign plurals, but there is a tendency, when a word has been long enough in the language, for it to conform to the ordinary rules. Thus we have *appendices* and *appendixes, cherubs* and *cherubim, indexes* and *indices.* Where there are two plurals, however, there is a tendency to differentiate between them in sense. Thus *indexes* refers to the indexes of books, and *indices* to algebraical signs. So, also, a difference of meaning arises between the two plurals *cloths* and *clothes, brothers* and *brethren.* Other nouns, again, have lost the singular form, as in *trowsers, breeches, scissors, scales,* etc. This is sometimes very troublesome, for if we wish to speak of a particular *scissors* or *breeches,* we have to do so in a roundabout way, by speaking of a *pair of scissors.* In other cases the singular has a different meaning from the plural, and ambiguities may again arise, as in *draughts, irons,* in which case we speak in the singular of a *set of draughts,* etc. Notice, also, *compass, compasses,* the singular of which, when we wish to distinguish one instrument from others, is a *pair of compasses.* Other forms, again, though plural by origin, are now only used as singulars, despite the plural form. Such are *news, gallows.* Other words, again, which look like plurals but are really singulars and are treated as such, are *riches* (Fr. *richesse*), *alms* (O.E. *œlmesse*).

§ 108. The inflection -'*s* is also used in Modern English to mark the possessive case, singular or plural. The plural inflection has been borrowed from the singular. There is one remarkable case development in Modern English which is known as the group-genitive, in which the inflectional -'*s* is added, not to the word to which it grammatically belongs, but to the last word of the group, as in *the King of England's*. This practice is just one more example of the triumph of meaning over grammar, for in such a phrase as *the King of England's*, we have in fact a compound in which the two elements of meaning indicated by *King* and *England,* have fused into a single and indivisible whole, and therefore all inflections are added to the end of the word just as if the word were *stockbroker* or any other normal compound. The construction is so convenient and accords so well with the logical spirit of English that we find the inflection added even to parts of speech other than nouns, as *The man we saw yesterday's house.*

THE ADJECTIVE

§ 109. In Old English the adjective, like the noun, had a strong and a weak declension, but in so far as the Modern English adjective has no inflections at all, we need not stop to survey the inflections of the adjective in Middle English. The only survival, even in Chaucer, is a final -*e* in the plural or to indicate the definite adjective and an occasional -*er* as in *alder*, which is a development of O.E. *eallra,* the genitive plural of *eall.*

§ 110. But if the inflections of number, gender and case have quite disappeared, the comparative and superlative suffixes have remained. In Old English the comparative was formed from the positive by the addition of *-ra*, as *heard, heardra,* "harder." The superlative was formed by the addition of the suffix *-osta, heardosta,* "hardest." Another method of forming the comparative and superlative was by means of the suffixes *-ra, -esta,* in which the earlier forms were *-ira, -ista.* These adjectives differed from those of the other group in having a changed or mutated stem vowel in the comparative and superlative, as O.E. *ieldra, ieldesta,* beside the positive *eald.* But already in Old English this method was disappearing, doubtless owing to the general tendency to simplify. It survives, however, in the Modern English, *old, elder, eldest,* though the second form is no longer a true comparative in function.

§ 111. Old English had also other methods of forming the comparative and superlative. One such which has survived in Modern English, though it is not common in Old English, is by means of the superlative suffix *-m-ost,* which is really a double superlative, consisting of the suffix *-m,* as in Latin *pri-m-us,* and the usual suffix *-ost.* Hence we have the modern English *utmost, outmost, hindmost, inmost,* etc. Other comparatives and superlatives, again, were formed from stems which are not identical with those of the positive, as, for example :

gōd	*betera*	*betest, betst*
yfel	*wiersa, wyrsa*	*wiersest, wyrsta*
micel	*māra*	*mǣst*
lȳtel	*lǣssa*	*lǣs(es)t*

The original positive of *māra* exists in the form *mā,* M.E. and early Mod. E. *mo,* which is an adverb, though it subsequently assumes adjectival function in Middle

English. In one or two cases the Old English forms
differ in the stems in the positive and the other forms,
the difference being due to phonetic laws. Thus O.E.
nēah, "nigh," has the comparative *nēara* and the superlative *nīehsta*, which forms regularly give *nigh, near, next*.

§ 112. The numerals in Old English are as follows :

1	*ān*	11	*end(d)lefan*
2	*twēgen, twā, tū*	12	*twelf*
3	*þrīe, þrēo*	13	*þrēotīene*
4	*fēower*	14	*fēowertīene*
5	*fīf*	15	*fīftīene*
6	*siex*	16	*siextīene*
7	*seofon*	17	*seofontīene*
8	*eahta*	18	*eahtatīene*
9	*nigon*	19	*nigontīene*
10	*tīen*	20	*twentig*

30	*þritig*
50	*fiftig*
60	*siextig*
70	*(hund)seofontig*
80	*(hund)eahtatig*
90	*(hund)nigontig*
100	*hundteontig, hund, hundred*

The numerals from *one* to *ten* correspond in their sounds
to the cognate forms in other Indo-Germanic languages,
cf. c. vii. Thus, *twā* corresponds exactly to the Latin *duo*,
eahta to Latin *octo*, etc. The form *tīen* corresponds to the
Latin *decem*, and is a contraction from an earlier *tehan*
(cf. German *zehn*). The numeral *twentig* in its second
syllable *-tig* contains another form of the numeral *ten*,
which is due to a special development explained in the
chapter on Sound Changes. *Twenty*, therefore, means
two tens, *thirty*=three tens, etc. The numerals *eleven*
and *twelve*, O.E. *endlefan, twelf* are composed of the

numerals *ān* and *twā*, followed by the stem *lif*, which means "left," that is to say, one, or two, more than ten.

§ 113. Of the whole system of adjectival inflections of Old English all that is left in late Middle English is a final *-e*. It disappeared soon after Chaucer. There also occur a few adjectives with an inflectional *-s* in the plural, but these are only French adjectives and the inflection did not spread beyond them. Thus Chaucer has *places delitables*. The survival of the genitive plural form *alder*, from Old English *eallra* has already been noticed, and is found as late as Shakespere.

§ 114. In regard to comparison, the Old English suffixes *-ra, -osta, -esta*, become in Middle English *-er*, *-est*. Of the older forms with a mutated stem vowel in the comparative and superlative the forms *ieldra* and *ieldesta* survive in Middle English, as in Modern English in the forms *elder, eldest*, though an unmutated comparative and superlative developed side by side with them : *older, oldest*.

§ 115. In Middle English, however, the analytic comparison by means of the adverbs *more* and *most* becomes more and more common. This mode of comparison is found as early as the twelfth century, but it is not until the fourteenth century that it becomes common. Its origin is perhaps to be found in the Norman-French comparison in *plus*, no doubt strongly aided by the native tendency to replace inflectional modes of expression by means of a periphrase. In Middle English we also notice the appearance of double comparatives and superlatives such as *more hotter*, *most noblest*, which persist in Modern English, and are quite common in Shakespere. This construction is not without parallel in Old English, where we find the comparative of *longlived*, to be *lenglifra*, in which both the adverb *long* and the adjective *lif* are compared.

§ 116. Among the irregular comparatives and superlatives there are several modifications in the Middle English period. Firstly, for the positive *ȳfel* there appears the form *bad*, which first occurs in the thirteenth century, with the comparison *badder* and *baddest* as well as *worse* and *worst*. Another positive, from Scandinavian, is *ill*. The Old English forms *nēah, nēara, nīehst* gave regularly in Middle English *nigh, near, next*, so that *near* is really a comparative and *next* a superlative. But *near* came to be used as a positive and then a new comparative *nearer*, and a new superlative *nearest*, were formed from it. Of the remaining irregular forms, *much* or *many, more, most ; good, better, best ; little, less, least* are regular developments of the Old English forms, as are also the superlatives in -*most*, as in *utmost, inmost*, etc., though a new, double comparative *lesser* was formed from *less*. Similarly, though the regular comparative of *late* is *latter*, with a shortened vowel, a new comparative *later* was formed from the positive. Middle English also loses the positive and superlative of *rather*, and the comparative becomes an adverb instead of an adjective. From the Old English superlative adverb in -*m, forma*, we find the form *forme* in Middle English, used still as a superlative, but there is formed from it a new comparative *former*.

§ 117. The Middle English ordinal and cardinal numerals are regularly developed from the Old English forms. But the following points may be noted. O.E. *ān* becomes M.E. *one*, but in an unstressed form it gives

rise to the indefinite article *an* or *a*.   The form *two* is
derived from the O.E. feminine form *twā*, while the M.E.
twain is from the O.E. masculine *twēgen*.   Middle
English has also a new cardinal, *million*, from French.
Among the ordinals the only special points of interest
are the forms *first* and *second*.   The former is derived
from the O.E. superlative of *fore, fyrest*, and the latter
is derived from French.

§ 118. Middle English has certain multiplicative
forms which are developments of Old English adverbial
forms of the numerals.   Thus *twice* or *twies* is a development of the O.E. genitive *twīges* from the stem *twi-*
meaning " two."   Similarly *thrice*.   A new form in
Middle English, derived from Scandinavian, is *both*.

§ 119. The Modern English forms of the numerals
are regularly developed from the Old English forms.
It may be noted, however, that in Old English the
numeral for *two* was declined :

	Masc.	Fem.	Neut.
Nom., Acc.	*twēgen*	*twā*	*tū, twā.*

From the fem. and neut. forms we derive Modern
English *two*, and from the original masculine our *twain*.
So also the numeral *ān* was declined, and from the
genitive, masc. or neuter, *ānes* we have our *once*.   The
ordinals of Old English were formed from the cardinals
by the addition of the suffix *-ta* or *-þa*, which gives
the Modern English *-th*.   The only exceptions are the
ordinals corresponding to *one* and *two* (O.E. *ān, twēgen,
twā, tū*) which were *forma, ǣrest, fyrmest* and *fyr(e)sta*,
all of them superlatives, and the last of which gives
Modern English *first*.   The O.E. ordinal for *second* was
ōþer.

THE PRONOUN

Personal Pronouns

§ 120. The personal pronouns in Old English were subject to the same tendencies as were the nouns. That is to say, there is visible early a tendency to reduce, as far as possible, the number of forms, and a parallel tendency to introduce the analytical method of expression by using prepositions instead of inflections.

§ 121. The first forms to disappear were the forms for the dual, *wit*, " we two," *git*, " you two," and their oblique cases. But there is also a tendency to replace the accusative by the dative, a tendency which is doubtless due to the use of prepositional cases, in which the preposition usually governed the dative. The forms in common use in Old English are these :

	SINGULAR.	PLURAL.
Nom.	*ic*	*wē*
Acc., Dat.	*mē*	*ūs*
Gen.	*mīn*	*ūser, ūre*
Nom.	*þū*	*gē*
Acc., Dat.	*þē*	*ēow*
Gen.	*þīn*	*ēower*

	Masc.	Fem.	Neut.	Masc.	Fem.	Neut.
Nom.	*hē*	*hēo*	*hit*		*hīe*	
Acc.	*hine*	*hīe*	*hit*		*hīe*	
Gen.	*his*	*hiere*	*his*		*hiera, heora*	
Dat.	*him*	*hiere*	*him*		*him*	

The simplification, by the end of the Old English period, had gone so far, then, as to obliterate the dual forms and the accusatives except those of the third person singular.

Of these forms the genitives were used as possessive adjectives and were inflected, except *his, hiere* and *hiera*, like any other adjectives, according to the strong declension. The personal pronouns were also used as reflexive pronouns. In this function they could combine with *self*, which was declined like a strong adjective. Thus : *ic self*, " myself," *þē selfne*, " thyself," acc. ; *him selfum*, " himself," dat. ; *ūre selfra*, " ourselves," gen.

§ 122. The number of pronominal forms in Middle English is considerably smaller than the number in Old English, as a consequence of the developments we have already noticed in surveying the more important syntactic changes of the period. The tendency is for all forms except the nominative, dative and genitive of the personal pronouns, and the nominative singular and plural of all other pronouns, to disappear.

First Person.

	SINGULAR.		PLURAL.	
	O.E.	M.E.	O.E.	M.E.
Nom.	*ic*	*I*	*wē*	*we*
Acc., Dat.	*mē*	*me*	*ūs*	*us*
Gen.	*mīn*	*mine*	*ūser, ūre*	*our(s)*

Second Person.

Nom.	*þū*	*thou*	*gē*	*ye*
Acc., Dat.	*þē*	*thee*	*ēow*	*yow*
Gen.	*þīn*	*thine*	*ēower*	*your(s)*

Third Person.

	SINGULAR.					PLURAL.	
	Masc.		Fem.		Neut.		
	O.E.	M.E.	O.E.	M.E.	O.E.	M.E.	O.E.	M.E.
Nom.	*hē*	*he*	*hēo*	*she*	*hit*	*it*	*hīe*	*(they)*
Acc., Dat	*him*	*him*	*hīe*	—	*hit*	*it*	*hīe*	*(them)*
Gen.	*his*	*his*	*hiere*	*her*	*his*	*his, its*	*hiera*	*(their)*
Dat.	*him*	*him*	*hiere*	*her*	*him*	*him*	*him*	*(them)*

§ 123. The development of the pronouns of the first and second persons is quite regular. The accusative forms are all really the Old English datives, *mē*, *þē*, *ūs*, *ēow*. The form *thou* is spelt with *ou* instead of *u*, owing to the influence of the Norman spelling, and the same spelling is seen in *our*. The form *you*, which, it will be noticed, was originally only an accusative form, and is kept distinct from the Nom. *ye* until comparatively modern times, is derived from O.E. *ēow* by a shifting of the stress from the first to the second element of the diphthong, *eów* from *éow*. The same applies to *your*. Of the genitive forms, *mine* and *thine* are still used as pronouns, but the plural forms *our* and *your* are not ; they have now become possessive adjectives and not pronouns. New pronominal forms *ours* and *yours* were derived from them, and the pronominal forms *mine* and *thine* were also used as possessive adjectives, together with the shortened forms *my* and *thy* before words beginning with a consonant.

§ 124. In Old English the form *ūre*—and *ēower*, *mīn*, etc.—was used only as a pronoun in the genitive, *weorþ þu ūre gemyndig*, " be thou mindful of us." When it was a possessive, either adjective or pronoun, it was inflected like an adjective, *ūrne gedæghwāmlican hlāf syle us todæg*, " give us our daily bread." In Middle English, however, the forms *our* and *your* were gradually restricted to the adjectival function, and the form *ours*, *yours* come into use with the pronominal function : *For wel ye woot that al this gold is vres* (Chaucer, *Pard. Tale*). The form is really a double genitive and is found again in the forms *hers*, *theirs*.

§ 125. Throughout Middle English the distinction between the nominative *ye* and the accusative *you* is carefully drawn, and it is not until the modern period that *you* is regularly used in the nominative.

§ 126. The pronouns of the third person are not all regularly developed from the Old English forms. *He* and *him* are quite regular developments, *it* has lost its initial *h-*, *his* and *her* (dat.) are also the regular representatives of the O.E. *his* and *hiere*. But *her* (gen.) as a pronoun becomes *hers*. The remaining forms are irregular and require special explanation. They are *she*, *its*, *they*, *their*, *them*.

§ 127. *she*, O.E. *hēo*. It is commonly supposed that the form *she* is derived, not from *hēo*, but from the feminine of the definite article, *sēo*, with the stress shifted to the second element of the diphthong so that *sēo* became *seó* (sjo or sje), which later, perhaps in conjunction with the form (hjo, hje) from O.E. *hēo, hīe*, became *she*.

§ 128. *it*. The accusative form *it* is derived from the O.E. acc. *hit*, and not, as in the other accusatives, from the O.E. dative forms.

§ 129. *they, them, their* replaced the O.E. forms *hīe, him, hiera*, quite early in the Northern dialect, from which they spread to the other dialects in late Middle and early Modern English. All three forms are derived from Scandinavian. Traces of the old dative *him* are perhaps still to be found in the dialect form *'em*.

Possessives

§ 130. We have already noticed that the possessive pronouns were originally the genitive cases of the personal pronouns. The forms of the third person, *his*, *hire*, were undeclinable in Old English, but the forms of the first and second persons, *mīn*, *þīn*, *ūre*, *ēower* were declined like adjectives when used conjointly with a noun. In Middle English, however, *his* and *hir* were also declined like the other forms and thus yield in the plural *hise* and *hire*. The forms *mine* and *thine* lose their final *-n* before a consonant. When used absolutely, the forms *our, your, her, their* take a final *-s, ours, yours, theirs, hers*.

Reflexive

§ 131. In Old English the personal pronouns were used as reflexive pronouns, and when so used might be emphasised by the addition of *self*, which was inflected like an adjective. Thus Old English would decline :

Dat. *him selfum.* Acc. *hine selfne,* etc.

In Middle English *self* came to be regarded as a noun and was therefore constructed with the genitive : *myself, thyself, ourself, ourselves, yourself, yourselves,* though traces of the older construction with the dative are to be seen in *himself, themself, themselves* or *themselven*.

Demonstratives

§ 132. There were two demonstratives in Old English. One of them, which develops the functions of the definite article, was *sē, sēo, þæt* and the other was *þes, þēos, þis*. The declension of these two pronouns was as follows :

	SINGULAR.			PLURAL.		
	Masc.	Fem.	Neut.	Masc.	Fem.	Neut.
Nom.	sē	sēo	þæt	þā		
Acc.	þone	þā	þæt	þā		
Gen.	þæs	þ̄ære	þ̄æs	þāra		
Dat.	þ̄æm	þ̄ære	þ̄æm	þ̄æm		
Nom.	þes	þēos	þis	þās		
Acc.	þisne	þās	þis	þās		
Gen.	þisses	þisse	þisses	þissa		
Dat.	þissum	þisse	þissum	þissum		

These forms were well preserved throughout the Old English period, but in the Middle English period not only did the inflections disappear, as in the case of the adjectives, but there were also considerable changes in their functions.

§ 133. Old English also had a demonstrative *swylc* or *swelc,* " such," derived from the pronominal stem *swā-* =" so " +*līc,* " so-like." It was declined like a strong adjective.

§ 134. A glance at the declension of the demonstratives above will show that of the thirty-two forms of the two articles only two, *sē* and *sēo,* begin with s- and all the rest begin with þ-. In Middle English th- is carried into these two forms also, giving *the, theo.* According to the general tendencies of development all the forms except those of the nominative gradually disappeared. There were then left :

	SINGULAR.		PLURAL.
O. E.	sē, sēo, þæt		þā
M. E.	the, ·	that	tho
O. E.	þes, þeos, þis		þās
M. E.		this	those

In the course of the Middle English period *the* became restricted in sense until it came to be used only as the -definite article, a function which it already had in Old English. *That*, on the other hand, came to be used only as a demonstrative, and with the disappearance of all inflections these two forms, *the* and *that* were used for all genders. The plural form *tho*, originally the plural of both *the* and *that* came to be used only as the plural of *that*. It appears then to have become confused with the plural *those*, which was really the plural of *this*, so that *those* became the regular plural of *that* and a new plural for *this* was formed, *these*. The definite article, on the other hand, being *only* an ordinary adjective and not a pronoun, had no need of any inflections and became indeclinable after the loss of gender and case in nouns. There are some traces of the older use of *that* as a definite article in Middle English, so especially when it was used in the neuter form *that, thet*. In such a M.E. phrase as *the tother*, for example, the original is *þæt ōþer*.

§ 135. The Old English *swylc* in M.E. becomes indeclinable, loses its -*l*- and appears as *swuch* or *such*.

Interrogatives and Relatives

§ 136. Old English possessed no special relative pronoun. It used for this purpose the article *sē* either with or without the indeclinable particle *þe*, or it used the particle *þe* alone or in combination with a personal pronoun. This lack of a suitable relative pronoun is one of the indications of an undeveloped syntax to which reference has already been made. Its absence very soon makes itself felt and in the Middle English period we find, in consequence, that numerous experiments were made in order to supply this deficiency of § 139.

§ 137. Old English had four interrogative pronouns : *hwā*," who " ; *hwæt*, " what " ; *hwæþer*, " which of two "; *hwylc*, " which." Of these *hwā* has no feminine forms. In regard to interrogatives and relatives Old English again shows a simplification of forms, for both Gothic and Old High German have fully declined relatives, and Gothic and Old Norse have fully declined interrogatives.

§ 138. The four Old English interrogatives *hwā*, *hwæt*, *hwylc*, *hwæþer* all survive in Middle English as *who, what, which, whether*. Of these, *what* was originally only a pronoun, but in Middle English came to be used adjectivally, irrespective of gender, *what man, what thing*, etc. As a pure pronoun in the masc. or fem. *what* (*hwæt syndon ge*=who are you) is later replaced by *who*. The pronoun *who* was originally, and still is, only used of persons. The genitive case *whose* is a re-formation of the Old English genitive *hwæs*, and the dative *whom* is derived from the Old English dative *hwām*, which supplants the Old English accusative *hwone*. The interrogative *which* is the regular development of O.E. *hwylc*, the inflected forms of which all disappear in Middle English. The interrogative *whether* was much more commonly used in Middle English than it is in Modern English, to signify one of two.

Relatives

§ 139. The Old English relatives *sē, sē þe*, etc., disappeared in Middle English and new substitutes were found. Of these perhaps the earliest and the one in most common use was *that*, originally the neuter of the demonstrative or definite article. Already in Old English, however, it was used for all genders and not merely as a neuter. The use of *that* as a relative, probably arose from its use in sentences in which demonstrative and relative functions were combined, as in, *he wile nu gelæstan þæt he lange gehet*, "he wished to perform that which he had long promised." In such a sentence *þæt*, though originally the pronominal object of the verb *gelæstan* might very easily be taken as a relative.

Two new relatives appear in Middle English : *who* and *which*. These two pronouns were originally only interrogative pronouns, but they were early used as relatives, especially when followed by the normal relative *that*, or preceded by *the* : *the which that, who that*. Subsequently they were used alone as relatives, though *who* did not come into regular use as a relative until the Modern English period. *Which* in Middle English was not restricted to neuters as in Modern English ; cf. *Our Father which art in heaven*. The less common relative *as*, derived from O.E. *alswa, eallswa*, also survives in Middle English and Modern English, commonly in combination with *such*.

Indefinite Pronouns

§ 140. The Old English indefinite pronouns are formed partly from older elements of the language, as in *āhwā*, "anyone," *gehwilc*, "each" ; partly they consist of uncompounded forms which have survived in the modern language, such as : *ælc*, "each," *ǣnig*, "any," *swylc,* "such," *sum,* "one"; partly they consist of new analytical formations with *swā,* "so," as in *swā hwā swā,* "whoso," *swā hwelc swā,* "whichso(ever)," and others. Of the older compound forms only *āhwæþer* or *æghwæþer* or *ægþer,* "either"; *nāhwæþer,* "neither"; *āwuht,* "aught"; *nāwuht,* "nought" and *nān,* "none," have survived.

Indefinite pronouns were often formed in Old English, as we have seen, by prefixing *ā-* to an interrogative, or by placing *swā-* both before and after an interrogative : *āhwā, āhwæþer, swā hwā swā, swā hwelc swā,* etc. This manner of formation was continued in Middle English and is seen in the formations *whoso, what-so.* To this method of formation was added another, likewise found in Old English, the addition of the word *ever,* giving rise to the indefinite forms *whoever, whatever.* Sometimes the two methods of word formation are combined, and the resulting forms are *whosoever, whatsoever,* etc.

Most of the numerous Old English indefinites which were formed by means of the prefix *-ā-* do not survive in Middle English. The most important survival is the form *aught,* from O.E. *ā-wiht, ō-wiht.* The negative form of this word was O.E. *nāwiht, nōwiht,* giving Modern English *naught, nought.* There were in Middle English two spellings of both of these words, one in *au,* the other in *ou.* In Modern English we write only *aught,* but we preserve both *naught* and *nought,* with specialised meanings. For the rest, these two words are obsolete in Modern English, having given way to *anything* and *nothing,* but it is interesting to note that *naught* survives in *naughty,* = " good for nothing."

some, O.E. *sum*.   In Old English this indefinite
pronoun was generally a singular ; in Middle English
it has become a plural, and in Modern English new
singulars have been formed, *somebody, something*.   In
Middle English *some* was also combined with the indefinite *what* to form *somewhat*, which in Modern English
has become an adverb.   Other compounds with *some*
are *some one* and, Middle English, *somdel*.   *Some* in
Middle and Modern English is also used as an adjective
in various senses.   It may mean " a certain" (*ther was sum
prest*=a certain priest), or " about," *some fifty men*, etc.

any, O.E. *ænig*, derived from the numeral *ān+ig*.
In Middle English there were two forms of this word,
eny and *any*, of which the former is retained in pronunciation and the latter in writing.   In the Modern
English period *any* has become an adjective and survives as a pronoun only in a few idioms such as *Have
you any?*   It has been replaced in this function by the
new compounds, *anyone, anybody, anything*.

other, O.E. *ōþer* (composed of the two elements *an* and
-thar, an alternative suffix, " of two ").   In Old English
ōþer was inflected like an ordinary adjective, and the
genitive form survives in *other's*.   From *other* various
compounds have been derived, such as *another* and the
reciprocal pronouns *each other, one another*.   The two
latter, though now inseparable compounds, were not originally so, for each of them was separately inflected according to its syntactical function.   Thus O.E. *æghwæþer
ōþerne ūtādrǣfde*, " each drove out the other," where
æghwæþer is a nominative and *ōþerne* an accusative.

each, O.E. *ælc* from *āgilic*, " ever alike."   As in
which and *such*, the O.E. *-l-* is lost in Middle English.

The word is now used either as an adjective or as a pronoun. In Middle English it is also constructed with *a, an* : *each a, each an,* hence Modern English *each one.*

every, M.E. *ever-ech,* is a new compound formed in Middle English. In Modern English it is only used as an adjective, and in the pronominal use new compounds have been formed, *everyone, everything, everybody.*

either, O.E. *ǣgþer, ǣghwæþer* or *āhwæþer.* There was originally a distinction of meaning between *ǣgþer* and *āhwæþer,* the former meaning " each of two " and the latter meaning " one or other of two." It is the latter sense which has survived. The O.E. form *āhwæþer* gave rise to M.E. *auther, outher* which in an unstressed form gives the conjunction *or.* The M.E. *either,* on the other hand, is derived from the O.E. *ǣgþer.*

neither. The development of this word is exactly parallel with that of *either.* It differs from it only in having the negative prefix *n-.* The conjunction *nor* is developed in the same way as *or,* with the prefix *n-.*

one, O.E. *ān,* is the numeral *one.* Its use as an indefinite pronoun arises in Middle English, when a plural form *ones* and a genitive *one's* were also found, *Some clerkes says that an sal come that sal hald the empire of Rome* (Hampole, *Pricke of Conscience*). It is used in a variety of senses. Thus in *a good one* it is used as a pronoun, it also enters into the compounds *anyone, some one, many a one,* etc. Formerly it was used with a superlative with the sense of " of all," *she was oon the faireste under sunne,* " the fairest of all."

none, O.E. *nān* from *ne+ān,* " not one." From *none* was formed *no,* by loss of *-n,* as in *my* from *mine, thy* from *thine. None* is used only as a pronoun or substantive, *no*, only as an adjective. This form should not be confused with the form *no* in *no longer*, *no sooner*, etc., where *no* is an adverb derived from O.E. *nā*.

Middle English and Modern English have three new indefinite pronouns derived from French, *several*, *certain*, *divers*, though these are now used as adjectives rather than as pronouns.

THE VERB

§ 141. The Old English verb shows several changes which distinguish its conjugation from the conjugation of the verb in the cognate Germanic languages. In comparison with Gothic it has lost several of its categories, as, for example, the whole of the medio-passive voice, represented by the Gothic *haitada*= "I am called," and the forms of the dual number. Of these, the latter is not replaced, and the former is expressed analytically by means of the auxiliary verbs *bēon*, *wesan*, "to be," or *weorþan*, "to become." In common with the other Germanic languages it has reduced the number of tenses to two: the present and the past tense. The future, conditional and the perfect tenses are formed analytically; the former with the help of the auxiliary verb *sculan*, "shall," and the latter with the help of the auxiliaries *habban* and *wesan*.

The Old English verb, then, consists of the following parts. In the finite verb it has an active voice with an indicative, imperative and subjunctive mood. In the indicative and subjunctive moods it has a present and a past tense, in the imperative mood only a present tense. In the infinitive mood it has a past participle passive, a present participle active, and a present infinitive. All other tenses and voices and moods are expressed analytically by the help of auxiliaries.

§ 142. According to the formation of the past tense and past participle, verbs in Old English are classified as *strong* or *weak* verbs. The strong verbs are those which form their past tense by a change of the vowel of the stem and their past participle by a change of stem vowel accompanied by the ending *-en*. Weak verbs, on the other hand, are those which form both their past tense and their past participle by means of an inflectional dental, *-de* (*-te*) in the past tense and *-d* (*-t*) in the past participle. But since some weak verbs have a change of stem vowel in the past tense it follows that the only sure distinguishing mark of the strong or weak verb is the absence or presence, respectively, of the dental inflection. The two (or three) types of verb may be illustrated as follows :

	Infinitive.	Sing. Past.	Plur. Past.	Past Part.
STRONG.	*bītan,* " bite "	*bāt*	*biton*	*biten*
WEAK.	{ *wēnan,* " suppose "	*wēnde*	*wēndon*	*gewēned*
	{ *tellan,* " tell "	*tealde*	*tealdon*	*geteald*

§ 143. Strong verbs, again, may be divided into reduplicating and non-reduplicating strong verbs. The former class originally had in the past tense a so-called reduplicating syllable consisting of the initial consonant of the verbal stem and a vowel *e*. In Old English there is nothing left of this reduplicating syllable, but it is clearly to be seen in Gothic. Thus, for example, the past tense of the Gothic verb *haitan* is *haihait,* in which the first syllable is a reduplication such as we see in Latin *do—dedi, curro—cucurri*, etc. The Old English equivalent for the Gothic *haihait* was *heht*, in which something of the reduplication is still visible, though this verb is exceptional in that respect.

§ 144. Concerning the classification of verbs into strong and weak, it is a point of some interest that the former are the older and the latter are a specially Germanic formation without any parallel in the other Indo-Germanic languages. The distinction is an important one, for it explains how it comes about that all new verbs are weak verbs and not strong. Only those verbs, with rare exceptions, which are as old as Indo-Germanic, and therefore were subject to the changes described in § 147, are strong.

§ 145. There are in Old English six classes of strong verbs, and we shall best be able to understand how they arose by first noting their peculiarities. The following scheme shows the vowels of the stem in the infinitive, past singular indicative, past plural and past participle respectively of the six classes of strong verbs:

	I.-G.	O.E.	I.-G.	O.E.	I.-G.	O.E.	I.-G.	O.E.
I.	$e+i$	$\bar{\imath}$	oi	$\bar{a}$	i	i	i	i
II.	$e+u$	$\bar{e}o$	ou	$\bar{e}a$	u	u	u	u, o
III.	$e+\begin{Bmatrix} n \\ m \\ l \\ r \end{Bmatrix}+$Con.	e, i	o	a	u	u	u	u, o
IV.	$e+\begin{Bmatrix} l, m, \\ n, r \end{Bmatrix}$	e	o	α	$\bar{e}$	$\bar{\alpha}$	u	u, o
V.	e	e	o	α	$\bar{e}$	α	e	e
VI.	o	a	$\bar{a}$	$\bar{o}$	$\bar{a}$	$\bar{o}$	o	a, α

These six classes may be illustrated by the following Old English verbs :

	Infinitive.	Past Sing.	Past Plural.	Past Part.
I.	*wrītan*	*wrāt*	*writon*	*writen*
	snīþan	*snāþ*	*snidon*	*sniden*
II.	*bēodan*	*bēad*	*budon*	*boden*
	lēosan	*lēas*	*luron*	*loren*
III.	*singan*	*sang*	*sungon*	*sungen*
	bindan	*band*	*bundon*	*bunden*
	helpan	*healp*	*hulpon*	*holpen*
	weorþan	*wearþ*	*wurdon*	*worden*
IV.	*beran*	*bœr*	*bǣron*	*boren*
V.	*tredan*	*trœd*	*trǣdon*	*treden*
	wesan	*wœs*	*wǣron*	
	cweþan	*cwœþ*	*cwǣdon*	*cweden*
VI.	*sc(e)acan*	*sc(e)ōc*	*sc(e)ōcon*	*sc(e)acen*
	faran	*fōr*	*fōron*	*faren*

§ 146. There was also a seventh class of verbs showing a change of stem vowel in the past tense, the so-called Reduplicating Verbs. These originally had a reduplicating syllable prefixed in the past tense, as in Latin, *do, dedi ; curro, cucurri ;* or Gothic *haitan, haihait.* The forms in Old English are as follows ;

1.	*cnāwan*	*cnēow*	*cnēowon*	*cnāwen*
2.	*grōwan*	*grēow*	*grēowon*	*grōwen*
3.	*lētan*	*lēt*	*lēton*	*lǣten*

§ 147. A glance at the table of Indo-Germanic vowel equivalents on p. 170 will show that there are in Indo-Germanic certain regular changes which are not so clearly visible in the Old English table. In the first place it may be noted that the Indo-Germanic classes I. to V. all have the vowel *e* in the infinitive and the vowel *o* in the singular of the past tense. The only difference between these five classes originally, so far as these two forms are concerned, was that the vowel *e* was followed in class I. by *i* ; in class II. by *u* ; in class III. by *l, m, n, r,* and another consonant ; in class IV. by *l, m, n,* or *r* without another consonant ; and in class V. by any consonant other than *l, m, n,* or *r*. It will further be noticed that in the past tense singular the stem vowel is always *o,* followed by the same sound, vowel or consonant, as in the infinitive. This vowel change of *e* to *o* is known as gradation, and it is this change of gradation which characterises the tense formation of all strong verbs. Gradation may consist in a change in the quality of a vowel, as in the change of *e* to *o,* or it may consist in a change of the quantity of a vowel. There is thus a qualitative and a quantitative gradation. Quantitative gradation is seen in the forms of the plural of the past tense and of the past participle. Looking once again at the Indo-Germanic vowels we find in these two forms that the *ei* of the present appears as *i,* and *eu* appears as *u*. In other words, the quantity of the *e* has changed to such an extent that it has entirely vanished. The same quantitative changes occurred also in the other classes, but the subsequent development of the sounds remaining after the loss of the *e* has become so obscured that it would not be profitable to discuss it here. It may be sufficient to point out that the verbs of the classes I. to V. originally belonged to one class only, and that the difference of development in Old English is due to special Germanic and Old English sound laws which affected the verbal stem differently according as the original stem vowel was followed by an *i* ; *u* ; *l, m, n, r,* +consonant ; *l, m, n, r*

without a succeeding consonant ; or some consonant
other than *l, m, n, r*.

§ 148. The cause of this vowel gradation is to be
found in the conditions of the stress in Indo-Germanic.
Speaking broadly, the forms of the plural past tense and
of the past participle, in which the stem vowel vanishes,
are due to the absence of stress on the stem syllable.
The change of vowel may be paralleled in Modern
English in the prononication of *phótogràph* with a stress
on the first and last syllables, and *photógrapher*, in
which the two syllables which were stressed in *photograph* become unstressed and the vowels are correspond-
ingly weakened. In Indo-Germanic this is exactly
what happened, for with the system of free accent the
stress was sometimes placed on the stem of the verb,
sometimes on the ending and sometimes on the reduplicating syllable. Such a shifting of the stress very well
explains the so-called quantitative gradation, but it
does not explain the qualitative gradation of *e* to *o*,
which is usually attributed to a variation of the
musical stress or tone in Indo-Germanic.

§ 149. It will also be noticed on looking at the parts
of the Old English verb that the two forms in which we
have just noticed the operation of quantitative gradation,
i.e. plural past tense and past participle, also show a
change of consonant in certain verbs. Thus we see :

lēas	*luron*	*loren*
snāþ	*snidon*	*sniden*

This change of consonant is due to exactly the same
cause as the quantitative gradation. Where, in Indo-
Germanic, the stress fell after the consonants *k, t, p,*
which it always did in these forms of the verb, then these

consonants instead of appearing in Old English as *h*, *th*, *f*
—the sounds which appear in the infinitive, pres. indic.
and past singular—appear as *g*, *d*, *b*.   In the same way
and under identical conditions an original *s* appears as *r*.

§ 150. There are very few survivals of the operation
of this consonant change in Modern English, because
one or other of the consonants has been carried through
in all forms of the verb, but it is still to be seen in *was*,
sing., and *were*, plural.

§ 151. From this brief sketch of the origin and history
of the so-called strong verbs it appears that they are the
result of very special causes operating in the Indo-
Germanic period, causes which are rooted in the special
nature and quality of the original accent and which were
dependent upon the sentence stress and syntax of the
original language.   It follows, therefore, that verbs
formed after these causes had ceased to operate ; when,
for example, the accent was no longer free ; when the
word order of the sentence became more rigid ; could
no longer form their tenses by gradation, unless they were
deliberately formed on the analogy of existing older
verbs.   As a matter of fact new verbs were not, as a
rule, in Germanic, forced into the older categories.
Instead, a quite new method of formation came into use
and gave rise to the so-called weak verbs, which are
peculiar to the Germanic languages.   These weak verbs
are again the result of the tendency to analytic expression
which we have so often noticed.   Instead of being formed
by means of gradation, the past tense was formed by
the addition of a part of the verb *do*, so that our Modern
English *I heard* is really the equivalent of *I hear did*=
I did hear.   This is most clearly seen in certain forms

of the Gothic past tense of weak verbs, thus Gothic *sōkidēdum*, " we sought," is the past tense of *sōkjan*, " to seek." The same analytic tendency, of which the tense formation of weak verbs is one of the earliest clear manifestations, is also to be seen in the formation of the future tense and the compound perfect tenses in the Germanic languages. Such Modern English forms as *I shall seek, I should seek, I have sought*, etc., appear to have been common to the various Germanic languages and are the result of the desire to indicate more clearly the exact time of the action of the verb. In Old English, it is true, as in Old High German and Gothic, it was possible to express future time by means of the present indicative tense, but only when the context made it clear that the future was intended. The same usage still exists in Modern English : *he comes to-morrow.* The motive for the development of the analytic future may have been the desire to emphasise the futurity of the action or else to express futurity where there was no word in the context, like *to-morrow* in the above sentence, to indicate futurity. The perfect compound tenses, on the other hand, must have arisen from a desire to express more precisely the manner, the time, both absolute and relative, of the action of the verb ; for the simple, indefinite time could already be expressed by the uncompounded tenses.

§ 152. Old English had three classes of weak verbs :

I. Those which originally ended *-jan* and therefore have *j* mutation (cf p. 228) and gemination (p. 227) wherever it is admissible ; the past tense is formed by the addition of *-ede*, or *-de* when the stem vowel is long.

cnyssan, " strike "   *cnyessede*   *gecnyssed*

II. Those verbs which originally ended in -*ōjan*. The past tense ends in -*ode* and the past participle in -*od*.

þancian   þancode   geþancod

III. A limited number of verbs with mutated vowel and geminated consonant in the infinitive, 1st sing. present indicative and plural present indicative. The past tense ends in -*de* and the past participle in -*d*.

secgan   sægde   gesægd
hæbban   hæfde   gehæfd

§ 153. In addition to strong, weak and reduplicating verbs, Old English also had certain Past-Present and anomalous verbs, the peculiar conjugation of which is retained in Modern English. The Past-Present verbs, or Preterite-Present as they are also called, are verbs which have the form of a strong past tense, but the meaning of a present tense. We give here the Old English forms which have survived :

Class.	Present.	Past.	Past Participle.
I.	*wāt*, " I know "	*wiste*	
	āh, " I possess "	*āhte*	*āgen*
III.	*conn*, " I can,"	*cūþe*	*cūþ* (adj.)
	" know "(how to)		
IV.	*sceal*, " I must "	*sceolde*	
V.	*mæg*, " I can "	*meahte, mihte*	
VI.	*mōt*, " I may "	*mōste*	

If one looks at any one of these forms one will see that it agrees with the corresponding form of the strong verb in two respects : firstly it has the vowel of the past tense of the strong verb and secondly it has the personal inflection of the strong past tense. Thus *can* is exactly the same in form as *band* or Modern English *sang*. Moreover, though a present tense, it has no inflection. We say in Modern English *he can* and not *he cans*, like *he walks* or *he sings*. Originally these verbs had perfect sense, thus *wāt* meant " I have seen " (cf. Lat. *video*) ; *can* meant " I have known " ; *mæg*," I have had the might." In all these forms the original element of present meaning developed until it completely supplanted the element of past meaning.

§ 154. The anomalous verbs in Old English are : *bēon, wesan*, " to be " ; *dōn*, " to do " ; *gān*, " to go " ; *willan*, " will, to wish." The verb *bēon* or *wesan* is conjugated from three original stems : *es* (Lat. *esse*), *bhu* (Lat. *fui*) and *wes*. Of these the stem *es* is only found in the present indicative and subjunctive. The conjugation is as follows :

INDICATIVE.

		PRESENT.	PAST.
Sing.	1.	*eom, bēo*	*wæs*
	2.	*eart, bist*	*wǣre*
	3.	*is, biþ*	*wæs*
Plural.	1, 2, 3.	*sind, sint, sindon, bēoþ.*	*wǣron*

SUBJUNCTIVE.

Sing.	1.	*sīe, bēo*	*wǣre*
Plural.	1, 2, 3.	*sīen, bēon*	*wǣren*

§ 155. Of the remaining anomalous verbs, *dōn* forms its past tense as *dyde*, and *willan* forms a past tense *wolde*. The verb *gān* forms a past tense *ēode* from a different stem.

§ 156. The changes in the development of the Modern English verb from its Old English forms illustrate more clearly than other series of changes the main

E.L. M

tendencies at work in the development of the language. We see here better than anywhere else three tendencies at work which we have already noticed : (1) The tendency to reduce the number and variety of grammatical forms. (2) The tendency to indicate a syntactic concord once only. (3) The tendency to analytic expression. The first of these is seen in the reduction of the three classes of weak verbs of Old English to one in Modern English ; in setting aside the difference of vowel and consonant in the singular and plural of the past tense : *he sang, we sang* and not *he sang, we sung*. The second tendency is seen in the loss of all personal inflections except -*s* of the third singular of the present indicative, the person and number being expressed either by the pronoun or the noun. The third tendency is seen in the development of numerous analytic tenses such as *I am reading, I have read, I have been reading, I shall have been reading, I am going to read, I was going to read, I do read, I did read,* etc.

§ 157. The first simplification to be made in the complicated conjugation of the Old English verb was to set aside the change of consonant in the past tense and to carry the consonant of the singular into the plural and the past participle. In Modern English the only survival in the verb of the original change of consonant is to be seen in the forms *was* and *were*. The change is also visible in the forms *sodden* and *lorn*, both of which are old participles. Somewhat later than this change, and belonging in the main to the Middle English period, is the setting aside of the difference of vowel in the singular of the past tense and the plural and past participle. This levelling out of forms began first in the

Northern dialect and spread from there to the South. In Modern English the vowel change is only preserved in *was* and *were*, but there are traces of its original presence in the confusion which exists in certain quarters as to whether one should say *he swam* or *he swum, he sang* or *he sung*, where in Old English the singular form was *sang* and the plural form *sung*. It was usually the vowel of the singular which was carried into the plural, but sometimes it was the vowel of the plural which was carried into the singular, especially where the vowel of the plural was the same as the vowel of the past participle, *e.g.* O.E. *findan—fand—funden—funden* gives Modern English *find—found—found—found*. The fact that the vowel of the past participle was the same as the vowel of the plural of the past tense does not necessarily, however, turn the decision in favour of that vowel, as may be seen from the development of O.E. *singan—sang—sungon—sungen* to Modern English *sing—sang—sang—sung*. In fact, various influences co-operated in determining in which direction analogy would work. The real causes underlying the choice of one form or another were doubtless those that underlie all analogical changes. The fundamental cause of analogy is always that one form is more strongly impressed on the mind than another. That which determines the impression on the mind of one form rather than of another is usually the frequency with which the form in question is used. In some verbs the plural form would be more used than the singular. Without in the least suggesting that such actually was the case, it is a theoretical possibility, for example, that *sang* may have been in commoner use than *sung*, on the assumption that collective singing was not as common as individual singing, or, to be more precise, was not the subject of conversation as much as was individual singing. There can be little doubt, for example, that a verb like *drink* would be used very much more in the singular than in the plural, and it is therefore natural that the vowel of the singular should prevail. Some verbs, again, would scarcely ever be used in the plural, *e.g. stride.* Or, again, in some verbs where the plural and past participle agreed in their vowels these forms together may have been more frequent than the singular forms. There are all sorts of possibilities which it would be impossible to unravel at this date, but the varying results which we perceive in Modern English must be the result of some mental process underlying the analogical formations.

§ 158. A levelling of a similar kind took place in those verbs in Old English which differed in the singular and the plural of the past tense only in the quantity of the vowel. Sometimes, too, the vowel of the past tense is carried into the past participle, as in O.E. *scīnan—scān—scinon—scinen,* but Modern English has instead *shine—shone—shone—shone.* Here, again, one might hazard the suggestion that the singular form would be in more common use.

Another change which has occurred since the Old English period is that which is to be seen in the conjugation of originally strong verbs as weak verbs. Such verbs are fairly common. Thus, for example, *melt—melted, climb—climbed,* though now weak, were once strong, as the obsolete *clomb* and the adjective *molten* show. *creep, leap, weep* were similarly once strong and have become weak. The general tendency when a verb changes its conjugation is for a strong verb to become weak and not *vice versa*, because, no doubt, the weak verbs are much more numerous.   There are, however, examples of the contrary change as, for example, *stick —stuck*, O.E. *stician—sticode ; wear—wore*, O.E. *werian werede*.   In the first case there is a strong sense analogy with *sting—stung*, and in the second case there is a strong form analogy with *swear—swore*.

§ 159. We may now turn to the regular development of the six classes of strong verbs and the seventh class of reduplicating verbs in Modern English.   They are represented by the following verbs :

I.	write	wrote	written
	drive	drove	driven
	rise	rose	risen
II.	choose	chose	chosen
	freeze	froze	frozen
III.	sing	sang	sung
	swim	swam	swum
	drink	drank	drunk
	bind	bound	bound
	find	found	found
IV.	bear	bore	born
	steal	stole	stolen
V.	give	gave	given
VI.	shake	shook	shaken
	take	took	taken
VII.	know	knew	known
	grow	grew	grown
	let	let	let
	fall	fell	fallen
	hold	held	(be)hold(en), held

CLASS I.

O.E.	*ī* ˙	*ā*	*ĭ*	*ĭ*
M.E.	*ī*	*ō*	*ĭ, ō*	*ĭ*
Mod. E.	*ī* [ai]	*ō*	*ō*	*ĭ*

§ 160. In this class *shone* takes its past participle vowel from the past tense. The verb *bite* has the past tense *bit*, instead of *bōt*, from the past participle. *chide* is now weak, as it was also in O.E., but cf. *chidden*; *slide* has the shortened past participle *slid* which gives also the past tense *slid*. The forms of the past tense *bit* and *slid* may, however, equally well be the O.E. plural forms *slidon, biton*. In earlier Modern English we find more forms of this kind such as *driv, writ, ris*, etc. The verb *strike* has its past tense *struck* and past participle *struck*, or, regularly, *stricken*; *strive* is an exceptional case of a loan verb being conjugated strong.

CLASS II.

O.E.	*ĕo*	*ĕa*	*ŭ*	*ŏ*
M.E.	*ē*	*ē*	*ō, ē*	*ō*
Mod. E.	*ee* [ij], *oo o*		*o*	*o*

§ 161. Many of the verbs belonging to this class have become weak, and none faithfully presents the normal development in Modern English. *shove, lock, suck, creep,* and others have become weak; *cleave, seethe* and *lose* have left traces of their original strong participles in the adjectives *cloven, sodden* and *forlorn*; *cleave* has also an earlier strong past tense *clave*, which has been replaced by *clove* or *cleaved*, the former with the vowel of the past participle; *shoot* is regular except that it has the short form of the past participle, *shot* and the past tense formed from it. Of the verbs *freeze* and *choose* the former represents the regular development of the O.E. vowel *ēo*, the latter is a dialect form. The past participle in both cases is regular and the past tenses are derived from them.

CLASS. III.

O.E.	*i, e,*	*a (ea)*	*u*	*u, o, ŏ, ŭ, ō*
M.E.	*ī, e,*	*a*	*ou, ŏ, ŭ*	*ou, u, ō*
Mod. E.	*i* [ɑi, i], *e*	*a,u* [a], *ou* [ɑu, ɔ]	*u* [a], *ou* [ɑu]	

§ 162. The verbs of this class are numerous. We distinguish those which have in Modern English preserved the three vowels of Old English such as :

(a)
sing	*sang*	*sung*
drink	*drank*	*drunk*
sink	*sank*	*sunk*
swing	*swang*	*swung*
begin	*began*	*begun*
shrink	*shrank*	*shrunk*
spring	*sprang*	*sprung*
ring	*rang*	*rung*
swim	*swam*	*swum*

(b) those which have carried the vowel of the plural of the past tense and the past participle into the singular :

fight	*fought*	*fought*
find	*found*	*found*
bind	*bound*	*bound*
grind	*ground*	*ground*
wind	*wound*	*wound*
slink	*slunk*	*slunk*
fling	*flung*	*flung*
spin	*spun*	*spun*
cling	*clung*	*clung*
sting	*stung*	*stung*
win	*won*	*won*
wring	*wrung*	*wrung*
swing	*swung*	*swung*

Those verbs which have -*nd* after the root vowel lengthened the short *u* already in Old English and the long *u* was then written *ou*, as in *house, thou*, etc. In *won* the *o* is a M.E. spelling for the sound *u*.

(*c*) Those which have become weak in Modern English. Such are *help, delve, yield, burn, carve, starve, climb, melt, swell*. However, these verbs have left traces of their strong forms in *molten* and *swollen*. Here also belongs the verb *run—ran—run*, the past forms of which are probably Scandinavian and the infinitive forms of which it is difficult to account for.

CLASS IV.

O.E.	*e*	*æ*	*ǣ*	*o*
M.E.	*ē*	*a*	*e, ō*	*ō, u*
Mod. E.	*ea* [ɛ, ij]	*ō*	*ō*	*o* [ou, ɔ]

§ 163. In this class the vowel of the past participle has usually replaced the original vowel of the past tense in Modern English :

steal	*stole*	*stolen*
tear	*tore*	*torn*
bear	*bore*	*born*
shear	*shore*	*shorn*
break	*broke*	*broken*

The verb *speak* has also come into this class, though originally in class v. In all the above verbs the final *e* is not inflectional, but merely marks the length of the stem vowel. *bear* has a second participle, *borne*, meaning " carried." There were, in early Modern English, some forms of these verbs derived from the Old English singular forms, *bare, spake, brake*, whereas the modern forms have taken the vowel of the original past participle. To this class also belongs the irregular *come— came—come*, O.E. *cuman—cōm—cumen*.

CLASS V.

O.E.	e	œ	ǣ	e
M.E.	i, ē	a	ē	ē
Mod. E.	e, ea, ee, i	a [ei], o	a [ei], o	various

§ 164.

give	gave	given
sit	sat	sat
spit	spat	spat
eat	ate	eaten
bid	bade	bidden
get	got	got(ten)
tread	trod	trodden
lie	lay	lain
see	saw	seen
weave	wove	woven

The regular vowel of the past tense is *a*, O.E. *œ*, *ea*, as in *sat*, *bade*. The long vowel in *ate* was present already in O.E. Modern English has two pronunciations : [ɛt] and [eit]. The former is probably a M.E. shortening of *ēt* and the latter would seem to represent a secondary O.E. form *ǣt* with short instead of long vowel. The regular vowel of the past participle should be *e* [ij] as in *eaten*. Under the influence of neighbouring sounds or of analogy it had become *i* in *bidden* and *given*. The *o* vowel in *got*, *gotten* (*forgot*, *forgotten*) is probably due to the analogy of verbs like *stole*, *stolen*, and the same is true of *trod*, *trodden*, and *weave*, *wove*. The verb *spit* was originally a weak verb. The *w* of *saw* is derived from the plural form of the O.E. past tense, *sāwon*. To this class belong the forms *was* and *were* which have not only faithfully preserved the Old English distinction of vowel in the singular and plural, but have also preserved the distinction of consonant.

Class VI.

O.E.	a	ō	ō	a
M.E.	ā	ō	ō	ā
Mod. E.	a [ei]	o, oo [u]	o, oo [u]	oo, a [ei]

§ 165. Some verbs have preserved the original vowels :

shake	shook	shaken
take	took	taken
forsake	forsook	forsaken

some have certain forms preserved, though others are now weak :

shape	(shaped)	shapen, adj.
engrave	(engraved)	engraven, (adj. engraved)

others have taken the vowel of the past tense into the past participle, perhaps on the analogy of *stole, stolen* :

swear	swore	sworn
stand	stood	stood
awake	awoke	awoke, awaken

Two verbs have *ew* in the past tense :

slay	slew	slain
draw	drew	drawn

The *w* of *draw* represents the development of an O.E. ʒ. The *e* of the past tense has come in on the analogy of verbs like *blew*, in which the *e* is original, O.E. *blēow*. In *slay* the vowel of the infinitive is taken from the past participle, and the *i* or *y* represents an O.E. ʒ, O.E. *slægen*. The formation of the past tense resembles that of *drew* (O.E. *drōh*). The form *stand* with *n* only in the present corresponds to the O.E. form, cf. Latin *linquo—liqui*.

To this class also belongs the verb *heave, hove*, though it now has the weak past form *heaved*.

Reduplicating Class

§ 166.

O.E.	$\bar{a}, \bar{o}, \breve{e}a,$	$\bar{e}, \breve{e}o$	$\bar{a}, \breve{o}, \bar{e}a$
Mod. E.	$a, o, ea,$	$e, ea,$ [ij, ɛ]	various

blow	blew	blown
know	knew	known
crow	crew	crown
grow	grew	grown
throw	threw	thrown
mow	(mowed)	mown
sow	(sowed)	sown
beat	beat	beaten
let	let	let
hew	(hewed)	hewn
fall	fell	fallen
hold	held	held (but beholden)
hang	hung	hung

To this class originally belonged *sleep, weep, leap,* which are now weak. The form *hight* is also an old reduplicating past tense, O.E. *heht. crow* now has a weak past tense, *crowed,* especially in the metaphorical sense. The past participle *held* has taken the vowel of the past tense ; *hang* has also the weak past forms *hanged.* The infinitive and the weak forms are derived from an O.E. weak intransitive verb *hangian, hangode.* The strong forms *hung* are not derived from the O.E. *heng,* but are formed on the analogy of *sung.*

A past participle possibly formed on the analogy of verbs of this class is *shown.*

It will be noticed that in Modern English some participles preserve the O.E. final *-en* and some do not. The broad rule is that in genuine participial forms, that is to say, in forms which are not analogy formations, such as *sat, held,* the *-en* is preserved in those stems which end in one consonant or a double consonant and is lost in those verbal stems which end in two (different) consonants, that is to say, in verbs of the third class.

Weak Verbs

§ 167. The three classes of Old English weak verbs were in Middle English reduced to a single class; the Old English inflections -(e)de, -ode being reduced to a uniform -d, except in those verbs whose stem ends in a dental, as *grafted*, *wafted*, etc., in which the inflection is still -ed. But although these are the only verbs in which Modern English pronounces the vowel (pronounced -id) yet there are many in which the full inflection -ed is preserved in the spelling, as for example in *dreamed*, *burned*, *loved* and many more. The actual pronunciation of the final -ed or -d varies according to the nature of the preceding sound; if it is a vowel or a voiced consonant then -d, -ed have the sound of -d, otherwise they have the sound of t: *loved*, *braised*, but *finished*, *crept*. There are a few exceptions to this rule: *felt*, *dealt*, *smelt*, *learnt*, *burnt*, *dreamt*. If the verbal stem already ends in a dental consonant, then in Modern English the inflectional -d is apparently missing, as in *lead*, *led*; *feed*, *fed*; *read*, *read*. Really the single -d in these words represents the simplification of earlier -dde, O.E. *lædde*, etc. In some verbs the final -d, which after a voiceless consonant is pronounced t, is also written t: *sleep*, *slept*; *lose*, *lost*; *creep*, *crept*. Some verbs ending in -ld, -nd-, -rd, change the d of the stem into t in the past forms: *build*, *built*; *bend*, *bent*; *rend*, *rent*, etc.

§ 168. In consequence of these special developments there are many verbs which have the same forms for

the present and past tense, so that it is only possible
from the context of one of these verbs to know which
tense is meant.   Such verbs are :

hit	*hit*	*hit*
cast	*cast*	*cast*
hurt	*hurt*	*hurt*
shut	*shut*	*shut*
put	*put*	*put*

In actual speech the present and past tenses are differentiated in the third person singular—the form most
commonly used—by the personal ending in the present
indicative and the absence of ending in the past tense,
he hurts, he hurt.

§ 169. There are some verbs in Modern English which
have the vowel of the past tense or the second and third
singular present indicative carried into the present tense.
Such are *say* and *lay*.   The O.E. forms of these verbs
were *secgan—sægde* and *lecgan—lægde*.   The past tenses
regularly give *said* and *laid*; the old infinitives should give
sedge and *ledge*, but they have been reformed on the model
of the past tense, since in most weak verbs the stem in
the infinitive and the past tense is the same.

§ 170. There are a few weak verbs which have modified their stem consonant in the past tense.   Such are :

leave	*left*
bereave	*bereft*
lose	*lost*
cleave	*cleft*

§ 171. In Old English there was also a special group
of weak verbs which had different vowels in the present
stem and the past stems.   These verbs always showed a
mutated vowel (and sometimes a double consonant)

in the former and an unmutated vowel in the latter.
Thus O.E.

sellan	*s(e)alde*
tellan	*t(e)alde*
sec(e)an	*sohte*
bycg(e)an	*bohte*

These verbs had originally an *i* or *j* attached to the stem
in the present tense, but not in the past tense. (cf. Lat.
capio). This *j* mutated the stem vowel so that an original
salj- became *sellj-*, *sōkj-* became *sēkj-*, etc. At the same
time the *j* doubled the preceding consonant, except *r*, if
the preceding stressed vowel was short. The result of these
changes was that we find in the present tense the forms
sell, tell, seek, but in the past participle the forms without
mutation, *s(e)ald, t(e)ald, soht* becoming in Modern English
sold, told, sought. In verbs like *sought, taught, thought*
and others it will also be noticed that there is a change
of consonant in the past tense. This is due to yet another sound law according to which an original *k* or *g*,
b or *p*, *d* or *t*, when followed by a dental, become respectively *h, f, s*. Hence in a verb like *seek*, when the dental
inflection of the past tense was added to the stem, the
consonant *k* changed to *h*, which originally was pronounced like the *ch* in *loch*. In Modern English it has
become silent in *sought, thought, brought*, and other verbs,
but is written *gh*.

§ 172. Two verbs in Modern English have the further
irregularity that in the past tense they have not only
changed the *g* of the present tense to *h* (*gh*) in the past
tense, but have also lost an *n* in the infinitive. This
change is due to the sound law mentioned on p. 226,
according to which the original group *anh* becomes *āh*

and then *ōh*. Thus the original infinitive stem *þanc-*,
O.E. *þenc* after the dental inflection *-ða* was added,
became **þanhða*, *þāhte*, *þōhte*, *thought*. This verb,
therefore, illustrates several sound laws.

§ 173. A special class of Old English verbs called causative verbs deserves special explanation. These causative
verbs were all derived from the past stem of the corresponding strong verb by the addition of *-j-* to the stem,
and this *-j-* caused mutation of the stem vowel wherever
possible. Thus from the strong verb *drincan* was formed
drencan, " to drench." The stem of the past tense was
dranc, the causative was therefore *drancjan*, which
by mutation became *drencan*, " drench." Similarly
rear is formed from *rise*, *set* from *sit*, *fell* from *fall*, *lay*
from *lie*, etc.

§ 174. The following verbs present special irregular-
ities in Modern English :

catch, caught. This verb, as we have seen, is a doublet·
of *chase* and is of French origin. Its past tense was
formed on the analogy of *teach*, or, as some say, of
laughed.

distract, distracted, distraught. The infinitive is of Latin
origin, though cognate with an Old English form *streccean*,
which regularly would give a past tense *straught* (surviving
in *straight*). Hence by confusion the form *distraught*.

work has an old past tense *wrought*, which shows a
metathesis from earlier *worhte*.

make, made. The form *made* is a contraction of
earlier *macode*. A similar loss of intermediate consonant is seen in *clothe, clad*. *clad* was earlier *clāþode*.

have, had. The past tense represents an assimilation
of O.E. *hœfde* to *hadde* and then *had*.

go, went. The past tense *went* is really the weak past tense of the old verb *wendan,* " to wend."

§ 175. In conclusion it may be noted that in many weak verbs in Modern English the vowel of the past tense is shortened in accordance with certain sound laws of the Middle English and Modern English period. Such, for example, are : *flee, fled ; shoe, shod ; sleep, slept ; lose, lost ; leave, left ;* etc.

Past-Present and Anomalous Verbs

§ 176. Several of the Old English Preterite-Present verbs have disappeared in Modern English, and of those which have survived some have lost certain forms and others have changed their meanings. The only one which has an infinitive in Modern English is *dare* ; and *must* and *ought* have only a single form for the present and past tenses, so that these two forms are, as it were, Preterite-Present verbs twice over, since the form of the present, though itself a past formation, has the meaning of a present tense.

wāt survives into early Modern English in the shortened form *wot.* The past tense, *wiste,* now obsolete, shows a change of the *t* of the stem to *s* before a dental (cf. § 208).

ought. The real present form *owe* shows the vowel of the O.E. infinitive *āgan* and not that of the O.E. present tense singular, *āh.* Its original sense of " possess," which it preserves in the form *own,* has been lost in Modern English. The form *owe* is now used as an independent weak verb, *owe, owed.* The original past tense *āhte* becomes regularly *ought,* and this form is now used with present meaning.

can, could. The singular *can* is found in all persons, as in other strong verbs. The Old English past tense *cūþe* has been replaced by *could*, which has *ld* on the analogy of *would* and *should*. The Old English form survives in the adjective *uncouþ*.

dare, durst. O.E. *dear, dorste.* The correct form *dare* is now only used before an infinitive. Otherwise it has taken the ordinary inflectional *-s* of other verbs, *dares*. The regular past tense is *durst*, but a new weak past tense *dared* has developed; originally with the sense of "to dare somebody to do something."

shall, should. O.E. *sceal, sc(e)olde.* This verb in Old English had the sense of "owe," "being under the obligation to do." In Modern English, though it has not this sense when used as an auxiliary in the formation of a future tense, it has developed new meanings when used independently. Thus *he shall do it* implies a determination on the part of the speaker. *should* is perhaps formed on the analogy of *would*.

may, might. O.E. *mæg, mihte.* The Modern English forms are regularly derived from the Old English forms.

must. O.E. *mōste.* The O.E. present tense *mōt* has disappeared from Modern English and its place has been taken by the past tense *must*, but *mote* is found in early Modern English, in Spenser and other writers.

will, would. O.E. *wille, wolde.* The form *would* shows a change of *o* to *u* under the influence of *w*. There is also an independent verb *will* in Modern English which is derived from O.E. *wilnian* or *willian*, e.g. *he wills it*; *will* has a negative form *won't* which shows a survival of a Middle English present stem *wol-*. In Middle English and Old English there was also another negative

form with the negative prefix, O.E. *nelle*, M.E. *nille*.
This form survives in *willy-nilly*. For the rest, it is
characteristic of all the Preterite-Present verbs that
they take a contracted form of the negative : *shan't*,
can't, etc., which is compounded with the verb. The
same composition is also found with the verbs *to be*
and *to have*.

§ 177. *be*. The modern forms of the present indicative
are regularly derived from the Old English *eom*, *is*, *earon*
(Northern). In Middle English and Modern English
the *be* forms were, however, quite common. The forms
of the past tense *was* and *were* are also regularly derived
from the O.E. forms *wæs*, *wǣron*. The modern forms of
the present subjunctive are derived from the O.E. *be*
forms, though they have practically disappeared from
the spoken language. The forms of the past subjunctive,
on the other hand, are fully preserved even in the
spoken language : *I was*, but, *if I were*. Modern English
has also developed a past participle *been*.

have. The forms of the first person singular and the
plural, *have*, do not correspond to the Old English forms
hæbbe and *habbaþ*, but take their consonant from the
forms which in Old English had a single *f*, *hæfþ*. The
third person *has* is from O.E. *hæfþ* with the substitution
of inflectional *-s* for *-th* and assimilation of *-fs* to *-s*.
The form *hath* represents a development of *hæfþ*.
In Modern English the word *behaviour* shows the
regular development of the stem vowel. In all the
forms of the verb the vowel *æ* is the consequence of
the lack of stress. Indeed in Modern English when the
parts of *have* are used as auxiliaries they are always
reduced or shortened as in *I'd*, *I've*, etc.

Inflections

§ 178. The Old English inflections already show a very considerable simplification as compared with the much more complex system of Primitive-Germanic. Thus the three persons of the plural have the same inflection, no matter whether the verb be strong or weak. So also the inflections of the singular present indicative are very much the same in strong and weak verbs, and also the inflections of the conjunctive present in the singular. The O.E. inflections were as follows :

STRONG VERBS.

		PRESENT.		PAST.	
		Indic.	Conj.	Indic.	Conj.
Sing.	1.	-e	-e	—	-e
	2.	-(e)s(t)	-e	-e	-e
	3.	-e(ð)	-e	—	-e
Plur.		-að	-en, -an, -on	-un, -on, -an	-en, an, -on

Infinitive.	Pres. Part.	Past Part.
-an	-ende	-en

WEAK VERBS.

		PRESENT.		PAST.	
		Indic.	Conj.	Indic.	Conj.
Sing.	1.	-e	-e	-de	-de
	2.	{ -(e)s(t)	-e	-des, -dest	-de
		{ -as, -ast	-e		
	3.	-(e)ð, -að		-de	-de
Plur.	1, 2, 3.	-að, iað	-en	-dun, -don, -dan	-den, -dan, -don

Infinitive.	Pres. Part.	Past Part.
-an	-ende	-ed, -od

§ 179. In Modern English all these inflections have disappeared with the sole exception of the inflection of the third person singular (-s), the dental inflection of the past tense of weak verbs, (-d, -t) and the -en of strong past participles. The -s of the third person is in all probability simply the -s of the second person carried into the third person. That the two persons should have come to have the same ending, first in the North and then in the Midlands is not strange, especially when we bear in mind that among the Scandinavian population such identity of ending in the second and third persons was already familiar in the ending -r. Nevertheless it is not to be supposed that they disappeared without a struggle or without leaving some trace behind. In Middle English in the plural of the present indicative we find two endings -eth and -en. Chaucer uses both. The ending -s in the third person was originally a Northern ending and side by side with it there existed the O.E. -eth, which is now archaic or confined to poetry. The ending of the past participle of strong verbs still survives, except in verbs of the bind class. The ending of the present participle in Modern English is -ing and not -ende as in Old English. This ending competed for some time in Middle English with the Northern ending -ande and the Midland ending -ende, but ultimately it prevailed over both of these. It is probably derived from the ending -ing which was common as a noun-forming suffix in Old English.

In the present infinitive we see once again the tendency to analytic expression in the forms with to; Modern English to sing, Old English singan, in which to sing has syntactically the function of an ordinary noun.

Modern English has developed a second noun-form in *-ing*, which is identical in form with the present participle, *singing*. Such verbal nouns arose from the identity as regards form of the participial form *singing* with older genuine nouns such as *learning*, O.E. *leornung*. Originally, however, such a participle was felt to be a noun and its syntax was that of a noun. Thus, for example, we find that it is constructed with the definite article and followed by a preposition just like any other noun, *e.g. the giving of alms*. Gradually, however, the use of the article disappeared as in, *they thanked him for giving them such a fight*, in which sentence *giving* has verbal function and governs an object. The identity in form of the true noun in *-ing* and the participle in *-ing* made it very easy, however, to form new nouns from any verb.

THE ADVERB

§ 180. The Old English adverb is partly composed of old material and partly it is a new formation. Numerous adverbs are nothing but adjectives with an adverbial inflection such as *-e*, *-a*. Thus side by side with the adjectives *dēop*, " deep," *riht*, " right," *sweotol*, " clear," *wīd*, " wide," *wēnung*, " hope," " chance," we find corresponding adverbs, *dēope*, *rihte*, *sweotole*, *wīde*, *wēnunga*, " deeply," " rightly," " clearly," " widely," " by chance." The comparative of such adverbs, was formed by the addition of the suffix *-or*, *dēopor*, etc. The superlative was formed by the addition of the suffix *-ost*, *dēopost*, etc.

§ 181. In addition to these regular comparatives and superlatives there were a number of irregular compara-

tives and superlatives, some of which have survived.
Thus :

yfle	*wiers*	*wierrest*
lyt	*lǣs*	*lǣst*
micle	*mā*	*mǣst*
nēah	*nēar*	*nīehst*

§ 182. A considerable number of Old English adverbs
are newer formations and represent a definite growth
in the material of the language. Many of these are
merely cases of nouns used as adverbs. Thus accusatives
are used in the adverbs "home," "west," "north," "west-
ward," *ealne weg, ealneg, alway.* Genitives are used in
hwīles, "whilst," *dæges,* "daily," *willes,* "willingly,"
nīedes, "needs," "of necessity," *nihtes,* "at night,"
hennes, "hence," *hwennes,* "whence," A genitive
plural is found in *gēara,* "of yore." Dative forms
are found in *wihte,* "at all," *nīede,* "necessarily,"
hwīlum, "sometimes" ("whilome"), *wundrum,* "wonder-
fully," *stundum,* "from time to time," *seldum* "seldom."

§ 183. A large number of new adverbs were also formed
by the composition of prepositions and nouns, as in
onweg, "away," *to-dæge,* "to-day," *underbæc,* "backwards," *underneoþan,* "underneath."

Some of these adverbs were subsequently replaced by
their analytical equivalents and new ones formed on
the model of them, such as *of necessity, of course, of right,*
etc. In others of the same kind the preposition was
weakened to *a,* which represented earlier *on* and *of,* so
that it is not always easy to tell which was the original
preposition. Such are *nowadays* (cf. *on Sundays*),
abed, afoot, alive, asleep, once a year. In *o'clock,* on the
other hand, *o'* is a shortening of *of.* Sometimes the

preposition used was *be* as in *beside, before.* Other prepositions used in these compound adverbs are *to, to-day, to-night, to-morrow; at* in *at night, at times, at last.*

§ 184. Another adverb-forming element was O.E. *weard* or *weardes,* seen in *forwards, backwards, home-wards,* etc.

§ 185. Forms ending in *-s* often developed a final *-t* as in *amidst, betwixt, whilst, amongst.*

§ 186. But the great majority of new adverbs were formed directly from adjectives. This facility for forming adverbs is said to be due to the fact that the normal adverbial ending *-e,* which was found in Old English adverbs otherwise similar to adjectives, weakened and disappeared. It is not necessary, however, to attribute it to this cause. It may be due equally well to the general tendency to discard inflections and to express syntactic concords by means of word order. Thus even before the adverbial *-e* was lost it would still have been possible to distinguish an adverb from an adjective by its position in the sentence, and this tendency was doubtless strengthened and supported by the parallel use of adjectives as adverbs in Old French.

§ 187. Another common adverbial suffix, still in use in the formation of adverbs, was the suffix *-lice,* which in Middle English fell together with the adjectival suffix *-lic,* Modern English *-ly.* Yet another adverbial suffix of Old English survives in the modern formations *headlong, sidelong.* Old English had an adverbial phrase *on oþre wisan,* which contracted in Middle English to *otherwise,* and the element *-wise* was then used to form new adverbs such as *likewise, nowise.* Similarly, *way* was used in *no way, some way, midway*, and with the inflectional *-s, noways.* *time* and *while* similarly entered into the composition of *meanwhile, sometime, sometimes.*

§ 188. Numerous adverbs were also formed from prepositional stems, such as *afterwards, before, forth, beforehand, behind, beneath, within, without, thorough* (from *through*), *upward, above* (from *bufan*), etc.

§ 189. From the pronominal stems of the pronouns *þe, hē* and *hwā* are derived the so-called pronominal adverbs. From *þe* are derived : *there, thither, then, thence* (containing the common adverbial inflection *-es*, written *-ce* as in French words), *thus.* From *hē* are derived : *here, hither, hence.* From *hwā* are derived : *where, whither, whence, when, why* and *how.* The forms *so* and *also* are also derived from a pronominal stem *swā.* *so* is regularly derived from O.E. *swā*, and *also* from a compound of it, O.E. *ealswā.* The negative adverb *not* is a weakened, unstressed form of *nought* from O.E. *nā wiht*=" not anything."

§ 190. In *nevertheless* there survives an Old English adverbial phrase *nā þȳ lǣs*, while another similar adverbial phrase, *þy lǣs the* has been contracted to the conjunction *lest*, with the development of a final *-t*, as in *whilst, amongst*, etc.

§ 191. A numerous class of adverbs consists of compounds formed from such adverbs as *here, there, where* and a preposition : *herein, therein, wherein, hereof, herewith, hereupon, hereby.* Others, again, are compounded with *so* or *soever* and *where, whither-, whence-, wheresoever*, etc.

PREPOSITIONS

§ 192. Prepositions were originally words placed before the verb with the object of expressing more precisely the manner of action of the verb. They were therefore originally adverbial in function. Something of this original function can still be seen in Modern English, where a word may be either adverb or preposition. Thus we can say in English : *the river overflowed its banks*, or *the river flowed over its banks*. The preposition, however, comes more and more to express the nature of the relationship, usually in time or space, between two things, rather than the relationship between a thing and an action. Where, however, the relation between a verb and a noun is expressed we have to deal rather with a prepositional adverb than with a pure preposition. The difference of function may be seen in the sentences : *Put it underneath the table ; put it underneath*, and, *the dog underneath the table*. In the first of these sentences the word *underneath* is still largely adverbial, in the second it is wholly adverbial, and in the third it is entirely prepositional.

One of the consequences of the original intimate association of the preposition with the verb was that the noun dependent upon that verb varied in respect of case with the precise modification of sense introduced by the preposition. Hence prepositions come to govern definite cases. This is what we find still in Old English, where prepositions may govern an accusative, a genitive or a dative or instrumental case according to the nature of the relationship which it expresses. In the earliest Old English the case of the noun was alone sufficient to

indicate the relation between the verb and the noun :
he hit dyde his agnum hondum, " he did it *with* his own
hands." Here the instrumental plural *agnum hondum*
already means " *with* his own hands." But in the
tendency to analytical expression this becomes, *mid
his agnum hondum*. The development from adverb to
preposition may be clearly seen in such a sentence as :
he him spræc to, " he spoke to him." Here the word
to was originally constructed with the verb, forming a
compound *tospræcan*. But in accordance with the older
syntax this prefix was separable and in simple sentences
was placed at the end of the sentence, just as it still
is in Modern German. However, with the development
of a fixed word order the word *to* came to be placed
immediately before the word which it governed, so that
the sentence became : *he spræc to him*. The older
usage, however, still survives in such sentences as *the
man whom he spoke to*.

§ 193. The prepositions in Old English were not fully
developed. Many of them had numerous meanings
which in Modern English are represented by different
words. Thus O.E. *æfter* in addition to its ordinary
meaning, " after," might mean " along," " according to,"
" for," as we can still see in such sentences as, " make
it after the pattern of," " to seek after gold," etc. O.E.
æt might mean " from," " with," " against," etc.

§ 194. Most of the simpler prepositions of Modern
English existed already in Old English, though not
always with the same meaning. Thus *in, of, for; from,
on, up, to, over, under, after* existed in the same form in
Old English ; *at, by, out, through* have changed very little
(O.E. *æt, bi, ut, þurh*, etc.). So also some of the com-

pounded prepositions existed in the same form : *toward*, *into*. The Modern *with*, O.E. *wiþ*, has changed its meaning from "against," a meaning which it still retains in *withstand* or *to fight with*. *but*, O.E. *būtan* from *be-ūtan*, originally meant "unless," "except," or "without." *among* is from O.E. *on gemang*, "in the multitude." With an inflectional *-s* it gave *amonges*, and then with the development of a final *-t*, *amongst*. *again* and *against* have had a similar development, O.E. *ongegn*, *ongegnes*. Similar are *amid* and *amidst*, O.E. *on middan*. *since* is from O.E. *siþþan* with inflectional *-s*. *along* is from O.E. *and*="against" and *long*. Other compounded prepositions are *betwixt*, *between*, both of which contain the same stem as is to be found in *two*, *toward*, "towards."

§ 195. Others, again, consist of prepositional phrases, as *on behalf of*, *by way of*, *for the sake of*, and yet others are participial phrases such as *owing to*, *notwithstanding* ; many of these latter are of Romance origin, as *during*, *concerning*, *regarding*, *including*, *except*. Finally, there are prepositions of Romance origin consisting of adjectives or substantives combined with native prepositions : *by means of*, *in case of*, *in spite of*, *in consequence of*, *on account of*, *with respect to*, *exclusive*, *inclusive of*, *prior to*. Of Latin origin are the common prepositions *plus*, *minus* and *versus*.

CONJUNCTIONS

§ 196. Some of the Modern English conjunctions existed already in Old English, though most of them are of more recent development. *either*, *and*, *eke*, *though*,

O.E. *ǣgther, and, ēac, þēah* are the surviving co-ordinating conjunctions, and *if, so . . . as, as soon as, so that, that, while,* O.E. *gif, swā . . . swā, swā sōna swā, swā þæt, þæt, þā hwīle þe* are the surviving subordinating conjunctions. There are also a number of conjunctions in Modern English which in Old English were used in combination with *þæt*; such are *ere, for, with.* In many cases Old English used phrases as conjunctions, and some of these have survived in *may be, were it not that, how be it.* In some cases these phrases were contracted into a single word in Middle English as in *lest* from *þȳ lǣs thē,* "nevertheless." Many conjunctions, again, are new formations from adverbs, as *sometimes . . . sometimes, partly . . . partly, now . . . now*; or they may consist of phrases such as *at one moment . . . at another moment, on the one hand . . . on the other hand.* Of adverbial or prepositional origin are *only, even, after, before.* Many, again, are of Romance origin, usually constructed with *that, in order that, provided that, considering that, because, finally, lastly, except.*

CHAPTER VII

THE DEVELOPMENT OF SOUNDS

§ 197. THE development of sounds is, as we have already said, the least significant of the changes which affect language and is very largely an effect of the other changes, such as those of syntax, word order, word meaning, which we have already discussed.

The causes of sound change are not yet fully known. But enough is known of the conditions under which they change to enable us to form a fairly accurate idea of the nature of the underlying causes. Sound changes are usually classified as being either isolative or combinatory. Isolative changes are those which appear to occur spontaneously, that is to say, not under the influence of other sounds. Combinatory sound changes are those which occur under the influence of other sounds, as, for example, the change known as i-mutation, in which a vowel is mutated under the influence of an i in the next syllable. It is very doubtful, however, whether this classification is valid, for it cannot be said with any certainty that any sound has not been influenced by a neighbouring sound. All that can be said is that in certain cases, i-mutation for example, the influence of one sound on another is

quite clear, while in other cases such an influence cannot
be proved.

We begin, then, with the consideration of the so-called
combinatory sound changes. These are most marked
where a word is pronounced not alone, but in a sentence.
Let us observe the pronunciation of the three words,
the last time, in ordinary speech. It is quite clear that
in speaking these three words one does not as a rule
pronounce the *t*-sound of *last* and *time* twice over.
There is an economy of effort by which a long or
double *t* is shortened or reduced to a short or single *t*.
In the same way, in pronouncing the word *postman*,
the *t*-sound is either very faintly pronounced or not at
all. We may say in this case that the *t*-sound is either
silent or that it is assimilated to the preceding *s*. But
in either case the change which occurs is a combinatory
change ; it is due to the combination of sounds *st* + *m*.
Notice that in *post-office* the *t* is quite clearly pronounced.
Now such combinatory changes do not necessarily
cause a change in a word where it is found in other
contexts, but we can quite readily conceive that if the
word *post* was never found alone, but only when followed
by *m* or some other consonant, there would be a marked
tendency to pronounce it as if it were written *pos*. Or
if the word were used a hundred times as often followed
by a consonant as when followed by a vowel the same
tendency would arise, because our pronunciation of any
word depends upon our memory of how it is pronounced,
and if one pronunciation outnumbers another by a
hundred to one there is always a chance that the pronunciation of the ninety-nine cases will spread to the
hundredth. In the word *adder* such a change has

occurred, for it was formerly pronounced *nadder* ; *a nadder* became *an adder* by a false division of syllables, so also *nick-name* has gained an *n* instead of losing one ; the proper name *Noll* has taken its *n* from a preceding *mine*. But though the number of words in which an independent word used independently has changed its form in this way is not great, yet there are very many words which have a double pronunciation as a result of the surrounding sounds, as in *postman* and *post-office*.

The combinatory sound changes which were discussed in the last paragraph are those in which the final sound of one word is influenced by or itself influences the initial sound of the next word. There are other combinatory sound changes in which the influence exerted is within the word itself, in which one sound of a word affects another which precedes or follows it. Thus if in Modern English we say *house* in the singular and *houses* in the plural, there is a change in the character of the *s* of the stem, and this change is a combinatory change. In the singular the *s* is final and is voiceless, but in the plural it comes between two voiced sounds, the vowel *ou* and the inflectional -*es*. Under these circumstances there is again an economy of effort in so far as the vocal cords are kept vibrating from the -*ou*- to the -*s* of the plural instead of being relaxed for the intervocalic -*s*-. Or, to take another example, if we cry out a prolonged *milk*, there is a tendency to bring forth a pronunciation *miulk* or *mielk*, but if we make the same experiment with the word *mid* there is no such tendency. The reason is that *l* is a sound which itself has much of the character of a vowel in English (cf. the word *handle*, in which *l* forms a syllable) and therefore there is a tendency to accentuate that vocalic element and for it to become an independent vowel under certain conditions. Thus in Old English the original word *milk* actually occurs with the form and pronunciation *miolc*. Now there are certain sound changes of this kind which occur with such regularity that they may be formulated in laws, but there are many more which are not so regular and which are therefore not known as combinatory sound changes. We may take as an example the case of the word *clean*. A careful observation of the pronunciation of this word will show immediately that the pronunciation of the sound which is here written *c* differs very considerably from the pronunciation of a *c* in a word like *coal*. In fact, if the word *clean* were to be deliberately pronounced as if it were spelt *tlean* most people would not notice the difference. Here again, then, is a case of the prununication of a sound being strongly influenced by its neighbour. We have deliberately selected extreme cases of such influence in order to emphasise the character of the influence which one sound exerts over another. But it would be no exaggeration to say that every sound exercises an influence more or less marked on every neighbouring sound, and that therefore all sound changes are by nature combinatory.

We turn finally to the sound changes which, nevertheless, are called isolative. Such a change as that from O.E. *hām* to Modern English *home*, or O.E. *cyrce* to Modern English *church* is called isolative because it is not possible to say that the neighbouring sounds have directly influenced the vowel *ā* in *hām* or the consonant *c* in *cyrce*. The majority of the sound changes noted in historical grammars are of this kind.

Before attempting to give any account of how and why sounds change it is still necessary to point to the influence which stress exerts in all sound changes. It is found that in all languages sounds in stressed syllables have not the same development as sounds in unstressed syllables. This is only another way of saying that all sounds are combinatory, since their development is bound up with stress. But setting aside this point for the moment, it is clear that a sound which is stressed will have more resistance to changes of a certain kind than a sound which is not stressed, for it will not be slurred over in pronunciation, it will be more clearly pronounced and any divergence from the normal will be more noticeable than if it were unstressed. On the other hand, an unstressed sound tends to be slurred and shortened, especially in those languages in which the stress tends to fall on the syllable which really conveys the meaning, for in such languages unstressed syllables are less important from the point of view of significance. Hence there is usually in language less variety of sound and quantity in unstressed syllables than in stressed ones.

If we now turn to enquire how and why sounds change we shall find that the cause is purely psychological. The cause is to be found in the mental processes which underlie all speech. In the first place it is to be noted that as between individuals there is a very considerable difference in the pronunciation of most sounds. The native of Aberdeen does not pronounce English in the same way as the native of London, and one Londoner does not pronounce it in the same way as another. In fact there is an infinite variety of pronunciations in every language as between one individual and another, a difference which is founded partly on differences of education, but partly also on the fact that the organs of speech in individuals differ just as much as shapes of noses or colour of eyes, and where the instruments which produce a sound are not the same we cannot expect the sound produced to be the same. But though these differences do exist, and though in some cases—the Londoner and the Aberdonian—the difference is most marked, yet there is no great difficulty in one individual understanding another. In other words, there is always a very considerable latitude possible in the pronunciation of any particular word. Our ears have become so reconciled to these minor differences that in everyday speech we scarcely notice any but the most marked variations, and we make no attempt to correct them. Now this fact is of very considerable importance when we come to consider how we learn our native language and how sounds change in the process.

A child, when it learns to speak, first of all hears its parents speak and retains a memory picture of the sound or word spoken. It hears that sound or word frequently until its memory picture of it is definitely settled. That is the starting point. But it should be noted, too, that there is always the possibility of the child hearing a sound imperfectly and of receiving a wrong memory picture. After the memory picture has been defined in the mind of the child it tries to reproduce the sound itself. Its first effort may be a poor one and the child will be corrected. It makes a second effort and a third until it manages to produce a sound to the satisfaction of its parent. That achieved, the child now has a second memory picture. It now knows exactly the position which the tongue, the lips, etc., have to take up for the production of certain sounds, and by reason of that memory picture it is able at any future time to produce those sounds at will. But here, too, it is to be noted that there is a possibility of error. The parent, in correcting the child, may have imperfect hearing and the correction may therefore be unjustified or insufficient. Already, therefore, there are two possibilities of error : in the pronunication of the child and in the hearing of the parent. Both of these may perpetuate themselves, since, as we have seen, a considerable variety in pronunciation is always permissible in the speech of adults. The first sounds learnt by the child, then, depend for their quality upon the care and the ability with which the parent corrects the child when it is learning to speak. It may be that peculiarities of pronunciation which have escaped the attention of the parent may be subsequently corrected at school or in adult life, but nevertheless there are, in the speech of the child, the potentialities of sound change. It is in this way that the child very soon learns the sounds of a language. When its vocabulary grows larger it uses the same sounds in the newly acquired words as it did in those which it first learnt, and it is for this reason that a sound change, whenever it occurs, is found to operate in all the words of a language containing that sound and not merely in some of them.

The imperfection of the hearing of either parent or child may vary infinitely in degree. Indeed there are such fine shades of difference in the pronunciation of individuals that the human ear, however sensitive, cannot catch them. Hence even in the ideal combination of a child with very sensitive hearing and a conscientious parent with equally sensitive hearing there is still ample room for a slight change in pronunciation from father to child, and if each subsequent generation advances the change a little further the final result will be an appreciable sound change.

It may rightly be objected to this view that the chances are very much in favour of such changes cancelling each other out and leaving the language as it was. But this is scarcely likely in fact. There would, in all probability, be a majority of individuals whose pronunciation would tend in a certain direction, or if there were no actual majority there would still be some whose speech would be imitated or copied by reason of their greater influence or higher social position. But quite apart from the probability or improbability of such a development, there are forces at work which determine in what direction the modifications in the speech of the child will tend. The force referred to is nothing more than the influence of the neighbouring sounds. For just as in Modern English the sound *c* has a special development when it is found before an *l*, so in the speech of the child each sound is learned in a given and limited number of sound contexts, and the particular quality of the sound which it first learns is the quality it has under the influence of the neighbouring sounds in those contexts in the words which it first hears. In this sense it would appear that sound changes are due primarily to an imperfect and uncorrected imitation or else to the influence of the sound groups which are first learned. Since a child does not learn sounds singly, but in words, it follows that its average sound, *i.e.* the sound which it will tend to produce in all new words, will be the sound which is learned in a particular context of other sounds. Thus, for example, if a child of the present generation learned its pronunication of the sound *c* in words in which it was usually followed by an *l*, as in *clean*, it is safe to say that the child would pronounce a *c* sound differing from that of its parents. The case is extreme, as we have said before, but nevertheless it represents a process which is going on with regard to all other sounds also.

If sound change is very largely determined by the influences which have just been mentioned it would appear that sound change, like all the other changes which we have noticed, is the result, though here somewhat indirectly, of the environment, the education, the institutions, etc., of the community which speaks a language. For it is these forces that determine which words are first spoken to the child and to what extent it is corrected. And it is the forces at work in the life of the adult members of the community which determine, as we have seen, the form which words take, and therefore their sound context : whether they are inflected forms or not, what the word order in the sentence is, and a hundred other changes which all ultimately modify the word before it is presented to the child for imitation. It must also be borne in mind that the same influences as are at work in modifying the quality of the sounds of the child are also at work in the adult.

PHONETICS

§ 198. Sounds are either vowels or consonants. Consonants are those sounds in which the breath in passing from the lungs to the outer atmosphere is interrupted at some point in such a way as to produce audible friction. In vowels the breath is allowed to pass unimpeded from the lungs to the outer atmosphere, without any such interruption or audible friction.

§ 199. Consonants are usually classified according to the place where the passage of the breath is impeded. The impediment may be such as completely to stop, momentarily, the passage of the breath; or it may only narrow the channels through which it passes without completely stopping it.

There are therefore two classes of consonants, (1) stops, (2) continuants. Stops (*k*, *t*, *p*, *g*, *d*, *b*) are also called explosives, because the impediment to the escape of the breath may be removed and the breath thus released escapes with a kind of explosion. Continuants are also called often breathed consonants or spirants. They may, unlike the stops, be continued as long as there is breath in the lungs.

Consonants may be further divided into voiced and voiceless. All consonants may be either one or the other, though in English some consonants are not usually found voiceless. A voiced consonant is one in which the vocal cords vibrate during the pronunciation of the consonant. Thus *b* and *p*, *g* and *k*, *d* and *t*, are respectively voiced and voiceless. The two varieties may be best distinguished in the continuants by stopping the ears and listening to the difference. In pronouncing a *v* a distinct buzzing sound will be heard, but in pronouncing *f* no sound will be audible when the ears are stopped. The buzzing sound proceeds from the vibration of the vocal cords.

§ 200. We may now examine the various consonants in order to see at what point the passage of the breath is interrupted or impeded. Phonetic symbols are, where necessary, printed in brackets.

We begin with those in which the breath is completely stopped for a moment, the stops or explosives.

b, p. In this sound the passage through the nose is closed by raising the uvula, and the passage through the mouth is stopped at the lips. The lips are then opened and the breath escapes with a mild explosion. At the same time the vocal cords vibrate. In *p* exactly the same thing happens, except that the cords do not vibrate. Hence *b* is called a voiced, and *p* a voiceless, bilabial stop.

d, t. In *d* and *t* the stoppage is made by pressing the blade of the tongue against some point behind the base or root of the teeth, or against the gum. They are therefore called dental stops or linguo-dental stops. *d* is voiced and *t* voiceless.

g, k. In *g* and *k* the stoppage is made by the tongue pressing against some point of the palate. If it is pressed against the soft palate the result is a velar *g* or *k*; if it is pressed against the hard palate the result is a palatal *g* or *k* [ǵ, ḱ]. *g* is therefore a voiced velar or palatal stop, and *k* is a voiceless velar or palatal stop.

We next consider the continuants.

m. In pronouncing *m* the lips are completely closed,

but the passage through the nose is left open and the vocal cords vibrate. *m* is therefore both nasal and labial. Its articulation only differs from that of *b* in that the nose passage is open. Hence, if for any reason the nose passage becomes stopped, any effort to pronounce *m* results in *b*. So when one has a cold in the head *Emma* becomes *Ebba*. It is for this reason, too, that a *b* or *p* so easily develops after a final *m*, as in *chamber* from *camera*, *empty* from *æmtig*.

n bears the same relation to *d* or *t* as *m* bears to *b* or *p*. It is formed by putting the tongue in the *d* position and leaving the nose passage open. Just as *Emma* becomes *Ebba* when one has a cold in the head, so also *and* becomes *ad*, and similarly a *d* develops often after final *n*, as in *sound*, Fr. *son*, M.E. *soun*.

ng. If the tongue is pressed against the soft palate, making a closure, and the nose passage is left open, the result is the sound produced in *thing* [ŋ]. Sometimes this sound is followed by a *g* or *k*, *finger*=fiŋger, *think*= thiŋk.

f, v. If the lower lip is pressed against the upper teeth and the breath forced between them, the result is *f*, or, with vibration of the vocal corbs, *v*. *f* and *v* are, there-fore, labio-dental continuants.

th. If the nose passage is closed and the tongue is placed between the teeth or just behind them and the breath allowed to escape, the result is þ, O.E. þ, or ð, with or without a vibration of the vocal cords. *th* is therefore a linguo-dental continuant and may be voiced or voiceless, as in *though* and *thin*.

s, z. If the tongue is placed behind the gum and the breath escapes through a narrowed aperture, the result is *s*, or, with vibration of the vocal cords, *z*.   *s* and *z* are, therefore, linguo-palatal continuants.

sh.   If the tongue is retracted a little from the *s* position and at the same time the channel between the tongue and the palate somewhat lengthened and the lips pouted, the result is the sound produced in *sh*un, fi*sh*, or, with vibration of the vocal cords, the sound found in *azure*. For these two sounds it is convenient to use the symbols [ʃ] and [ž].

y.   If in approximately the same position as for ʃ the breath escapes over a wider surface of the tongue but without any pouting of the lips, and the tongue is a little lowered, the result is the initial sound produced in *year*. We represent this sound by [j]. The corresponding voiceless sound [j̥] is scarcely known in Modern English, but was very common in the older language.   There is an approximation to it in certain pronunciations of *humour*.

χ.   If the narrowing is made still further back, by the tongue opposite the soft palate, the result is χ which may either be voiced or voiceless. The sound does not exist in Modern English, but was common in Old English, written ʒ [ʒ], voiced, and *h* [χ] voiceless.

w.   If the back of the tongue is raised and the lips are pouted, the resulting sound is *w*, which may be voiced or voiceless.

l.   If the point of the tongue is pressed against the upper gum and the breath is allowed to escape at the sides, the result is *l*, which may be voiced or voiceless. *l* is commonly called a liquid, either because the sound is felt to have a liquid quality or because the breath in escaping passes over the salivary glands and promotes the flow of saliva. The English *l* is a dull and full sound, resembling a vowel, and for that reason it has powerfully influenced neighbouring vowels, tending to form diphthongs with them.

r. If the point of the tongue is slightly trilled, the result is *r*, which may be voiced or voiceless.

There are also compound consonants in English which are sometimes represented by a single symbol. Thus the sound represented by *j* in *joy* is really [d+ž] and the sound of *ch* in *church* is the corresponding voiceless sound [t+ʃ]. This combination is called an affricate. We should also notice the combination of *g, d, b, +h,* which combinations are called aspirates.

VOWELS

§ 201. Since in vowels the breath is allowed to escape freely without interruption in the pronunciation, it is not so easy to determine exactly how they are formed. The quality of a vowel depends upon the shape of the oral and nasal cavity, which can be modified by the movements of the tongue and jaws. A sound can also be modified to some extent by the position of the lips. The quality is further modified by the length and the tenseness of the vocal cords.

Vowels may be rounded or unrounded. That is to say, in every tongue position the lips may be pouted or not, though such rounding is much more difficult in the so-called "low" vowels. In the pronunciation of the vowel in *who* the lips are distinctly pouted, in the pronunciation of the vowel of *he* the lips are drawn

Table of Consonants.

	Bilabials. Voiced.	Bilabials. Voiceless.	Labio-Dental. Voiced.	Labio-Dental. Voiceless.	Linguo-Dental. Voiced.	Linguo-Dental. Voiceless.	Palatal. Voiced.	Palatal. Voiceless.	Velar. Voiced.	Velar. Voiceless.
Stops - -	b	p			d	t	ǵ	ḱ	g	k
Continuants -			v	f	ð	þ	j, z, ž	j̊, s, ʃ	ȝ	χ
Labials or Liquids }							l	l̥		
Nasals - -	m	m̥			n	n̥	ń		ŋ	ŋ̇
Trills - -					r	r̥				

tight across the teeth and there is no pouting. The vowel of *who* is thus a rounded vowel, and the vowel of *he* an unrounded vowel.

Vowels are also divided into slack and tense vowels. Any vowel may exist in either variety. In the tense vowels the muscles of the tongue are contracted tensely, and in the slack vowels they are relaxed or slackened. The difference between the two kinds of vowel may best be heard by pronouncing in rapid succession the vowel produced in *he* and the vowel produced in *it*. The continual tightening and slackening of tongue muscles will soon make the tongue tired. In *he* we have a tense vowel, and in *it* a slack vowel.

With regard to the shape of the oral cavity, in so far as it is determined by the tongue position, it is usual, for convenience, to distinguish three horizontal positions, *high*, *mid* and *low*, and three vertical positions, *front*, *mixed* and *back*. There are, therefore, nine normal positions, and since of each of these nine vowels has both a tense and slack variety and a rounded and un-rounded variety, there are thirty-six theoretical vowels. In fact, of course, there are very many more, since there are innumerable positions of the tongue intermediate between the nine positions mentioned, and the actual position in any given word depends upon the nature of the surrounding sounds.

It requires a considerable amount of practice to determine the exact nature of a vowel, and phoneticians themselves are not always in agreement, but it may help to determine the tongue position of the commoner vowels if the following experiments are made. If the tongue is slightly lowered from the position taken up for the pronunciation of the sound of *y* in *yes*, so that there is no longer audible friction, it will be found that the vowel produced is *i* as in *it* or *he*. Or the converse may be done : the tongue may be gradually raised while pronouncing the vowel *i*, and the sound will gradually merge into [j]. Thus in the pronunciation of *i* the tongue is raised and advanced as much as possible without actually pronouncing a consonant. The sounds *i* and *y* [j] are thus very near, and that is the reason why when another vowel follows *i*, especially after dentals, the *i* becomes (j) and then [dž]. Cf. *soldier*=souldžə, *Dewsbury* and *Jewsbury*, Lat. *diurnum* and *journal* =džʌnəl.

If, again, the tongue is lowered as far as it will go, then the result will be an *a* sound. The proof of this is the doctor's request to say *ah* when he wishes to examine the throat, for he knows that in the pronunciation of this sound the tongue is depressed as much as possible.

If the tongue is raised and drawn back to the extreme limit attainable without coming so near to the soft palate as to produce audible friction, then the result is the sound produced in *who*, [u], though this sound is accompanied by lip-rounding. Between these extreme limits fall the remaining vowels, which may be conveniently, though not accurately, presented in the form of a triangle, thus :

The English vowels may be more accurately shown in a table thus :

§ 202.

	UNROUNDED.					
	FRONT.		**MIXED.**		**BACK.**	
	Tense.	Slack.	Tense.	Slack.	Tense.	Slack.
High -	i he			*i* bit		
Mid -	e day	ε bell		ə better	a but	ɑ father
Low -		æ hat	ʌ bird			

	ROUNDED.					
	FRONT.		**MIXED.**		**BACK.**	
	Tense.	Slack.	Tense.	Slack.	Tense.	Slack.
High -	u, O.E. y				u who	*u* put
Mid -						
Low -					ɔ hall	o not

Diphthongs are compounded of two vowels. Thus in Modern English we have o +u in *home,* ɑ +i in *mine,* e +i in *day,* o +i in *boy,* ɑ +u in *how,* ε +ə in *there,* i +ə in *here,* u +ə in *poor.*

§ 203. In the following pages are presented some of the more important sound changes which have occurred in the history of the English language. It would be impossible here to give more than a fraction of all the changes which have taken place. Nor is it necessary to do so, for it is our present intention only to explain historically those features of Modern English which require a knowledge of the older state of the language, and not to explain forms and changes of which there is no trace in the modern language. Moreover, the sound changes here given are only those which have occurred in stressed syllables and not those which have occurred in unstressed or inflectional syllables. The changes in the latter, amounting in most cases to a complete loss, are due, moreover, to other causes which have already been discussed elsewhere.

§ 204. We begin with the more important changes which took place in the transition from Indo-Germanic to Old English. These, it is true, are not necessary to an explanation of Modern English forms, but they help to give perspective and to show the grounds on which English is called an Indo-Germanic language. The first and most important of these changes is that which goes under the name of The First Sound-shifting or Grimm's Law. The sounds affected by this law are the Indo-Germanic voiceless stops: *k, t, p*; the voiced stops: *g, d, b*; and the voiced aspirates: *gh, dh, bh*. Their development in Old English is as follows.

I.-G.	k	t	p	gh	dh	bh	g	d	b
O. E.	h	þ	f	g (ȝ)	d	b (f)	k	t	p

Examples.—*k.* Lat. *quod,* O.E. *hwæt,* "what"; Lat. *cord-,* O.E. *heorte,* "heart"; Lat. *decem,* O.E. *teon* from **tehan,* "ten"; Lat. *centum,* O.E. *hund(red);* Lat. *caput,* O.E. *heafod,* "head."

t. Lat. *tres,* O.E. *þreo,* "three"; Lat. *tenuis,* O.E. *þynne;* Lat. *frater,* O.E. *brōþor,* "brother"; Lat. *tu,* O.E. *þū,* "thou"; Lat. *dentem,* O.E. *tōþ* from **tanth.*

p. Lat. *pater,* O.E. *fœder,* "father"; Lat. *pedem,* O.E. *fōt,* "foot"; Lat. *capio,* O.E. *hebban,* "heave"; Lat. *pro,* O.E. *for.*

dh. In Latin *dh* also usually appears as *f* or *d.* Lat. *fa-cere,* O.E. *dōn,* "do"; Lat. *fores,* O.E. *duru,* "door"; Lat. *medius,* O.E. *midd,* "middle"; Lat. *rufus,* O.E. *read.*

bh. In Latin, Indo-Germanic *bh* is usually represented by *f.* Lat. *fagus,* O.E. *bōc, bēc,* "book," "beech"; Lat. *fero,* O.E. *beran,* "bear"; Lat. *frater,* O.E. *brōþor*

gh. In Latin *gh* appears as *f, g* or *h.* Lat. *anser,* from *hanser,* O.E. *gōs,* "goose"; Lat. *(præ)hendo,* O.E. *gietan,* "get"; Lat. *hostis,* O.E. *giest,* "guest"; Lat. *veho,* O.E. *wegan,* "weigh."

g. Lat. *tego,* O.E. *þæc,* "thatch"; Lat. *jugum,* O.E. *geoc,* "yoke"; Lat. *gelidus,* O.E. *ceald,* "cold"; Lat. *gnosco,* Eng. *know;* Lat. *ego,* O.E. *ic,* "I"; Lat. *genu,* O.E. *cneo,* "knee; Lat. *genus,* O.E. *cynn,* "kin."

d. Lat. *id,* Eng. *it;* Lat. *quod,* O.E. *hwæt,* "what"; Lat. *dentem,* O.E. *tōþ;* Lat. *edo,* O.E. *etan,* "eat"; Lat. *duo,* O.E. *twā,* "two"; Lat. *video,* O.E. *witan;* Lat. *sudare,* Eng. *sweat.*

b. Lat. *labium.* Eng. *lip;* Lat. *lubricus,* from *slubricus,* Eng. *slip;* Greek, *cannabis,* O.E. *hœnep,* "hemp."

§ 205. The change of *k, t, p,* to *h, þ, f,* does not occur, however, when any of the respective consonants is immediately preceded or followed by a spirant. O.E. *fisc*, Lat. *piscis*, the *k* is unshifted ; so also in *spurn*, Lat. *spernere*, the *p* is unshifted ; also Lat. *est*, O.E. *ist*, " is." Moreover, if two of the above consonants follow one another only the first is shifted if it be *k*, *t*, or *p*. Lat. *octo* is O.E. *eahta* and not *eahþa*, Lat. *noctem* is O.E. *nieht* and not *niehþ*.

§ 206. After Grimm had discovered this law it was found that there were a number of words which did not conform to it, and on further investigation it was found that these exceptions were due to the free accent of Indo-Germanic. It was discovered that Grimm's law was only operative in those cases in which the accent originally fell on the same syllable as the consonant. Where it was further removed it was found that the voiceless stops, *k*, *t*, *p* became, in English, the voiced stops, *g*, *d*, *b*, instead of *h*, *þ*, *f*. For this reason there are words in Old English, and some even in Modern English, in which there are two forms of the same word, one with *h*, *þ*, *f*, and another with *g*, *d*, *b*. Sometimes the two forms are found side by side, sometimes only one of the two forms has survived.

Examples.—*k* becomes *g* instead of *h*. Lat. *décem* gives Germanic **tehan*, but Greek *dekás* gives Germanic *tig*, cf. *twenty* = twice ten. The change is most clearly seen in the conjugation of the Old English verb, where regularly the singular of the past tense has *h* and the plural and past participle *g* ; O.E. *seah*, " saw " (sing.) *sǣgon*, " saw " (plur.).

t becomes *d* instead of *th*. Lat. *centum*, O.E. *hund*, with *d* instead of *th* ; Greek *patér*, O.E. *fœder* with *d* instead of *th* as in *brōþor*, Lat. *frater*. This change may still be seen in *seethe* and *sodden*.

p becomes *b* instead of *f*.

§ 207. A similar change, under identical conditions, affected an original *s*, which was first voiced [z] in Germanic and then in English became *r*. Hence *s* in English interchanges with *r*, as in *was* and *were*. The same change may be seen in Latin *genesis* and *generis*, or in English *lose* and (*for*)*lorn*.

§ 208. The next important sound change which has left its mark on Modern English is that which occurs when original labials (*b*, *p*), velars (*g*, *k*) and dentals (*d*, *t*) were followed by a dental. Under such conditions the labials became *f*, the velars became *h* (pronounced in O.E. as in *loch*) and the dentals became *s*, *ss*.

Examples.—*b*, *p*. Original *weban* (verb), Eng. *weft*; German *geben* (verb), Eng. *gift*.

g, *k*. O.E. *sēcean*, " seek " past tense *sōhte*, " sought " ; O.E. *þencean*, " think," *þōhte*, " thought " ; O.E. *bringan*, past tense *brōhte*, " brought " ; O.E. *wyrcan*, past tense O.E. *worhte*, " wrought."

d, *t*. O.E. *witan*, past tense *wiste*.

§ 209. Another important consonant change occurred when *n* was followed by *h*. Under such circumstances *n* is lost. Thus in the past tense of *bringan*, " to bring," the *g* became *h* before the dental inflexion of the past tense, giving a stem **branht-*. The *n* then disappeared, so that we have in Old English the form *brōhte* in which *-ōh-* comes from *anh*. Similarly, in *thought* beside *think*. In the Old English period *n* also disappeared when followed by other spirants than *h*, particularly before *þ*, *f* and *s*.

Examples.—Before *th*. O.E. *ōþer* is from earlier *anþer* ; *cūþ* beside *cann* ; *tōþ* beside Lat. *dentem* ; *mūþ* beside Lat. *mund*. Before *s*. O.E. *gōs*, " goose " beside *gander* ; O.E. *ūs*, from *uns*, cf. Lat. *nos*.

Before *f*. O.E. *fīf*, " five," Greek *pente*, Lat. *quinque*.

§ 210. Another important sound change is known as the West Germanic consonant gemination, according to which any consonant except *r* was doubled after a short stressed vowel when followed by a *j*, sometimes also by *r* or *l*. Thus from the stem of the past tense of strong verbs causative verbs were formed by adding -*j*- to the stem : *sittan*, " to sit," past tense *sat*, causative **sat-j-an*, became by gemination and mutation, *settan*.

VOWELS

§ 211. The Indo-Germanic vowel system suffered very little change in the transition to Old English. The only important changes were those of *ŏ* to *ă* as in Latin *hostis*, P.G. *gast* ; Lat. *hortus*, O.E. *geard*, from *gard*, " garden " : *ā* to *ō*, as in Lat. *frater*, O.E. *brōþor*, Lat. *mater*, O.E. *mōdor*, " mother " : *ē* to *ǣ*, *ā*, Lat. *edimus*, O.E. *ǣton*, " ate." The diphthongs show greater changes. Thus the original six diphthongs *ai, oi, ei, au, ou, eu* are reduced to two in Old English : *ai* and *oi* become first *ai* and then *ā* ; *au* and *ou* become first *au* and then in Old English *ēa* ; *eu* becomes *eo* and *ei* becomes *ī*. The regular development of the Indo-Germanic vowels and diphthongs in Old English, therefore, yields the following series :

Short - -	*a, e, i, u*	
Long - -	*ā, ē, ī, ū, ō*	
Diphthongs	*ēa, ēo, īo*	

This series was expanded, however, in the Primitive-Germanic and Old English period by the development under special conditions of a new *o* from the original *u*, and a new diphthong *ïo* from the original *eu*. This vowel system was, however, further developed in the Old English period in accordance with special Old English sound laws :

When followed by a nasal, *a*, *e* and *o* became respectively *o*, *i*, *u*. Thus *camb* became *comb*, *man* became *mon*, *lang* became *long*. It will be noticed that in Modern English the *a* sound has usually come back except in words in -*ng* and a few more such as *on, from, bond*.

When followed by *h*, or by *l* or *r* and another consonant the vowels *ï*, *ĕ*, *ǣ* suffered the change knowing as " Breaking," that is to say, they were diphthongated to *io*, *eo* and *ea* respectively. Since, however, none of these diphthongs survives in Modern English it is unnecessary for our present purpose to adduce examples. In the same way these vowels were also diphthongated to *ie* and *ea* after such palatal consonants as *ǵ*, *sc*, *ĉ*.

When followed by an *i* or *j* in the next syllable most of the Old English vowels suffered the change known as *i*-mutation :

ǣ, *ă* became *e*, *man*, *men*.

ŏ   „   *e*, Lat. *oleum*, O.E. *ele*.

ŭ   „   *y*, Lat. *moneta* becomes first *munita* with the change of *o* to *u* before *n*, and then *mynt*; Modern English *mint*.

ā   „   *ǣ*, *ē*, O.E. *hǣlan*, " to heal " beside *hāl*, " whole."

ō   „   *ē*, O.E. *fōt* beside *fēt*, *tōþ* beside *tēþ*, " teeth."

ū   „   *ȳ*, O.E. *mūs*, "mouse" beside *mȳs*, "mice"; *cū* beside *cȳ*, ki(ne).

Similarly the diphthongs *eo, io, ea* were all mutated in West Saxon to *ie*. Short vowels were also lengthened in late O.E. before certain combinations of liquid or nasal followed by a voiced stop of similar articulation : *-nd, -mb, -ld,* e.g. *ăld* > *āld, cĭld* > *cīld,* etc. The Old English vowel system therefore consisted of the following vowels :

Short - - -	*a, ̆œ, i, e, o, u, y*	
Long - - -	*a, œ, i, e, o, u, y*	
Diphthongs : Long or Short }	*ea, eo, io, ie*	

We may now sketch in outline the development in Modern English of these Old English vowels and consonants.

DEVELOPMENTS IN ENGLISH

CONSONANTS

b

§ 212. O.E. *b* normally remains unchanged in Modern English. In a number of words a *b* has developed after an *m*, as M.E. *slumber* from O.E. *slumrian*; cf. also *bramble, thimble.* This is a very common development and is caused by opening the lips after the pronunciation of the *m* and before the organs of speech are ready for the pronunciation of the next sound; cf. *chamber* from Lat. *camera.*

b has become *p* in the final unstressed syllable of *gossip,* from *godsib,* and also in the French loan word *purse,* from *bourse.*

b has been reintroduced in writing into a number of Latin words in which it had regularly disappeared : *debt, subtle,* etc.

p

§ 213. O.E. *p* normally remains in Modern English. An etymological *p* has reappeared in *receipt, psalm,* M.E. *recette, salme.* An original *p* has been assimilated in pronunciation to *b* in *cupboard, raspberry,* and has become *b* in *lobster,* O.E. *lopestere.* After *m* a *p* often develops before a voiceless consonant: *empty,* O.E. *œmtig.*

v, f

§ 214. In Old English there was only one symbol, *f,* for these two sounds. Both normally remain as in Old English. But analogy has often effected changes. Thus in Old English *f* was pronounced when final, but *v* between vowels. In the declension of the noun *f* would therefore have a double pronunciation. This is reflected in Modern English *wolf, wolves.* As a rule, however, one or other of the two consonants has been carried through the whole declension. Thus we have *roof, roofs,* and not *rooves,* where the consonant of the singular has been taken into the plural ; but in *glove, gloves,* the consonant of the plural has been carried into the singular.

O.E. *f, v* has been assimilated in a number of words : *lady* from *hlœfdige, had* from *hadde* from *hœfde, woman* from O.E. *wīfmon,* etc.

f or *v* is sometimes lost before a consonant of the next word, as in *man o' war, o'clock.* This shortened *o'* was then confused with the *o'* which was a shortening of *on,* and hence we find it wrongly filled out in *think on* for *think of.*

f has been lost in a number of words such as *jolly* from

jolif, tardy from *tardif,* and also in *halfpenny.* In the
word *five* the *v* is exceptional. Being final, it ought to
be *f* as in Old English. The *v* probably arose from a
frequent combination of the numeral with a word beginning with a vowel or voiced consonant.

O.E. initial *f* was voiced in a part of the Southern
territory in M.E., and from this source we still have the
words *vixen* (cf. *fox*), *vat, vane.*

t, d

§ 215. O.E. *t* and *d* normally remain in Modern English.
Middle English *t* in Greek words which had come in
through French was often rewritten *th* as in the original,
and from being written *th* it has come to be pronounced
also (so-called spelling pronunciations). Thus M.E.
trone becomes *throne*; similarly, *theme, panther,* etc.
In some cases, however, the pronunciation of words
written with *th* is unaffected : *Thames, Anthony.*

O.E. *d* between a vowel and a syllable containing *r*
often becomes *th* : *father* from O.E. *fœder, mother* from
mōdor; so also *gather, weather.* This change does not
occur in loan words or derivatives, or if the *d* is preceded
by a consonant : *consider, leader, wonder.* Both *t* and
d tend to disappear between two other consonants :
*grandfather, handkerchief, handsome, chestnut, castle,
must not,* etc.

d final becomes *t* in pronunciation after a voiceless
consonant : *asked, passed.*

d has been lost in one or two words ending in *-nd* :
lime from *lind, wood-bine* from *wood-bind, scan* from
scand. On the other hand it has been added to one or

two words ending in -*n* : *sound*, Lat. *sonem*, Fr. *son* ;
hind (servant) from O.E. *hyne*.
t has become *d* in *diamond* and *card*.

th

§ 216. O.E. *þ* and *ð* interchanged in the declension
of nouns just like *f* and *v*, but one form has usually been
carried through. Thus *births* has its voiceless *th* from
the singular *birth*, whereas in *clothes th* is voiced.

th has become *d* under circumstances similar to those
under which the converse change from *d* to *th* took
place : *burthen* becomes *burden* ; *murther*, *murder* ; and we
have *swaddle* beside *swathe*.   *th* tends to disappear before
s : *sixths*, *clothes*, *Wordsworth's*.   *th* has become *t* in
nostril from *nōsþyrel* (*þyrel* is connected with the same
stem as *through*, *nostril* means therefore *nose hole*) ; in
lest from *þȳ lǣs þe*, and in *sight* from *gesihþ*.

s, z

§ 217. In Old English *s* was written for voiced and
voiceless *s* and is still so written though sometimes we
also write *z* for voiced *s* : *last, rose, glaze*.

The voiced sound in Old English was found between
vowels or voiced consonants, and the voiceless sound
elsewhere. This remains true of Modern English. But
in the declension either the voiced or the voiceless sound
is carried through. Thus we have *glass*, and *glasses*
with the voiceless *s* sound of the singular carried into
the plural, but *wise*, O.E. *wīs*, with the voiced *s* of the
inflected cases carried into the nominative. In *house*,
houses we find both voiceless and voiced *s*.

s was often written in Middle English with the French symbol *c*. This survives in *ice* from O.E. *īs*, *mice* from *mȳs*, etc., and in Romance words such as *face*, *place*, etc. Sometimes, on the other hand, *s* was written in Romance words for original *c* as in *search* for *cercher*.

The difference between voiced and voiceless *s* has sometimes been preserved and turned to account in the development of meaning. Thus we have *re-sign* and *resign*, *excuse* (noun) and *excuse* (verb). Notice also *advice* and *advise*.

s in loan words was often written *sc*, as in *science*, *scene*, etc. Sometimes this spelling is found in native words, *scythe* from O.E. *sigithe*.

In French, *s* had been lost before consonants under certain conditions, but it is preserved in *isle*. This spelling then extended to the native word *īland* from *igland* and thus gave *island*.

In a number of words the pronunciation of the *s* or [ʃ] appears to depend on the position of the stress. If the stress follows the *s* or [ʃ] then the *s* or [ʃ] is voiced [=z or ž], if it precedes then the *s* is voiceless. Compare *absolve* and *absolute*, *executor* and *execute*, *exert* and *exercise*, *exhibit* and *exhibition*, *anxiety* and *anxious*.

Middle English voiceless *s* when followed by *i* in loan words has become [ʃ] in pronunciation in Modern English : *ancient, version, vicious, gracious*. In the same way voiced *s* under identical conditions has become in Modern English [ž] as in *azure*: *confusion, vision, occasion*.

French *-ss-* in the syllable *-iss-* has become *sh* [ʃ] in English : *punish, flourish*, etc., Fr. *puniss-*, etc.

g, c [k]

§ 218. O.E. *g* before a velar vowel (*a, o, u*) remains in Modern English as in *go, good*. Before a palatal vowel (*e, i*) it developed into the sound which we have in Modern English *year* [j], O.E. *gēar*; *young*, O.E. *geong*; *yellow*, O.E. *geolwe*. O.E. *cg* (*gg*) after palatal vowels developed into the sound which is now represented by -*dge* [dž], as in *bridge*, O.E. *brycg*; *ridge*, O.E. *rycg*; *edge*, O.E. *ecg*, etc. For this last sound, however, French had also the symbol *j* which appears in Romance words such as *joy, join, jolly*.

In Romance words where the sound *g* as in *go* existed before palatal vowels it was spelt *gu*, as in *guise, guide*. This spelling is also found in a few native words : *guess, guest, tongue*.

In *ghost* and *ghostly* the sound of the stop *g* is written *gh*. In some words where we should expect O.E. *g* to appear as *y* it actually appears as *g*, under Scandinavian influence. Thus, for O.E. *giefan* Chaucer has regularly *yive*, but this has been superseded by the Northern and Scandinavian *give*. The same applies to *get, forget* and some more words.

A *g* has been lost in a number of contractions O.E. *stigel* > *style*, *stīgrap* > *stirrup*. *g* has become silent in the combination *gn* : *gnaw*.

c [k]

§ 219. O.E. *c*, according as it was followed by a palatal vowel on the one hand or a velar vowel or consonant on the other hand, developed into *c* as in *cat*, or into *ch* as in *child*; *come* from O.E. *cuman, creep* from

crēopan, cow from *cū* ; or *child* from *cīld, cheap* from *cēap*.
Hence we find in Modern English *seek* and *beseech, speak*
and *speech* according to the character of the vowel which
originally followed the *c*. A similar development
occurred in French, in which a Latin *c* appeared either
as *ch* or as *c* according to the dialect. We have therefore
double forms such as *cattle* and *chattel, pocket* and *poach,
attack* and *attach*. There were also differences in English
dialects, so that we have forms like *chester* and *caster*
side by side, and *kirk* beside *church*, the unshifted *c*
being the Northern form.

In Modern English *c* is written before *a, o, u, l, r, t.*
as in *can, corn, cup, clean, creep, act* ; *k* is written before
e, i, n, and when final : *kin, keen, know, book* ; *ck* is
often written for final *c* : *knock, crack*. *q* is sometimes
written before *u* or *w* : *quick, queen, quill*, and *qu* in loan
words, *coquette, burlesque*. *c* is usually written in the
suffix *ic* : *comic, tragic, frolic*, etc., though we also find
the French spelling *-ique* in *technique*, etc. In a few loan
words we find the spelling *ch* for the stop *c*: *choir, chorus*.

O.E. *c* has become silent in *know, knee*, etc., from
cnāwan, cnēo.

l

§ 220. O.E. *l* usually remains in Modern English. It
has been lost before or after *ch* in *much, such* and *which*,
O.E. *mycel, swylc* and *hwylc*, also in pronunciation before
k in *yolk, folk, talk*, and in the contractions *won't shan't*.

In a number of words where *l* is the result of an etymological spelling it has also come to be pronounced :
fault, realm, assault, earlier *faute, reme, assaute*.

In some words by a process of dissimilation it appears

instead of an earlier *r*, *purple*, Fr. *pourpre*; so also in *marble, laurel.*

In a few words a final *l* has been added in English : *chronicle, participle, principle, syllable.*

Though normally the French palatal *l* in words like *bataille* appears in English as *l*, *battle*, yet in a few words we find *li, brilliant, pavilion.*

l has become silent in *palm, salmon.*

r

§ 221. O.E. *r* has disappeared in Modern English except before a vowel : *worth, hurt, star*, etc., but *starry*, etc.

m

§ 222. O.E. *m* is preserved in Modern English. Modern *m* has replaced original *n* in *pilgrim*, Lat. *peregrinus*, and in *perform* (cf. *furnish*) ; *random*, Fr. *randon*; *venom*, Fr. *venin.*

m in *Stamford, Pomfret* and other place-names represents an assimilation from original *n*, cf. *Stanford* and *Pontefract.*

n

§ 223. O.E. *n* remains in Modern English. In a few cases we find an *n* where it did not exist in earlier forms : *nightingale*, O.E. *nihtegale*; *passenger*, Fr. *passager.* So also in *messenger, harbinger, scavenger.*

Final *n* is lost in pronunciation in loan words in the combination *-mn* : *condemn, solemn, column* ; but it is preserved when intervocalic : *solemnity, columnar, condemnation.*

n has been assimilated to *l* in *mill*, O.E. *myln*, Lat. *molina* (cf. the proper name *Milne*).

n has been lost in *adder* and *apron* owing to a false division of syllables in the context *a nadder, a napron.* Conversely, and for the same reason, *n* has been added to *nick-name* from *an ick* (*eke*=also) *name, the nonce* from *then ones, Noll* from *mine Oliver.*

The French palatal *n* [ɲ], written *gn*, was so written in English also, though its pronunciation soon became simply *n.* We find both spellings in *sign, reign*, but *vine* from *vigne, line* from *ligne.* Other variants are seen in *Spain* and *mountain* ; *ni* in *companion* where there is in fact a palatal pronunciation of the *n.*

w

§ 224. O.E. *w* remains in Modern English as a rule. The O.E. group *hw* is now written *wh-* but is pronounced either *hw* or *w.* O.E. *w* disappeared before *o* and *u*, sometimes in pronunciation though not always in the spelling : *sword, two.* It was also lost in an unstressed syllable : *answer, boatswain, gunwale.* It is also lost in pronunciation before *r* : *write, wrong, wring.*

O.E. *w* in final unstressed syllables appears in Modern English as *ow* : *medwe* becomes *meadow, halwe* becomes *hallow, morwe* becomes *morrow.* In *banquet, language* and other Romance words the spelling has influenced the pronunciation so that the *u*, though originally silent, is now pronounced as a *w.*

h

§ 225. *h* as in *have* has remained where it existed in Old English. In French words it was silent and remains so still in many words such as *heir, honour, hour, honest.* In other words it has been sometimes pronounced and sometimes not : *humble, herb, humour, hospital, hotel,* etc.

VOWELS

§ 226. The Old English vowel system, as we have seen on p. 229, consisted of the following vowels :

Long   - - $\bar{a}$, $\bar{æ}$, $\bar{\imath}$, $\bar{e}$, $\bar{o}$, $\bar{u}$, $\bar{y}$.
Short   - - a, $æ$, i, e, o, u, y.
Diphthongs :   } ea, eo, io, ie.
(long or short)

Of the diphthongs *eo* and *io* fell together in West-Saxon and *ie* existed only in West-Saxon.

§ 227. In the development of the Old English vowels the first thing we have to notice is that under certain conditions original short vowels were lengthened and long vowels shortened. Original long vowels were shortened before two consonants in Middle English. Thus :

O.E.	M.E.
lǽdde	*lĕdde*
lǽsse	*lĕsse*
wīsdom	*wĭsdom*
fīftīene	*fĭfteen*
hālge	*hălwe*
clāþde	*clădde*
hūsbonda	*hŭsband*

The change did not take place before -*ld*, -*nd*, -*mb*, -*rd*. Before -*st* we find both long and short vowels : *priest*, *least*, but *breast*, *lest*, *must*.

§ 228. Originally short vowels were lengthened before -*ld*, -*nd*, -*mb*, -*rd*, but were often subsequently shortened.

O.E.	M.E.	Mod. E.
fŭnden	*fōunde*	*found*
fĭndan	*fīnde*	*find*
cĭld	*chīld*	*child*
ĕald	*ōld*	*old*

The lengthening did not take place, however, (1) if a third consonant followed any of these groups : *children, hundred* ; (2) when these groups are followed by a syllable containing *m, n, l, r*: *wonder, alderman, wilderness* (cf. *wild*).

§ 229. The vowels *a, e, o* were lengthened before a single consonant followed by a vowel :

O.E.	M.E.	Mod. E.
ĕalu	*āle*	*ale*
năma	*nāme*	*name*
hŏpian	*hōpe*	*hope*
bĕran	*bēre*	*bear*
mĕte	*mēte*	*meat*
ĕtan	*ēte*	*eat*

§ 230. The vowels *u* and *i* may have been lengthened in this position. The lengthening did not take place, however, (1) if in Old English the next syllable had a secondary stress : O.E. *bodig, body* ; O.E. *pening, penny* ; O.E. *hefig, heavy* ; (2) sometimes if the next syllable contained *m, n, l, r*: *saddle, hammer, heaven*. But notice that *father* from *fœder* has a long vowel and that the spelling with *ea* of *heaven* and *heavy* seems to point to an earlier long vowel.

§ 231. Long vowels in the first syllable of trisyllabic words and in the second element of compounds are shortened. Compare *holy* and *holiday, white* and *Whittaker, Kingston* from *cyngestūn.*

§ 232. The Old English diphthongs all disappear in Middle English; *ĕa* becomes *a*, and *ĕo* and *īo* normally become *e*; *ēa* becomes *ē*. The *ē* which was derived from *eo* (or *e*), *io*, was sometimes written *ee* ; the *ē* which was derived from O.E. *ea* (or *ǣ*) was sometimes written *ea* : cf. *see* from O.E. *sēon, sea* from O.E. *sǣ*.

§ 233. In Middle English, however, there arose new diphthongs from the coalescence of vowels with certain consonants :

O.E.	M.E.
æ + g, dæg	ay, ai, day, dai
ǣ + g, grǣg	ei, ey, grey
e + g, weg, legde, regn	ey, ei, wey, wei, rain
ēa + g, ēage	ey, eye
ĕa + h, eahta	ei, eihte
ēa + w, scēawian	ew, shewe (shew)
ĕo + w, trēowe	eu, treu (true)
ĕ + f, efete	ew, ewt
a + g + velar vowel, dagan, lagu	aw, dawn, law
ō + h, plōh	ou, plough
ā + g, āgan	ow, own
ŏ + g, boga, flogen	ow, bow, flown
ā or ō + w, blōwan, cnāwan	ow, blow, know

§ 234. There also arose numerous **diphthongs** in words of French origin : *eo, ie, oi, ai*, etc.

§ 235. Apart from lengthenings and shortenings and the formation of new diphthongs the O.E. vowels, both long and short, remained in Middle English, the only changes being that of ǣ to *a* and *y* becomes usually *i*, though in Kent it becomes *e* and in the South-west *u*. Cf. *church* and *kirk*, *dint* and *dent*. O.E. ā becomes ō, except in the North. Thus we have *home* from *hām*, *stone* from *stān*, *bone* from *bān*. Also the ă which was lengthened became *o*, as in *old* from *āld* (*eald*).

The ō which was derived from ă was often written *oa*, and the ō which came from the O.E. ō was often written *oo*.

We may now notice some special developments in Modern English of the Old and Middle English vowels.

a

§ 236. This vowel has been slightly raised in pronunciation in Modern English to a sound approaching *e* : *have*, [hæv].

a + l + consonant becomes ɔ : *all, stall*; sometimes written *au* : *maul.*

a + voiceless spirant is lengthened [ɑ] : *glass, last.*

w + a becomes [o] : *want, wash.*

w + a + r becomes [ɔ] : *war.*

w + a + g or *k* remains [æ] : *quack, wax, waggon.*

i

§ 237. The sound *i* is written *e* in *England.* It is sometimes written *y* as in Middle English, when final : *happy, sorry.*

It is written *u* in *busy.* This is a Southern form.

In the combination *-igh-* it has become a diphthong [ɑi] : *might, sight, light.*

e

§ 238. The M.E. sound *e* is pronounced [ɑ] when followed by *r.* Thus *far* is from *ferre, star* from *sterre.* The old spelling survives in *clerk.* The words *certain* and *servant* were once pronounced *cartain* and *sarvant.* Notice also *sergeant.* The change to [ɑ] does not occur in later loan words. The M.E. sound *e* is pronounced *i* in *England* and *pretty.* An old spelling is preserved in *friend.*

o

§ 239. Short *o* has become a diphthong in some words in which it is followed by *l* : *bowl, toll.*   Note the change of pronunciation in *among.*

u

§ 240. In Middle English this vowel had the sound which it still has in *bush, push, cushion, sugar, put,* [*u*], but in most words it has now the sound which is found in *gun, shun, sun,* [a].   This sound is sometimes written *o* in the neighbourhood of letters with down strokes, *son, come.*

It usually preserves its original pronunciation before *l* : *bull, pull, full,* and before [ʃ] or after a labial : *push, put.*

LONG VOWELS

§ 241. Middle English long *ā* has become a diphthong [ei] in Modern English : *name, fame, lady able, hate.*

ī

§ 242. Middle English *ī* had the sound of [i] in *machine.* In Modern English it has regularly become a diphthong [ɑi] as in *mine, time, climb, bind.*   Where it has been shortened, however, it keeps its [*i*] sound ; cf. *vineyard* and *vine, wind.*   The long original sound is also found in some late loan words : *machine, police.*

ē

§ 243. Middle English *ē*, whether open (ę, ea), [ɛ] or close, (ẹ, ee), [ē] has developed in Modern English into the sound which we have in *beat, need,* [ij]. It is variously written, *ee, ea, ie, eo : creep, seek, agree, stream, ease, leave, receive, achieve, fiend, field, people.*

In *break* and *great* the pronunciation is nearer to the original, though it has developed into the diphthong [ei].

ō

§ 244. Middle English had two long *ō* sounds, one open, derived from O.E. *ā* and one close, derived from O.E. *ō*. The former becomes in Modern English the diphthong [ou] which is found in *bone, stone, home, go, nose.* This *o* was often written *oa*, as in *broad, loaf.* The other *o* has become in Modern English the sound which is heard in *shoe, school, too, do, loose* [u].

The former has been shortened in *hot* and *gone.* The shortening of the latter was first to *ŭ*, and this shortened vowel developed just like an original short *u*, that is, it gave the sound which we see in *blood, flood, done, mother* [a]. The intermediate stage of the shortening is seen in *foot, good, stood, took* [u].

ū

§ 245. Middle English *ū* has become a diphthong in Modern English [ɑu] : *brown, crown, mouth, pound.* When shortened it has the development of original short *u : dove, southern* beside *south.* The original pronunciation is sometimes kept before labials : *coop, room, tomb.*

DIPHTHONGS

ai

§ 246. This diphthong has developed into the sound found in *day, say, fail, nail*, [ei]. It has become a short monophthong in the forms *says, said* and *again*.

oi, ui

§ 247. These are of French origin and have developed into the diphthong found in *noise*.

eu, ew

§ 248. The first element of this diphthong has become consonantal, as in *new, knew, nephew*, [ju]. The same sound is also found after dentals and labials in French words : *due, tube, future, pure, view*. After *l, r* the diphthong has become a monophthong : *blew, crew, brew*.

au, aw

§ 249. This diphthong has also become a monophthong as in *awe, claw, draw, law, fought, aught*.

In Middle English this diphthong was frequently found before *l*, and has been simplified in Modern English : *fault*. It has been shortened in *sausage* and *laudanum*, and has become *œ* in *savage* (cf. Fr. *sauvage*). In *laugh* it has become *ā*, [ā]. In some words we find a double pronunciation : *launch, laundry, haunt*.

ou

§ 250. This diphthong remains in Modern English, *know, grow, slow*. In late M.E. *eu* became *ou* in the word *sew*, O.E. *sēowan*, possibly on the analogy of *sow*, O.E. *sāwan*.

In *ought, sought, thought, brought* and *four*, the diphthong has become a monophthong, also in *daughter* and in *cough, trough*. It has been shortened in *knowledge*.

§ 251. Finally, it should be noticed that vowels in Modern English have been much modified in quality by a following *r* when the latter has become silent. The developments are shown in the following table :

Normal Development			Development + *r*
ū	*hūs*	*house*	*court*
ĕ	*etan*	*eat*	*here*
ǣ	*sǣ*	*sea*	*there*
ō	*gōd, stān*	*good, stone*	*lore, for, soar*
ă	*nama*	*name*	*care, fare*
ĭ	*hit*	*it*	*birch*
ĕ	*bedd*	*bed*	*herd*
ŭ	*hnutu*	*nut*	*fur*

§ 252. We may now summarise in tabular form the development of the Old English and Middle English vowels in Modern English :

O.E.	M.E.	Mod. E.
a : crabba	*a : crabbe*	[æ] *crab*
a lengthened : *nacod*	*ā : naked*	[ei] *naked*
a/o + nasal : *man, mon*	*a/o : man, mon*	[æ/o] *sang, song*
a + ld, nd etc. : *ald*	*ō : old*	[ou] *old*
a + g : lagu	*aw : law*	[ɔ] *law*
æ : hæfde	*a : hadde*	[æ] *had*
æ + g : dæg	*ai, ay : day*	[ei] *day*
	a + l : all	[ɔ] *all*
	a + (s): glass	[ɑ] *glass*
	w + a : want	[o] *want*
	w + a + r : war	[ɔə] *war*
	w + a + g, k : wax	[æ] *wax*
i : sittan	*i : sitte*	[i] *sit*

O.E.	M.E.	Mod. E.
i + ld, nd, etc. : *findan*	*i : finde*	[ɑi] *find*
e : betst	*e : best*	[e] *best*
e lengthened : *etan*	*ē : ete*	[ij] *eat*
e + f : efete	*ew : ewt*	[ju] *ewt*
e + g : weg, regn	*ey, ay : wey, way*	[ei] *way, rain*
	e + r : sterre	[ɑ(ə)] *star*
o : god	*o : god*	[o] *God*
o lengthened : *hopian*	*ō : hope*	[ou] *hope*
o + g : boga	*ow : bowe*	[ou] *bow*
	o + l : toll	[æu] *toll*
u : sunu	*u/o : son*	[a] *son, sun*
u + nd, etc. : *funden*	*ou : founde*	[ɑu] *found*
	u + l : full	[u] *full*
	⎧ *i : bridge*	[i] *bridge*
y : brycg, cyrce, dynt	⎨ *u : church*	[ʌ] *church*
	⎩ *e : dent, evil*	[e] *dent*

LONG VOWELS

ǣ : hǣlan	*ē : heal*	[ij] *heal*
æ shortened : *lædde*	*e/a : ledde, ladde*	[e] *led*
ǣ + g : grǣg	*ey : grey*	[ei] *grey, gray*
ā : hām	*ō : home*	[ou] *home*
ā shortened : *hālge*	*a : halwe*	[æ] *hallow*
ā + g : āgan	*ōw : owen*	[ou] *own*
ā + w : cnāwan	*ōw : knowe*	[ou] *know*
ī : fīf	*ī : five*	[ɑi] *five*
ī + g : stīgrāp	*i : stirrup*	[i] *stirrup*
ī shortened : *fiftiene*	*i : fifteen*	[i] *fifteen*
ē : sēcean	*ē : seeke*	[ij] *seek*
ē shortened : *slēpte*	*e : slepte*	[e] *slept*
ō : scōle	*oo : schole*	[ŭ] *school*
	o shortened	[u, a] *foot, blood*
ō shortened : *gosling*	*o : gosling*	[o] *gosling*
ō + g, h : plōh	*ou : plough*	[ɑu] *plough*
ō + w : blōwan	*ōw : blowe*	[ou] *blow*
ū : hūs	*ōu : house*	[ɑu] *house*
ū shortened : *hūsbonde*	*u : husbond*	[a] *husband*
ȳ : fȳr	*i : fire*	[ɑi] *fire*

DIPHTHONGS

§ 253. All the Old English diphthongs disappear in M.E. as has been noted above under the various sounds into which they develop. The following points might be noted :

ēa + g : ēage	*ɜy : eye*	[ɑi] *eye*
ēa + w : scēawian	*ew : shewe*	[ou] *shew*
ea + h : eahta	*ei : eighte*	[ei] *eight*
ēo + w : blēow	*ew : blew*	[ū] *blew*

CHAPTER VIII

STANDARD ENGLISH, CORRECT ENGLISH

§ 254. When we speak of Modern English we mean the language spoken by Englishmen wherever they may be. Such a language is not, and never has been, uniform. It consists of many local dialects differing not only in individual sounds but also in vocabulary and syntax and accent. Frequently such dialects differ so greatly one from another that they are not everywhere understood. In addition to these local dialects there also exist, and probably always have existed, dialects which depend upon social rank and breeding rather than upon locality. They cut right through the geographical divisions. Even within these class dialects there are further dialect divisions which constitute what have been called occupational dialects. The differences which thus arise are everywhere the consequences of the peculiar circumstances of life, environment and tradition of those who speak them. It is common knowledge, to take only one particular illustration, that the language of the sailor is full of phrases, idioms, words, word meanings, metaphors and similes which are derived from his experience of the sea and of ships. So also the language of the miner, the farmer, the stockbroker is coloured

248

by his peculiar experiences and his habitual attitude towards the facts of life. In all such cases there is a closer bond of union and a quicker mental and emotional sympathy between individuals with common pursuits than between individuals who have nothing in common in their ways of life. The same causes, much magnified, are responsible for the differentiation of languages as well as of dialects.

But embracing and enfolding all these smaller variations there is an English which, while assimilating from time to time elements from these various dialects, yet on the whole discards everything which is only in purely local or professional use. Such a language is called Standard English. Such Standard English does not always consciously reject dialect peculiarities ; frequently it does not know them. If they seek entrance into the standard language they will be judged like all other new-comers—on their merits.

The conception of a standard language is one which is exposed to some misunderstanding, for it may be interpreted as a language which sets a standard which everybody ought to strive to attain, or it may be interpreted as a language which is actually spoken, as a matter of fact, by certain members of the community, irrespective of its claim to any sort of pre-eminence. Which of these two interpretations should be adopted it is not easy to say off-hand, for there are weighty considerations which should affect the choice either way.

It will be easier to approach this question, perhaps, if we first enquire what is meant by a standard language. By Standard English is commonly meant that English which is spoken by educated Englishmen speaking the

language of London. It is, however, by no means restricted to that district, but is found in all parts of the
country and in different social classes. There is in many
cases a conscious imitation of this standard speech by
people to whom it is not native, for it is felt to be one of
the marks of education, breeding and social position. If
we look in the *New English Dictionary* we shall find
that certain pronunciations are marked as " Standard,"
as, for example that *last* is pronounced with a long [ɑ]
sound, whereas in Northern English it is pronounced
as [æ̆] ; we shall find that certain words are
only found in dialects. There are other marks of the
standard speech which do not find a place in dictionaries,
such as peculiarities of idiom or syntax. The Irishman
says " will you be coming ? " when he means " are you
coming ? " and has many other delightful ways of
expressing himself which are not found in Standard
English.

If we are to decide whether such a standard language
is desirable and should be imitated we must decide on the
general grounds of the nature of language itself. Looked
at from this point of view a standard language, as imply-
ing an ideal, should either serve its purpose as a means
for the communication of thought better than a language
which it seeks to supersede, or else it should have some
advantages based on the fundamental principles of art
which are absent from that other non-standard language.

In fact, a standard language has some advantages as
an instrument for the communication of thought. The
more widespread a language is the more easy it is to
reach those who speak and write and read it. But it is
not merely a question of understanding what is written

or spoken ; there are other considerations than that.
For the fact that two individuals habitually use the same
language makes it possible for those two individuals to
come into much closer contact than would otherwise
be possible. The fact that two persons speak the
same language is only another way of saying that their
thoughts run in the same channels and that therefore a potential sympathy between them is already
in existence, a sympathy which may be awakened immediately by the spoken or written word. A standard
language, therefore, renders the communication of thought
easier, and it fulfils its function better than a language
which is not standard. That is its chief advantage.
Hence the deliberate and conscious endeavour to acquire
the standard language, though it may appear sometimes
to be merely a snobbish desire to acquire the external
marks of culture and education, may in reality spring
from a deeper-seated impulse to share the intellectual
and imaginative sympathies of a community. Indeed,
it is usually on such grounds that standard or " literary "
languages have gained currency, for it is only another
phase of the same impulse which makes a writer use
that language which will ensure for him the largest
circle of readers. It is characteristic, too, of the same
forces that standard languages usually have their origin
in the dialect of a capital where are centred all the culture
and all the best traditions of the people.

But if a standard language has the advantage of being
widely, immediately and sympathetically understood ;
if it is the result of one of the vital forces in language,
yet that very force tends always to its disintegration.
For if it is true that the case for a standard language

rests upon the universal desire to communicate thought in the form in which it will be best understood, yet it is also true that it is the desire to communicate thought which lies at the bottom of all innovations in language. There is, therefore, always a tendency to expand and develop language, which must be repressed by the existence of a standard language. In other words, conformity to any standard implies a certain restraint upon individuality, a certain forcing of the individual temperament into a conventional mould, and that is a disadvantage which should not be underestimated. In fact, however, the forces of individuality and spontaneity have always placed a limit to the sway of any conventionality in language.

Standard languages afford just one more example of the observation that language, wherever we find it, is the mirror of the peculiar civilisation, history and institutions of the people which speaks it. In England it has been the paramount influence of the capital, London, which has raised its dialect to the rank of a standard language, and much the same has occurred in France. In Germany, on the other hand, with different institutions and a different history, the language of the capital is not the standard language of the country— if there be one at all.

There is, moreover, an important difference between a written and a spoken standard language. There are many Scotchmen and many Welshmen and Irishmen who write standard English, but who are far from speaking it, and there are many Englishmen of whom the same can be said. The reason is not far to seek. Such men, though they may be anxious that their written work

should be as widely read as possible, yet have no fear
that the circle of their audience will be in any way limited
by their speaking their native dialect, and they know, too,
that the spoken word is spoken and is gone, while the
written word persists.

§ 255. We may now briefly sketch the rise and development of standard or literary English. In the Old English
period, although most of the poetic literature is probably
of Northern or Mercian origin, yet it has come down to us
in the language of Wessex. From the year 829, when
King Egbert of Wessex subdued the whole of the territory south of the Humber, and even compelled North-
umbria to pay tribute to him, Wessex was the chief
kingdom of the heptarchy. At the end of the ninth
century, that is to say, at the beginning of the reign
of King Alfred, West-Saxon had already risen to the
dignity of a literary language, in the sense that hence-
forth all writers seek to use only the forms of that dialect.
In that century poems composed in Mercia or North-
umbria were nevertheless written down in the language
of Wessex. Whether or not at this early date there
existed a standard spoken language as well as a standard
literary language it is impossible to say.

That the language of Wessex should have been pre-
ferred to that of the Midlands or the North is in itself
quite natural; for Wessex was politically and also,
especially after the Danish wars, in point of culture, the
most advanced of the kingdoms of England. Added
to this fact it must not be forgotten that from the court
of Wessex at Winchester there came a very strong
impetus to a new culture. The King himself busily
translated into the language of Wessex numerous Latin

works and circulated these translations throughout the country, so that it is only to be expected that his language should have been imitated wherever his influence was felt.

Alfred established a literary tradition, then, but it was not long-lived. In the eleventh century there are already signs of those momentous changes in the form and structure of the language which lead on to Middle English, and at the same time it becomes clear that the old uniformity of speech is disappearing. After the Conquest, indeed, the old tradition was lost and the various dialects of the country reappear in literature. For the early Middle English period we have the testimony of Ranulph Higden for the existence of three main types of dialect, the Northern, the Southern and the Midland. He tells us that people of the Midlands could understand both their northern and their southern neighbours, but that Northerners could not understand Southerners, and Southerners could not understand Northerners. But already in the early fourteenth century there are indications that the dialect of the South enjoys a higher prestige than any other, and Northern writers borrow from it words and forms which are not native to their own dialect. The Southern dialect thus favoured was not, however, the old dialect of Winchester, but with the change of the political and social centre of the country to London, that of London. It was this language of London which was used by Chaucer, who was himself a Londoner, and by Wyclif, who came from Yorkshire and lived at Oxford. It is clear, therefore, that this dialect already had a widespread influence and enjoyed some sort of special prestige. We may assume, therefore, that in the second half of the fourteenth century the speech of the educated Londoner, and more especially the speech of the Court had spread to other parts of the country and was there imitated because it was felt to be the " best English." This London dialect, or as we should perhaps now say, language, was given a wider currency by the writings of Chaucer and Wyclif. They did not, of course, create it, on the contrary it was Chaucer's native speech, but they made it current as the language of literature by their writings.

The language of London was originally predominantly Southern in vocabulary and form and pronunciation. But the people of London were the near neighbours of the people of the Midlands and of Kent. In the course of the fourteenth and fifteenth centuries there appear more and more elements from those dialects, especially from the Midland dialect, though there also appeared elements from the Northern dialect. Hence there arose many double forms in the language. Chaucer, for example, has verbal forms ending in -*en*, which is Midland, or -*eth*, which is Southern ; he has nouns with -*s* plurals or with -*en* plurals. This nascent literary language was, however, only standard so far as the language of literature was concerned, there was no corresponding standard spoken language. Indeed, even in the language of literature there existed great diversity, despite the existence of the more uniform language of Chaucer. Caxton tells us of some of the difficulties which he experienced in selecting words or forms for his translations. He, however, was responsible for the selection in many cases of one or other of two alterna-

tive words or forms, and he did much to introduce
uniformity into our spelling.

From Caxton's day until the present day London
English, though it has frequently taken up isolated
forms and expressions from other dialects, yet remains
Standard English.

§ 256. The discussion of the nature of Standard English
naturally leads to the broader question as to what is
correct and what is incorrect in language: The terms
"correct" and "incorrect," if taken with too narrow an
interpretation, are misleading when applied to language ;
for correctness implies a rigid standard from which
it is impossible to depart, and such a standard does not
and cannot exist in language. If it did it would be
impossible for language to develop in the least degree.
Since, however, language must develop, it can only do so
by some departure from what is at a given moment
accepted usage. The departure consists always in some
change in the meaning of a word or in a syntactic construction or in the introduction of a new word. Every
such innovation has at first only the authority of its
author, and whether it will win the approval of the rest
of the community depends upon many considerations.
But since language is always in a state of flux, since
there are always in progress certain experiments in
constructions or in word meaning or in word formation,
it is impossible to speak of any hard and fast standard
in any language.

In respect of vocabulary these innovations may consist in the use of slang words, of neologisms, or of foreign
words. Concerning the last of these, foreign words,
English has at all times been prone to borrow freely,

as has been seen in the chapter on vocabulary. Such foreign words still enter the language from time to time, and it is not possible without special consideration in each particular case to determine whether or not the use of such a word violates any canon of correctness. Generally speaking, a word which really supplies a need that cannot conveniently be supplied by a native word finds a very ready acceptance, more particularly if it is derived from a Romance language, for the history of our tongue has familiarised us with such words and predisposes us to accept them. Thus of recent times the word *camouflage* has not only been promptly accepted, but is already being used in a variety of figurative senses which demonstrate its usefulness and the completeness of its acclimatisation. It is used not only as a noun but also as a verb, which is additional evidence that it is regarded already as a native word. On the other hand, such a word as *penchant* has not the same merit of usefulness and irreplaceability as has *camouflage*, and has therefore never gained entrance into the language.

Neologisms, again, are the subject of much contention before they take up a fixed place in the language. Some of them, like the names given by inventors to their inventions, are accepted without further parley, though some of them promptly find rivals in popular speech or are in one way or another mutilated. Thus *cinematograph*, after having definitely ousted *electric theatre* and *biograph* and other terms has been reduced to *cinema*, and has as its most serious rival *pictures*. It is obvious that the language of a progressive people must from year to year accept a number of such neologisms ; for they are the record of the march of civilisation

among that people and the absence of them would
be evidence of a stationary or decaying civilisation.
But there are also new words coined by individual writers
who seek by means of them to give expression to some
particular shade of thought. Many, again, are introduced with the desire of replacing some foreign word,
though this does not happen so often in English as in
some other languages. Still we have an example of the
process in the use of *foreword* for *preface*.

Apart from the use of loan words and neologisms or
of slang words—to which technical words are closely
related—any assumed standard of correctness is liable
to be slighted by the use of words with a new meaning
or by the use of new syntactic constructions. If it were
possible—which it is not—to compile an absolutely
complete grammar of English, complete as regards
accidence and syntax, and also to define all the possible
forms and meanings of words, then we might deduce
from it a standard of correct English. But it so happens
that in every generation there are thousands of experiments in the use of language, slight variations in the
meanings of words, in the order of words and in the
syntax of the sentence, which may or may not become an
accepted part of the language, and of which the grammarian knows nothing and can know nothing because
their fate is undecided. If they conform to the spirit of
the language, if they are useful and if their usefulness is
generally appreciated, they may be taken up into the
language in spite of the grammarian. They are usually
the result, as we have seen, of an effort to give precise
expression to thought. If they represent some definite
departure from previously accepted grammatical rules,

-they will appear in future grammars as exceptions. But when once they have been accepted they serve as precedents for new departures, and thus the living language outstrips the grammarian. Indeed one might say that one half of the so-called " exceptions " in our grammars are survivals of older linguistic phenomena, and the other half are innovations which mark the amount of progress which any language has made. The standard of correctness is therefore very largely illusory, for it is a standard which must, in the nature of things, be constantly changing. To the extent that innovations or departures from the assumed standard of correctness are the result of a conscious effort to enrich and widen the range of expression of a language, all such innovations as find general acceptance are a benefit conferred on the language. There may be also, it is true, changes of a totally different character, changes which arise from ignorance or carelessness, and such changes must necessarily tend to blur the finer outlines of expression and to lead to indistinctness and ambiguity. Doubtless the existence of some authoritative body such as the *Académie* in France tends to check all such undesirable changes, but it may be doubted whether the gain would not be more than counterbalanced by the loss, for such a body is *ex hypothesi* conservative in function and would set its face against other changes than those which arose from ignorance or carelessness ; it would hamper and restrict the operations of the creative mind and deny to genius its supreme right of self-expression.

§ 257. In any endeavour to characterise the Modern English language it is instructive to observe the opinion which a foreigner entertains concerning it, for such an opinion at least has the merit of not being unduly biassed in its favour. By common consent the opinion of the foreigner concerning English is that it is a very practical language, easy to learn, and one in which one can with the utmost ease and convenience give expression to fine shades of thought. Now, although the foreigner very often gravely underestimates the difficulties of mastering English, yet his opinion that it readily lends itself to the expression of new turns of thought, and that it is a most flexible and adaptable instrument, is probably just, whilst his view that it is easy to learn holds promise of its future as a world language.

Its flexibility and adaptability are in the main the results of the tendency to analytic expression which we have noticed throughout the various periods of its development, a tendency which has caused it to dispense with almost all inflections ; which has rendered it possible to use a word at will as one part of speech or another ; and which has thrown so much of the duty of expressing meaning upon word order. These three features of Modern English, closely interdependent as they are in origin and purpose, explain very largely the peculiar excellences of the mother tongue. For in the first place the fact that actual word order and context play such a large rôle in indicating the meaning of words and their connection one with another, is responsible for that epigrammatic brevity and pregnant suggestiveness which is characteristic of Modern English. Where the plan of a sentence is not clearly and precisely marked out by inflections ; where the mind is not, as it were, in leading-strings from the beginning of the sentence to the end ; there is naturally more liberty for the mind to interpret the sentence as a whole instead of being fettered at each stage to the meaning of the single word. It is true that the large possibilities of suggestion which are present in the English sentence may be a source of ambiguity, but, on the other hand, they are the cause of much of the fineness and sensitiveness of expression which are to be found in English, and the language has the means, when necessary, of being perfectly precise.

Indeed the dependence of meaning upon the context in English implies a certain activity of thought on the part of the reader or the hearer in order to perceive it, and requires that the reader or hearer should be alive not only to the context of words but even to the context of events and external happenings. Nobody, for example, could, from the words alone, understand the notice which recently appeared in a shop-window : *Closed down, joined up.* There is in such a laconic phrase a brevity which it would not be easy to parallel outside English, and such a phrase is only possible in English because it is of the nature of our language that we must be constantly on the look-out for elements of suggestion not only from the verbal context, but also from the circumstantial context, whether it be emotional, political, social or of any other kind. Moreover, this tendency to take for granted a mental or emotional sympathy between the speaker and the hearer, or the writer and the reader, is becoming more and more marked in Modern English. It underlies much of our ironic humour, and by inducing brevity gives to it point and suggestion. Nothing could be in stronger contrast than the leisurely explanatoriness of a Fielding, which tells you everything and leaves little to the intelligence or the imagination, and the almost niggardly economy, coupled with brilliant suggestion, of a Meredith.

The early Modern English period was mainly occupied with the building up of the vocabulary of the language and the clarification of its syntax. Shakespere coined words lavishly, and Dryden and Addison were at pains to purify and elucidate the language which they had inherited. After the creative luxuriance of the Elizabethan age there came a period of repose, of organisation and of contented *laissez-faire*. But in the nineteenth and twentieth centuries there are visible experiments in language which take a new direction and which tend to exploit to the utmost the peculiar advantages of an uninflected tongue. The difference between the earlier and the later period may best be seen by a comparison between two writers whose style is often called obscure. The obscurity of Milton, in his prose writings, is the obscurity which arises from ill-constructed, badly-jointed, overweighted sentences in which it is difficult to follow the sense. It is not because the sense is not expressed with sufficient fulness ; it is not because any element of the sense is omitted from the sentence and left to the intelligence of the reader ; but it is because the elements of the sentence are badly co-ordinated or sub-ordinated. So, too, in the prose of Bacon the obscurity arises partly from defective syntax and a slovenly sentence structure, and partly from confused thought. But the obscurity of Browning or Meredith is of a very different kind. It springs from a constant demand on the reader to exercise his intelligence ; it springs from the fact that the writer is content merely to suggest his thought, and to suggest it with the least expenditure possible, rather than to paint it out in full in the manner of Richardson. Such obscurity is due to the fact that the reader is given only an inadequate clue to the association of ideas which is present in the mind of the writer, and not in any way to a merely technical defect of syntax.

For the rest, the English language reflects many of the special characteristics of the English people. We are a very reserved race, very conservative, and we dislike any ostentation either in manner, dress or speech. Our language is not rich in expressions of cordial welcome; a " glad to see you " is as much as we can place against the Frenchman's " enchanted " or " charmed." Our terms of praise are restrained, and lest we should be thought too emotional in giving even moderate expression to our feelings, we seek safety as often as not in a non-committal negative phrase such as " not bad " for " good," " I don't mind if I do " for " I should like to," and so on. The same dislike of assertiveness is responsible for much of the characteristic brevity of expression in English, and for the frequency of such short pregnant phrases as, " first come, first served," " first up, best dressed," " better late than never," and many more. On the other hand, much of our English humour depends for its point upon the rapid perception of concealed resemblances between things, and this rapid perception is certainly fostered and developed by the ordinary tendency of the language already referred to, to convey meaning by suggestion.

English shows in its vocabulary and phraseology a stronger influence of the Bible than do other European languages. We find in common speech and writing such phrases as "the powers that be," "to wash one's hands of," "a still small voice," "whited sepulchres," "a howling wilderness." So, too, "holy of holies" has been the model of many new formations such as "heart of hearts," "life of life." So, also, there are few languages which have incorporated into everyday speech so much of the technical language of sport as has English. Shakespere has many references to the sport of archery, most of which have now disappeared with the disappearance of that sport, but others have replaced them. "To have one's innings," "to hit below the belt," "to pull a good oar," "straight from the shoulder," "neck and neck," "to play the game," "to throw up the sponge" are only a few of the numerous idioms which have come into common use from this source.

CHAPTER IX

THE WRITING OF ENGLISH

§ 258. THE history of the English people is reflected in its spelling not less clearly than in its vocabulary and syntax. In the earliest period of English, when the number of those who could read and write was very small, words were written more or less phonetically, and since there was no accepted spelling there was more room for private initiative in this respect. We find, therefore, that even in one and the same dialect there was not the same absolute uniformity of spelling as we find to-day. But when we consider that there were no models of writing and no printed texts—nothing, in fact, to impose uniformity—it is most surprising that there was not a much greater variety of spelling than we actually find. Indeed we can only account for this fact on the ground that scribes wrote phonetically and, therefore, in so far as they spoke the same dialect, they achieved approximately the same results in spelling.

The earliest script of the Anglo-Saxons was the runic script, which they brought with them from the Continent. The runic alphabet was an adaptation of the Latin alphabet with certain modifications which were necessary, owing to the nature of the writing materials then in use.

Carving letters in wood or stone requires considerable skill if there are many curves, and for that reason the curves of an *s* or *r*, for example, were straightened out. Writing in runes did not long survive the coming of Christianity and is found, indeed, mainly in inscriptions on hard materials such as stone, horn or silver. Surviving manuscripts of paper or parchment are written in the Latin alphabet, which was probably introduced with Christianity. The Latin alphabet, however, lacked symbols for some of the commonest sounds of Germanic. In order to supply them, runic symbols were retained for the sounds represented in Modern English by *th* and by *w*. These symbols were þ and ƿ. A new symbol, ð, was also introduced for *th*, but even so there were not symbols enough for all sounds. Thus, for example, there was no symbol for voiced *f* [v]. *f* did duty for both sounds. So also the symbol ȝ might stand either for a stop or a spirant.

It was natural that the Norman Conquest, which had so profound an influence on the English vocabulary, should also have exercised an influence on the spelling of English, the more so as the majority of the scribes were Normans. In the twelfth century the continental or Carolingian variety of the Latin script began to influence the English script. The general effect of this influence was to give to the English symbols the values which they had in French, and to introduce new symbols with their French values. One of the earliest of the new symbols was *g*, which appears side by side with the older ȝ and has the value either of a stop, as in *good*, or of an affricate, as in *brycg*, "bridge." The old symbol ð was replaced by *th* and by degrees þ also yielded to *th*, though from the fact that it had come to resemble *y* in writing *y* was often written for it. A survival of this spelling is still to be seen in the inscriptions on sign-boards such as *Ye olde English*, etc., in which *ye* really stands for *þe*. In the same way the O.E. symbol ȝ had come to be written very like *y*, with the consequence that *y* was often written instead of ȝ as in M.E. *year*, O.E. ȝ*ear*. The second runic symbol *þ* preserved in Old English was quite unfamiliar to the Normans, and was early replaced by *w*, which was really nothing more than two *v*'s interlaced. The Old English sounds rendered by the symbol *f* were also differentiated by the use of *v* for the voiced and *f* for the voiceless consonant.

In the above change in spelling, either an old symbol has been repressed or a new one introduced. The Norman scribes, however, did much more than this. Not being familiar with some of the sounds of English, they tried to render them in their own way. They were not always successful. The O.E. palatal or velar spirant, *h*, especially, seems to have given them difficulty, if we may judge by the curious result of their efforts *gh*, as in *sight*, *light*, etc. Similarly, the O.E. *sc* appears to have given trouble, for we find in Middle English various attempts to render it : *ss*, *sss*, *sch*, *sh*, etc. Initial *h* seems also to have been a source of difficulty, for we find in Middle English texts that it is frequently omitted, or inserted in the wrong place, though this has not led to any modification of the normal spelling in Modern English.

Frequently the Norman scribes gave to existing symbols the sound values which attached to them in French. Especially noteworthy in this respect was their treatment of the O.E. *y*, which was always a vowel. The corresponding vowel sound in French was rendered by the symbol *u*, and the Norman scribes therefore replaced the symbol *y* in English by *u*, whilst the symbol *y* was either used as a consonant, because of its resemblance to O.E. ȝ as in *yer*, or else it was used to represent the vowel *i*, in which case it interchanged in Middle English freely with *i*.   Thus the O.E. *cyrce* appears as Middle English *church*.   In the majority of words the Old English sound represented by *y* developed in Middle English into the sound *i*, however, so that the number of words with *u* is not very great.   In other cases the Middle English development of O.E. *y* was *e*, and both sounds are to be seen in the two words *dint* and *dent*, and the difference is also seen in the pronunciation, though not in the spelling, of -*borough* and -*bury*. Another important change which was due to French influence, though the modern practice was only slowly arrived at, was the distinction between the use of *c* and *k*, according to which *c* when it had the sound *ch* [tʃ] was written *ch* ; when it had the value of a stop it was written *c* before *a*, *o*, and *u*, as in *came, cut, cot* ; and *k* before *e*, *i* or *n*, as in *kill, kettle, know*.   On the other hand, in the group *cw*, *c* was written *q* as in *queen*. French influence was also at work in the spelling of such words as *ice*, *mice*, (sing. *mouse*) and others.   In these words *c* has the value of *s*, which had developed from earlier *ts* in French words, from which it spread to native words.   Further, the spelling *sh*, for O.E. *sc* is likewise due to the Norman scribes, as in *shall, shun*, etc.

Just as the Norman scribes had substituted the French symbol *u* for the O.E. *y*, so also they substituted the

French *ou* for the O.E. *ū*, in words like *hūs, nū, hū*, etc., which now retain this spelling in *house, thou, now, how*. The spelling was sometimes *ow*, and for a long time the two spellings were interchangeable, but in Modern English *ow* is reserved for the final position in the word ; *thou* is exceptional in this respect.

In one or two cases the conditions under which manuscripts were written were responsible for changes in spelling. Thus, for example, the difficulty of reading certain sound groups such as *im, mi, um, mu, mun*, etc., in MS. led to certain changes which aimed at rendering the letters more easily legible. The letters chiefly affected were *i* and *u*, which presented special difficulties in the neighbourhood of letters with short down-strokes such as *m, n, w, v*. One simple way of distinguishing *i* was to place a dot over it, and another was to prolong it below the line, thus giving an undotted *j* ; the dotted *j* is the result of a combination of these methods. Yet a third, and earlier, method of distinguishing *i* was to prolong it above the line, especially when initial, and a survival of this practice is still to be seen in the writing of the pronoun *I* with a capital. For the same reasons *u* was often written *o*, which is preserved in numerous Modern English words, though the sound is that of *u*. Thus Modern English *wonder, come, love* were in Old English *wundor, cuman, lufe*. Sometimes both spellings are to be seen, as in *son* and *sun*, both of which had *u* in Old English.

French influence is also to be seen in the spelling of words in *gu*. This *gu* in Central French corresponded to Picardic *w*, and hence we have doublets such as *warden* and *guardian, warrant* and *guarantee*, etc. In French the *u* of *gu* was once pronounced, but later became silent, and the spelling with *u* was retained in order to show that the *g* was a stop before the vowels *e* and *i*. This practice was imitated in English both in the spelling of words taken from French, as *guise* and *guide*, and also in native words such as *guest*, *guilt*. Another innovation which was due to French influence was the introduction of the symbol *v*. In Old English the sound represented by this symbol was always written *f*. After the Conquest the symbol *u* became common and interchanged freely with *v*, which two symbols were regarded throughout the Middle Ages as being the same letter, both being used either as vowels or as consonants. It was not until the sixteenth century that efforts were made to restrict *v* to consonants and *u* to vowels. The sound [dž], as in *bridge*, came to be written *dg* in Middle English, but in French the same sound existed and was written *g*. This spelling with *g* was also introduced into English in French loan words such as *gentle*, *legend*, *danger*. Another method of representing the same sound was found in French in *journey*, etc., and this spelling is also to be found in numerous words such as *judge*, *joy*, *join*, etc.

We may mention one more important change in spelling which occurred in Middle English and which still remains, though its significance has been lost. It represents one of the latest deliberate attempts to represent in writing differences of pronunciation. In Middle English there existed two distinct long *e* sounds and two long *o* sounds. One was open and the other was close, and the two did not as a rule rime. The close vowel was written *ee* or simply *e*, and the open vowel was written *ea*. The close long *o* was written *oo* or *o* and the open

vowel was written *oa*. The two *e* sounds have fallen
together in Modern English, so that the vowel sounds
in *sea* and *be* are the same. But originally they were
different, and the difference is indicated by the spelling.
Thus we have *sea* and *see*, *stream* and *tree*. The two *o*
vowels have not, however, fallen together in Modern
English, but have developed into different sounds. The
close *o*, which corresponds to an O.E. *o*, has developed into
a *u* sound in Modern English, as in *too*, *shoe*, *goose*, etc.,
but the open sound has developed into the sound which
we now have in *rope*, and is developed from O.E. *ā*,
as in *boat*, *oath*, *oak*. There is thus a difference of spelling, the former sound being spelled *oo* or *o*, and the
latter *oa*. But this distinction was never consistently
carried through, and hence there are numerous words
in *oa* which should have *oo*, and *vice versa*.

The next important series of changes in English
spelling was occasioned by the revival of learning, when
the study of the classical tongues led to a perverted
desire to re-establish the etymological connection between English (French) words and their classical originals.
In this way large numbers of words which had been
borrowed from French, and which had been long in
the language in the form in which they had naturally
developed in French, were reconstructed on their classical
models—often quite mistakenly. Thus an older *dette*
was re-spelled *debt* on the model of the Latin *debitum*,
and *doute* became *doubt*, *descrive* became *describe*, and
vittailles became *victuals*. It should be noticed, too,
that whereas in the great majority of such cases the
reformed spelling did not in any way affect the
pronunciations, yet in some words the new spelling

occasioned a revised pronunciation (so-called spelling pronunciations). Thus the older *faute* was re-spelled *fault* and then the *l* was pronounced. The same applies to *describe*. In the same way the old suffix -*cioun* was rewritten -*tion*. Other words in which an etymological consonant has been introduced in spelling and yet does not affect the pronunciation are : *psalm, palm,* etc. Further examples of spelling pronunciations are : *vault, assault, altar, herald, falcon, realm,* etc. The revival of learning was also responsible for the introduction of certain new symbols for existing sounds. For example, we find *ph* for earlier *f* in words like *phantasy,* earlier *fantasy* ; *phantom* for earlier *fantom,* etc. *ch* appears for *k* in *echo* and *anchor,* and *sch* for *sc* in words like *school* (earlier *scole*) and *scholar*.

These examples from Modern English will suffice to show of what a composite character is the English system of spelling, though they only touch the surface of the subject. It appears that during the Old English period spelling was fairly uniform, thanks partly to the fact that it was to a great extent untrammelled and phonetic, and thanks partly to the fact that West Saxon had risen to the dignity of a standard literary language. In the Middle English period, though writers no doubt still sought to write phonetically, uniformity was impossible because the dialects had again come to their own, and it was not until Chaucer's example created a standard language for literature that there was again an approach to uniformity. At the end of the fifteenth century came the first printed books, and with them spelling became to a large extent fixed. But even when Caxton printed his first book in English, he experienced considerable difficulty in deciding upon a uniform system of spelling, for despite the influence of Chaucer there still existed great uncertainty as to the rendering of certain sounds and the spelling of many words. Thus, for example, *u* and *v* could both be used either as vowels or as consonants, and a similar confusion of function existed with regard to *i* and *y*. Gradually *v* was restricted to consonantic use, and the practice grew up of using *y* in the final position and in the neighbourhood of letters with down-strokes, such as *m, n, w*, etc.

The introduction of printing put an end to arbitrary spelling, but it also checked the developments of phonetic spelling. On the whole the effect of the new invention was to stereotype spelling and to make it uniform. In this there lay all the positive advantages which flow from uniformity and system, but on the other hand there was the disadvantage that the spelling from this time onward ceased to represent the pronunciation of the spoken language. Hence our Modern English spelling really represents the sounds of the fifteenth or sixteenth century. The extraordinary discrepancy which exists in Modern English between the spelling and the pronunciation of such words as *laugh, bough, sight, eight*, etc., is due to the fact that the spelling of these words was fixed by the early printers, and that they were themselves somewhat behind the times and adopted a spelling already to some extent traditional. During the sixteenth and seventeenth centuries experiments were still made with the purpose of finding the most acceptable spelling system. In the eighteenth century spelling became practically fixed after the publication of Dr. Johnson's *Dictionary*.

The first printed characters were naturally enough modelled upon those already in existence in the written script. The old symbol þ which had come to be written very like a *y*, appeared in print as *y*, as we have already noted. The old symbol ʒ, again, had come to be written like a *z*, and appeared as such, at least in Scotland, in the printed character. It survives in such proper names as *Mackenzie* and *Dalziel*, in which words it remains a consonant. It was after the introduction of printing, also, that the use of the symbols *j* and *v* was restricted to consonants and *i* and *u* to vowels. During the sixteenth and seventeenth centuries occurred most of the revised spellings under the influence of Latin and Greek. Some of these have already been noted, and to them we may add such typical spellings as *perfect* for older *parfit*, and *island* for older *iland*.

The effect of these learned spellings in English, together with the fact that the spelling of native words is, in the main, the same to-day as it was three hundred years ago, and has very often no relation at all to the actual pronunciation, has been that the spelling of Modern English is extraordinarily irregular and capricious, and a great burden is imposed on all who have to learn it. The positive disadvantages of our antiquated spelling are not confined, however, to the difficulties which Englishmen experience in learning it. They are also to be seen in the added difficulties which he experiences in learning foreign languages, where symbols have values quite different from those which they have in English.

APPENDIX

THE Gospel of St. Matthew in the Old English version of
the tenth century, in Wycliffe's version of 1389, and in
Tyndale's version of 1526.

THE GOSPEL OF ST. MATTHEW.

ANGLO-SAXON, 995.

CHAPTER VIII.

1. Soþlice ða se Hælend of ðam munte nyðer astah, ða fyligdon hym mycle mænio.

2. Ða genealæhte an hreofla to him and hine to him geað-medde, and ðus cwæþ, Drih-ten, gyf þu wylt, ðu miht me geclænsian.

3. Ða astrehte se Hælend hys hand, and hrepode hyne, and ðus cwæþ, Ic wylle, beo geclænsod. And hys hreofla wæs hrædlice geclænsod.

WYCLIFFE, 1389.

CHAPTER VIII.

1. Forsothe when Jhesus hadde comen doun fro the hil, many cumpanyes fole-widen hym.

2. And loo! a leprouse man cummynge worshipide hym, sayinge, Lord, ȝif thou wolt, thou maist make me clene.

3. And Jhesus, holdinge forthe the hond touchide hym, sayinge, I wole, be thou maad clene. And anoon the lepre of hym was clensid.

TYNDALE, 1526.

CHAPTER VIII.

1. When Jesus was come downe from the mountayne, moch people folowed him.

2. And lo! there cam a lepre and worsheped him, saynge, Master, if thou wylt, thou canst make me clene.

3. He putt forthe his hond, and touched him, saynge, I wyll, be clene. And immed-iatly his leprosy was clensed.

4. And Jesus said vnto him, Se, thou tell no man; but go, and shewe thysilf to the preste, and offer the gyfte that Moses comaunded to be offred, in witness to them.

5. When Jesus was entered into Capernaum, there cam vnto him a certayne Centurion, besechyng him,

6. And saynge, Master, my servaunt lyeth sicke att home off the palsye, and is grevously payned.

7. And Jesus sayd vnto him, I wyll come, and cure him.

8. The Centurion answered and saide, Syr, I am not worthy, that thou shuldest com vnder the rofe of my housse; but speake the worde only, and my servaunt shal be healed.

4. And Jhesus saith to hym, See, say þou to no man; but go shewe thee to prestis, and offre that ȝifte that Moyses comaundide, in to witnessing to hem.

5. Soþely when he hadde entride in to Capharnaum, centurio neiȝide to hym, preyinge hym,

6. And saide, Lord, my child lyeth in the hous sike on the palsie, and is yuel tourmentid.

7. And Jhesus saith to hym, I shal cume, and shal hele hym.

8. And centurio answerynge saith to hym, lord, I am not worthi, that thou entre vndir my roof; but oonly say bi word, and my child shal be helid.

4. Ða cwæþ se Hælend to him, Warna ðe, ðæt ðu hyt nænegum men ne secge; ac gang, æteowe ðe ðam sacerde, and bring hym ða lac ðe Moyses bebead, on hyra gecyðnesse.

5. Soþlice ða se Hælend ineode on Capharnaum, ða genealæhte hym an hundredes ealdor, hyne biddende,

6. And ðus cweðende, Drihten, min cnapa liþ on minum huse lama, and mid yfle gepread.

7. Ða cwæþ se Hælend to him, Ic cume, and hyne gehæle.

8. Ða andswarode se hundredes ealdor and ðus cwæþ, Drihten, ne eom ic wyrðe, ðæt ðu ingange under mine þecene; ac cweþ ðin an word, and min cnapa biþ gehæled.

ANGLO-SAXON, 995.

9. Soþlice ic eom man under anwealde geset, and ic hæbbe þegnas under me; and ic cweþe to þysum, Gang, and he gæþ; and ic cweþe to oðrum, Cum, and he cymþ; to minum þeowe, Wyrc ðis, and he wyrcþ.

10. Witodlice ða se Hælend, ðis gehyrde, ða wundrode he, and cweþ to ðam ðe hym fyligdon, Soþ ic secge eow, ne gemette ic swa mycelne geleafan on Israhel.

11. To soþum ic secge eow, ðæt manige cumaþ fram eastdæle and west-dæle, and wuniaþ mid Abrahame and Isahace and Iacobe on heofena rice.

12. Witodlice ðises rices bearn beoþ aworpene on ða ytemestan þystro; ðær biþ woþ, and toþa gristbitung.

WYCLIFFE, 1389.

9. For whi and I am a man ordeynd vnder power, hauynge vndir me kniȝtis; and I say to this, Go, and he goth; and to an other, Come thou, and he cometh; and to my seruaunt, Do thou this thing, and he doth.

10. Sothely Jhesus, heerynge these thingis, wondride, and saide to men suynge hym, Trewly I saye to ȝou, I fonde nat so grete feith in Yrael.

11. Sothely Y say to ȝou, that manye shulen come fro the est and west, and shulen rest with Abraham and Ysaac and Jacob in the kyngdam of heuenes;

12. Forsothe the sonys of the rewme shulen be cast out in to vttremest derknessis; there shal be weepynge, and beetynge togidre of teeth.

TYNDALE, 1526.

9. For Y also my selfe am a man vndre power, and have sowdeeres vndre me; and Y saye to one, Go, and he goeth; and to anothre, Come, and he cometh; and to my servaunt, Do this, and he doeth it.

10. When Jesus herde these saynges, he marveyled, and said to them that folowed him, Verely y say vnto you, I have not founde so great fayth, no, not in Israell.

11. I say therefore vnto you, that many shall come from the eest and weest, and shall rest with Abraham Ysaac and Jacob in the kyngdom of heven;

12. And the children of the kingdom shal be cast out in to the vtmoost dercknes; there shal be wepinge, and gnasshing of tethe.

13. Then Jesus said vnto the Centurion, Go thy waye, and as thou hast beleued, so be it vnto the. And his servaunt was healed that same houre. 14. And Jesus went into Peter's housse, and sawe his wyues mother lyinge sicke of a fevre. 15. And he thouched her hande, and the fevre leeft her; and she arose and ministred vnto them. 16. When the even was come, they brought vnto him many that were possessed with devylles, and he cast out the spirits with a worde, and healed all that were sicke. 17. To fulfill that which was spoken by Esay, the prophet, sainge, He toke on him oure infirmytees, and bare oure sicknesses.

13. And Jhesus saide to centurio, Go, and as thou hast bileeued, be it don to thee. And the child was helid fro that houre. 14. And when Jhesus hadde comen in to the hous of Symond Petre, he say his wyues moder liggynge, and shakun with feueris. 15. And he touchide hir hond, and the feuer lefte hir; and she roose; and seruyde him. 16. Sothely whan the euenyng was maad, thei broujte to hym many hauynge deuelys, and he castide out spiritis by word, and helide alle hauynge yuel; 17. That it shulde be fulfillid, that thing that was said by Ysaie, the prophete, sayinge, He toke oure infirmytees, and bere oure sykenessis.

13. And se Hælend cwæþ to ðam hundrydes ealdre, Ga, and gewurðe ðe, swa swa ðu gelyfdest. And se cnapa wæs gehæled on ðære tide. 14. Ða se Hælend com on Petres huse, ða geseah he hys swegre licgende and hriþigende. 15. And he æthran hyre hand, and se fefor hig forlet; ða aras heo, and þenode him. 16. Soþlice ða hyt æfen wæs, hig brohton him manege deofol-seoce, ond he ut-adræfde ða unclænan gastas mid hys worde, and he ealle gehælde ða yfel-hæbbendan; 17. Ðæt wære gefylled, ðæt ðe geoweden is þurh Esaiam, ðone witegan, ðus cweðende, He ongeng ure untrumnesse, ond he abær ure adla.

ANGLO-SAXON, 995.

18. Ða geseah se Hælend mycle menigeo ymbutan hine, ða het he hig faran ofer ðone muþan.

19. Ða genealæhte him an bocere, and cwæþ, Lareow, ic fylige ðe, swa hwæder swa ðu færst.

20. Ða cwæþ se Hælend to him, Foxas habbaþ holu, and heofenan fuglas nest, soþlice mannes sunu næfþ hwær he hys heafod ahylde.

21. Ða cwæþ to him oþer of hys leorning-cnihtum, Drihten, alyfe me ærest to farenne, and bebyrigean minne fæder.

22. Ða cwæþ se Hælend to him, Fylig me, and læt deade bebyrigean hyra deadan.

WYCLIFFE, 1389.

18. Sothely Jhesus seeynge many cumpanyes about hym, bad his disciplis go ouer the water.

19. And oo scribe commynge to, saide to hym, Maistre, I shal sue thee, whider euer thou shalt go.

20. And Jhesus said to hym, Foxis han dichis, and briddis of the eir han nestis, but mannes sone hath nat wher he reste his heued.

21. Sotheli an other of his disciplis saide to hym, Lord, suffre me go first, and birye my fadir.

22. Forsothe Jhesus saide to hym, Sue thou me, and late dede men birye her dead men.

TYNDALE, 1526.

18. When Jesus saw moche people about him, he commaunded to go over the water.

19. And there cam a scribe, and said vnto him, Master, I woll folowe the, whythersumever thou goest.

20. And Jesus said vnto him, The Foxes have holes, and the bryd of the aier have nestes, but the sonne of the man hath not where on to leye his heede.

21. Anothre that was one of hys disciples seyd vnto him, Master, suffre me fyrst to go, and burye my father.

22. But Jesus said vnto him, Folowe me, and let the deed burie their deed

23. And he astah on scyp, and hys leorning-cnyhtas hym fyligdon.

24. Ða wearð mycel styrung geworden on ðære sæ, swa ðæt ðæt scyp wearð ofergoten mid yðum; witodlice he slep.

25. And hig genealæhton, and hy awehton hyne, ðus cweðende, Drihten, hæle us, we moton forwurðan.

26. Ða cweþ he to him, To hwi synt ge forhte ge lytles geleafan? Ða aras he and be-bead ðam winde and ðære sæ, and ðær wearð geworden mycel smyltness.

27. Gewisslice ða men wun-drodun, and ðus cwædon, Hwæt is ðes, ðæt windas and sæ him hyrsumiaþ?

23. And Jhesu steyinge vp into a litel ship, his disciplis sueden hym.

24. And loo! a grete ster-yng was maad in the see, so that the litil ship was hilid with wawis; but he slepte.

25. And his disciplis camen niȝ to hym, and raysiden hym, sayinge, Lord, saue us; we perishen.

26. And Jhesus seith to hem, What ben ȝee of litil feith agast? Thanne he rys-ynge comaundide to the wyndis and the see, and a grete pesiblenesse is maad.

27. Forsothe men won-dreden, sayinge, What manere man is he, for the wyndis and the see obeishen to hym?

23. And he entred in to a shyppe, and his disciples fol-owed him.

24. And lo! there arose a great storme in the see, in so moche that the shippe was hyd with waves; and he was aslepe.

25. And his disciples cam vnto him, and awocke hym, sayinge, Master, save vs; we perishe.

26. And he said vnto them, Why are ye fearfull o ye en-dewed with lytell faithe? Then he arose and rebuked the wyndes and the see, and there folowed a greate calme.

27. And men marveyled, and said, What man is this, that bothe wyndes and see obey him?

ANGLO-SAXON, 995.

28. Ða se Hælend com ofer ðone muþan on Geraseniscra rice, ða urnon him togenes twegen ðe hæfdon deofol-seocnesse, of byrgenum utgan-gende, ða wæron swiðe reðe, swa ðæt nan man ne mihte faran þurh ðone weg.

29. And hig hrymdon, and cwædon, La! Hælend, Godes sunu, hwæt ys ðe and us gemæne? come ðu hider ær tide us to þreagenne?

30. Ðær wæs soþlice un-feorran swyna heord manegra manna læswiende.

31. Ða deofla soþlice hyne bædon, ðus cwæðende, Gyf ðu us ut adrifst, asende us on ðas swina heorde.

WYCLIFFE, 1389.

28. And whan Jhesus hadde comen ouer the water in to the cuntre of men of Gena-zereth, twey men hauynge deuelis runnen to hym, goynge out fro birielis, ful feerse, so that no man miȝte passe by that wey.

29. And loo! thei crieden, sayinge, What to us and to thee, Jhesu, the sone of God? hast thou comen hidir befoe the tyme for to tourmente vs?

30. Sothely a floc of many hoggis lesewynge was nat fer from hem.

31. But the deuelis prey-eden him, seyinge, ȝif thou castist out us hennes, sende vs in to the droue of hoggis.

TYNDALE, 1526.

28. And when he was come to the other syde in to the countre of the Gergesens, there met him two possessed of devylles, which cam out off the graves, and were out off measure fearce, so that no man myght go by that waye.

29. And lo! they cryed out, saynge, O Jesu, the sonne off God, what have we to do with thee? Art thou come hyther to torment vs before the tyme be come?

30. There was a good waye off from them a greate heerd of swyne fedinge.

31. Then the devyles be-sought him, saynge, If thou cast vs out, suffre vs to go oure waye into the heerd of swyne.

32. Ða cwæþ he to hym, Faraþ. And hig ða utgangende ferdon on ða swin ; and ðær rihte ferde eall seo heord myclum onræse niwel on ða sæ, and hig wurdon deade on ðam wætere.

33. Ða hyrdas witodlice flugon, and comun on ða ceastre, and cyddon ealle ðas þing, and be ðam ðe ða deoful-seocnyssa hæfdon.

34. Ða eode eall seo ceaster-waru togeanes ðam Hælende ; and ða ða hig hyne gesawun, ða bædon hig hyne, ðæt he ferde fram heora genærum.

32. And he saith to hem, Go ȝee. And thei goynge out wente in to the hoggis ; and loo! in a greet bire al the droue wente heedlynge in to the see, and thei ben dead in watris.

33. Forsoþe the hirdes fledden awey, and cummynge in to the citee, tolden alle these thingis, and of hem that hadden the fendis.

34. And loo! al the citee wente aȝeinis Jhesu, metynge hym ; and hym seen, thei preiden hym, that he shulde passe fro her coostis.

32. And he said vnto them, Go youre wayes. Then went they out and departed into the heerd of swyne ; and lo! all the heerd of swyne was caryed with violence hedlinge into the see, and perisshed in the water.

33. Then the heerdmen fleed, and went there ways into the cite, and tolde every thinge, and what had fortuned vnto them that were possessed of the devyls.

34. And lo! all the cite cam out, and met Jesus ; and when they sawe him, they besought him to departe out off there costies.